The Literature of Cinema

ADVISORY EDITOR: **MARTIN S. DWORKIN**
INSTITUTE OF PHILOSOPHY AND POLITICS OF EDUCATION
TEACHER'S COLLEGE, COLUMBIA UNIVERSITY

THE LITERATURE OF CINEMA presents a comprehensive selection from the multitude of writings about cinema, rediscovering materials on its origins, history, theoretical principles and techniques, aesthetics, economics, and effects on societies and individuals. Included are works of inherent, lasting merit and others of primarily historical significance. These provide essential resources for serious study and critical enjoyment of the "magic shadows" that became one of the decisive cultural forces of modern times.

Movies and Conduct

Herbert Blumer

ARNO PRESS & THE NEW YORK TIMES

New York • 1970

Reprint Edition 1970 by Arno Press Inc.
Library of Congress Catalog Card Number: 76-124023
ISBN 0-405-01640-9
ISBN for complete set: 0-405-01600-X
Manufactured in the United States of America

MOVIES AND CONDUCT

MOVIES AND CONDUCT

❖

HERBERT BLUMER
ASSOCIATE PROFESSOR OF SOCIOLOGY
UNIVERSITY OF CHICAGO

NEW YORK
THE MACMILLAN COMPANY
1933

THIS SERIES OF TWELVE STUDIES OF THE
INFLUENCE OF MOTION PICTURES UPON
CHILDREN AND YOUTH HAS BEEN MADE BY
THE COMMITTEE ON EDUCATIONAL RE-
SEARCH OF THE PAYNE FUND AT THE RE-
QUEST OF THE NATIONAL COMMITTEE FOR
THE STUDY OF SOCIAL VALUES IN MOTION
PICTURES, NOW THE MOTION PICTURE RE-
SEARCH COUNCIL, 366 MADISON AVENUE,
NEW YORK CITY. THE STUDIES WERE DE-
SIGNED TO SECURE AUTHORITATIVE AND
IMPERSONAL DATA WHICH WOULD MAKE
POSSIBLE A MORE COMPLETE EVALUATION
OF MOTION PICTURES AND THEIR SOCIAL
POTENTIALITIES

TO

RICHARD GEORGE BLUMER,

FATHER AND FRIEND

CHAIRMAN'S PREFACE

Motion pictures are not understood by the present generation of adults. They are new; they make an enormous appeal to children; and they present ideas and situations which parents may not like. Consequently when parents think of the welfare of their children who are exposed to these compelling situations, they wonder about the effect of the pictures upon the ideals and behavior of the children. Do the pictures really influence children in any direction? Are their conduct, ideals, and attitudes affected by the movies? Are the scenes which are objectionable to adults understood by children, or at least by very young children? Do children eventually become sophisticated and grow superior to pictures? Are the emotions of children harmfully excited? In short, just what effect do motion pictures have upon children of different ages?

Each individual has his answer to these questions. He knows of this or that incident in his own experience, and upon these he bases his conclusions. Consequently opinions differ widely. No one in this country up to the present time has known in any general and impersonal manner just what effect motion pictures have upon children. Meanwhile children clamor to attend the movies as often as they are allowed to go. Moving pictures make a profound appeal to children of all ages. In such a situation it is obvious that a comprehensive study of the influence of motion pictures upon children and youth is appropriate.

To measure these influences the investigators who co-operated to make this series of studies analyzed the problem

vii

to discover the most significant questions involved. They set up individual studies to ascertain the answer to the questions and to provide a composite answer to the central question of the nature and extent of these influences. In using this technique the answers must inevitably be sketches without all the details filled in; but when the details are added the picture will not be changed in any essential manner. Parents, educators, and physicians will have little difficulty in fitting concrete details of their own into the outlines which these studies supply.

Specifically, the studies were designed to form a series to answer the following questions: What sorts of scenes do the children of America see when they attend the theaters? How do the mores depicted in these scenes compare with those of the community? How often do children attend? How much of what they see do they remember? What effect does what they witness have upon their ideals and attitudes? Upon their sleep and health? Upon their emotions? Do motion pictures directly or indirectly affect the conduct of children? Are they related to delinquency and crime, and, finally, how can we teach children to discriminate between movies that are artistically and morally good and bad?

The history of the investigations is brief. In 1928 William H. Short, Executive Director of the Motion Picture Research Council, invited a group of university psychologists, sociologists, and educators to meet with the members of the Council to confer about the possibility of discovering just what effect motion pictures have upon children, a subject, as has been indicated, upon which many conflicting opinions and few substantial facts were in existence. The university men proposed a program of study. When Mr. Short appealed to The Payne Fund for a grant to support such an investigation, he found the foundation receptive because of its well-known interest in motion pictures as one of the major influences in the lives of modern youth. When the appropriation had been made the investigators organized themselves into a Committee on Educational Research of The Payne Fund with the following membership: L. L. Thurstone, Frank N. Freeman, R. E. Park, Herbert Blumer, Philip M. Hauser of the University of Chicago; George D. Stoddard, Christian A. Ruckmick, P. W. Holaday, and Wendell Dysinger of the University of Iowa; Mark A. May and Frank K. Shuttleworth of Yale University; Frederick M. Thrasher and Paul G. Cressey of New York University; Charles C. Peters of Pennsylvania State College; Ben D. Wood of Columbia University; and Samuel Renshaw, Edgar Dale, and W. W. Charters of Ohio State University. The investigations have extended through four years, 1929–1932 inclusive.

The committee's work is an illustration of an interesting technique for studying any social problem. The distinctive characteristic of this technique is to analyze a complex social problem into a series of subordinate problems, to select competent investigators to work upon each of the subordinate projects and to integrate the findings of all the investigators as a solution of the initial problem. Such a program yields a skeleton framework, which, while somewhat lacking in detail, is substantially correct if the contributing investigations have been validly conducted. To provide this framework or outline is the task of research. To fill in the detail and to provide the interpretations are the natural and easy tasks of those who use the data.

W. W. C.

Ohio State University
June, 1933

AUTHOR'S PREFACE

THE present study is an exploration into a field of conduct which, while intriguing, has deterred investigation because of its intangible character. The customary methods of study used in social and psychological science have not seemed to be of much promise. In this investigation the writer has dispensed with sophisticated techniques. He has simply asked people to relate or write as carefully as possible their experiences with motion pictures.[1] Typical sets of these accounts furnish the bulk of the report and are allowed in the main to convey their own significance. With the accounts at hand the reader may judge for himself the reasonableness of the interpretations made by the author.

No treatment is given in this volume to the influence of motion pictures on sex conduct and life. Materials collected in the course of the study show this influence to be considerable, but their inclusion has been found inadvisable. The omission is not to be construed as implying the absence of the influence.

The writer wishes to make recognition of the appreciated assistance of Mr. Paul G. Cressey, Mrs. Ada J. Davis, Mr. C. Walker Hayes, Mr. Frederick Hurd, and Miss Laura Pederson in securing a number of the motion-picture autobiographies used in this study. An acknowledgment of indebtedness for generous aid is due the principals and teachers of the grade schools and high schools in which questionnaire and autobiographical material was obtained. Finally the writer wishes to thank the many high-school and college

---

[1] A complete statement of the procedure appears in the first chapter.

xi

students who wrote their motion-picture experiences. Their fine spirit of coöperation and their good sportsmanship have done much to lighten and make pleasant this investigation.

In writing the report, the writer is indebted to Professor Louis Wirth for valuable comments and suggestions.

H. B.

Chicago, Ill.
December, 1931

TABLE OF CONTENTS

MOVIES AND CONDUCT

MOVIES AND CONDUCT

CHAPTER I
PROBLEM AND PROCEDURE

PROBLEM

DURING the three past decades motion pictures have become one of the chief forms of amusement in the lives of the American people and have given birth to a giant industry with a formidable financial structure. Corresponding with this growth there has been developing a belief that motion pictures have become one of the largest influences on contemporary life. Touching as they do the daily experience of millions of people in an appealing and magnetic way, it is but natural that many should regard them as wielding a powerful influence on conduct. A perusal of the discussions of motion pictures, however, discloses a singular lack of consensus on the nature of these effects on conduct.

On one side there are many who regard motion pictures as a meliorator of the hard character of modern life, as a surcease to sorrow, as a chief means of infusing romance into a dull world and thereby adding compensation to the ordinary routine of life. This contention is expressed frequently in a more scientific fashion by psychologists and other students of human behavior in the declaration that motion pictures are a means of satisfying in a vicarious and harmless fashion pent-up impulses which might otherwise take a more dangerous expression. By relieving strain, by occasioning a sort of emotional catharsis, motion pictures, it has been asserted, play a genuinely beneficial rôle.

1

As opposed to this point of view, there is the charge
expressed even more vigorously that motion pictures con-
stitute a harmful influence on the lives of people, particularly on the lives of youths. They have been held account-
able by many for crime and delinquency and, indeed, for a
supposed general weakening of moral standards; the spo-
radic yet persistent efforts at censorship in some sense may
be interpreted as an expression of this belief.

These opposing interpretations make vivid the problem
as to the effects of motion pictures. It is to this problem
that the present study has devoted itself. Reference may
be made in passing to the character of the studies which
hitherto have sought to deal with the question. Most of
them are frankly not direct studies of the influence of motion pictures, but rather collections of the opinions of people
on the supposed effects of motion pictures. These studies,
however interesting they may be in revealing the attitudes
of different groups of people such as ministers, school teachers, law enforcement officials, etc., are still far removed from
showing what motion pictures are actually doing.

There is another kind of study of a more scientific and
penetrating character. The investigations of this type have
sought to ascertain the influence of motion pictures under
experimental and control situations. The attempt usually
has been to introduce a number of subjects to a given kind
of picture and through the use of questionnaires and other
devices to test their reactions. Sometimes summaires of
the content of pictures have been presented to people to
rate or list in terms of one's feelings. It is not the purpose
of this investigation to make an evaluation of these studies;
but rather to point out their different character from that
which is given in the present volume.

This study is based chiefly on personal accounts given

by people of their experiences with motion pictures. The study aims to ascertain the kinds of influence wielded by motion pictures on conduct, in so far as these can be determined from personal accounts. The study assumes that one way to find out about the experiences of people is to inquire into those experiences. The effort has been always to secure accounts of actual incidents, episodes, and experiences with motion pictures, rather than judgments from the people as to how they believe they were affected by them. Such expressions of judgment, while of interest, have not been accepted as data for this study. As careful safeguards as could be devised were taken to secure reliable accounts. A description of the measures taken to assure reliability is provided in the statements which follow on the procedure employed in this investigation.

The accounts of experiences used in this study have been collected mainly from young men and women, adolescents, and children. No attempt has been made in this study either to compare or contrast motion-picture experiences with experiences from other sources, such as newspapers, fiction, or the theater.

PROCEDURE

IN seeking to throw light on the general problem as to how conduct is influenced by motion pictures the chief reliance was placed on the use of the written life history or the motion-picture autobiography. The subjects and informants from whom information was secured were asked to write in narrative form their motion-picture experiences.

Such motion-picture autobiographies were secured from 634 university students in two universities,[1] from 481 college and junior college students in four colleges, from 583

---

[1] In the designation of the documents which are cited in this study the term *college student* is used throughout to refer to both university and college students.

high school students, from 67 office workers, and from 58 factory workers. The university students were chosen from classes in Social Science and English. The colleges from whose students motion-picture autobiographies were secured are located in Arkansas, in North Carolina, in New York, and in Illinois. All four colleges were girls' colleges. The high-school students writing the documents were from ten public high schools located in Chicago. The high schools were chosen to represent different levels of economic and social status. The office workers and factory workers were chosen from two concerns located in Chicago.

Some mention should be made of the instructions given to those who wrote the motion-picture autobiographies. In the beginning of the study two classes of university students were asked merely to write in as natural and truthful manner as possible accounts of their experiences with "movies" as far as they could recall them. No further instructions were given. The accounts were written out of class. Usually six to eight weeks were allowed for the writing of the documents. From these and from subsequent documents recurrent experiences were selected as separate items; and from these items there was constructed a form or guidance sheet for the writing of the later motion-picture autobiographies. A copy of this form appears in Appendix A.

It was soon discovered in the course of the initial investigation that there were certain kinds of experiences which the students were reluctant to record in writing. It became advisable to devise some scheme whereby the anonymity of the writer could be provided for, so that he could feel free to write fully about his experiences of an intimate and personal character. At the same time it was desirable to hold the students responsible for serious accounts. Accordingly the following scheme was devised and employed in securing the greater proportion of the life histories used in this study.

The students of a class chose a small committee of their own who assigned to each student in the class a code number. To prevent the teacher from identifying the author of the documents, they were turned in under the code number. The teacher gave credit to those documents which showed signs of having been seriously written, turned back to the committee a list of the code numbers with the accompanying credit given, and received from the committee a list of the names of the students with the credit given to each. In this way the committee alone knew the names of the students corresponding to the code numbers, yet the committee had no opportunity to read the papers. Each document came to the teacher as anonymous, yet each student received credit for his or her work. This device proved to be especially helpful in giving to the student a sense of protection and inducing in him a greater readiness to write those experiences which he would ordinarily be reluctant to disclose as his own.

The utmost care and attention were devoted to gaining full coöperation from the students. For this purpose it was necessary to build up *rapport*. A very frank statement of the purpose of the investigation was always made so as to avoid suspicion that the investigator was seeking to get "something on the student." To this explicit statement of the purpose of the study was added a request for honest coöperation. Out of this effort to build up mutual confidence came the experience, confirmed on a succession of occasions, that students respond very favorably when asked to be "good sports" and to write freely about the kind of experiences concerned. Stress was also placed on the security in describing private and confidential experience which each student enjoyed under the arrangement which gave anonymity to his document. The student was asked to be honest with himself in writing his account, not to exaggerate and not to "dress up" his statement.

Certain questions inevitably arise concerning the truthfulness and reliability of the accounts which were secured in this fashion. Several ways of checking this reliability were used in the present study. It was possible in a number of cases to compare the document written by a student with the statement of his experiences secured later through a personal interview. At the time of writing their documents the students had no intimation of the possibility of a subsequent interview covering their motion-picture experiences. In some sixty or seventy cases male university students who had turned in documents were interviewed six months later. In each instance at the end of the interview, when asked, the student volunteered the code number under which his written document had been given to the teacher. This provided an opportunity to compare the content of the written document with the content of the interview. It is assumed that the period of six months elapsing between the two was sufficient for the individual to forget any fictitious or false incidents which he may have given in the motion-picture autobiography. In no instance was there discovered any discrepancy of importance between the experiences related in the document and those in the interview.

The accounts were also checked for internal consistency. In a few, numbering less than twenty, there was evidence of contradiction in the experiences given. These documents, accordingly, were not used in this study. All of the remaining accounts, as far as could be determined by careful scrutiny, were internally consistent.

The chief means of checking the character of the experiences given in the written documents was in the comparison of document with document. The motion-picture autobiographies were written independently by students in different schools and localities. With the exception of the students in the same class, there was little possibility for the exchange of experiences. The comparison of large numbers of documents coming from different groups of people with no knowledge of each other made it possible to ascertain the general run of experiences. The contents of documents coming from different sources yielded substantially the same general kind of experiences. Unless there be some fault in the manner in which students were asked to write, this massing of experiences on a number of outstanding facts points to the reliability of the accounts.

Another source of verification is yielded by the comparison of the content of the motion-picture autobiographies with the content of motion-picture conversations collected from other groups of people. The kinds of experiences which are described in the autobiographies were found to be similar to those dwelt on or alluded to in the motion-picture conversations of different groups. Since these conversations, recorded verbatim as far as possible, were collected in natural and naïve situtations, the conformity between them and the autobiographical materials strongly suggests the accuracy of both.

The reliability which has been revealed by the four kinds of checks above considered warrants the conclusion that the subjects did not tend to conscious falsification in writing their motion-picture autobiographies. In instructing the individuals the request was always made to write only those experiences which were recalled vividly. This request seems to have been adhered to consistently. The whole

character of the data collected as well as the conditions under which they were secured shows convincingly that there
was little tendency to exaggerate or falsify; if anything,
there was a tendency to withhold information. Many
kinds of intimate experiences, such as the influence of motion pictures on the sex life of the individual, came forth
in the interviews although frequently not mentioned in the
autobiographies.

The main use of these autobiographical materials has
been to show and illuminate the different kinds of ways
in which motion pictures touch the lives of young people.
Experiences which recurred with a high rate of frequency
in the separate documents have been selected and are
presented in this report. A few documents in their entirety
are also given, to indicate the types of material from which
the quoted experiences have been chosen.[1] It has also been
found possible to tabulate statistically many of the experiences spoken of in the documents. These counts can in
no sense be thought of as conclusive since individuals
were not required to write either one way or another about
many forms of experience. Yet since no formal questions
were asked and therefore no arbitrary answers solicited,
the tabulations may be thought of as having greater value
than as if they were based on material secured by a formal
questionnaire. As far as possible an effort has been made
to secure a numerical statement of the frequency with
which a given kind of experience has been described in
the mass of documents, whenever that kind of experience
has been considered.

Another major source of the information used in this
report has been gathered through the personal interview.
Eighty-one university students and fifty-four high-school

[1] See Appendixes C, D, E, and F.

students were interviewed on their motion-picture experiences. The college students had previously written motion picture autobiographies; the high-school students had not. These interviews were usually from an hour to an hour and a half in length. A number of grade-school children were interviewed for shorter periods, usually while in the classroom.

The procedure used in arranging for and carrying on these interviews was designed to enlist the fullest coöperation on the part of the subjects. In each case permission to be interviewed was first obtained from the subjects. There was no obligation to submit to an interview. The subject was always told in advance that he might be asked a number of delicate questions referring to intimate phases of his experience. It was found that the subject so forewarned was not disturbed by personal questions asked in the interview. A full stenographic account of the interview was taken. The subject had full knowledge of the presence in the room of the male stenographer. The stenographer, however, was placed at some point behind the subject so as to be out of the subject's range of vision. The interview frequently took the character of a free exchange of experiences, the interviewer talking of his own experience as a means of inducing the subject to talk freely of his. The purpose of the interview was mainly to inquire into intimate experiences which the ordinary student hesitates to write about even under guarantees of anonymity.

No fixed set of questions was followed in the interview; the line of inquiry was allowed to develop in accordance with the nature of the responses of the subject. For this reason the material provided by the interview has been found suitable for illuminating the more intimate effects of motion pictures, although because of this very character it has not lent itself to statistical tabulation.

A third method of securing information for the study has been the collection of conversations on the subject of motion pictures. These accounts, taken as nearly verbatim as possible, were almost always secured by participants of the groups engaged in the conversations. The purpose of this form of investigation was to secure as natural a picture as possible of the kind of conversation which ordinarily goes on concerning motion pictures. It was felt that the content of these conversations would in some sense reflect interests and attitudes and would serve also to show how, through such discussions, an individual may be led to particular interpretations of motion pictures.

These accounts of motion-picture conversations were secured from several fraternities of university students, a number of sororities and girls' groups, and from several "cliques" of high-school boys and girls. Accounts were also secured of conversations of high-school boys and girls at parties. Accounts, further, were secured from boys' gangs, play groups, office girls, and factory workers.

Ordinarily these accounts of conversations were collected by individuals working in pairs and seeking in this fashion to supplement each other. With very few exceptions the reporters were all members of the groups whose conversations were written down. In some instances remarks were taken as they were spoken; in other instances reliance had to be placed on memory. The reporters were instructed not to give any intimation to their groups that they were engaged in recording the conversations which went on. This precaution was taken in order to prevent the introduction of artifice into the remarks of the group. So far as it is possible to determine the workers faithfully obeyed this instruction.

In addition to the use of the motion-picture autobiographies supplemented by interviews and accounts of conversations, a considerable amount of material was collected through the use of direct questionnaires. These were given mainly to children. The principal questionnaire employed is given in Appendix B. It was distributed to 1200 grade-school children in the fifth and sixth grades of twelve public grade schools in the city of Chicago. Three of these schools were located in areas with very high rates of delinquency, four in areas with medium rates of delinquency, and four in areas with low rates of delinquency.[1] The other school was a special school for truants and boys with behavior problems. The questionnaire was simple, and the manner of its presentation raised no unforeseen problems.

It should be mentioned, finally, that use was made of direct observation of children. The behavior of children in small neighborhood motion-picture theaters was watched as far as time and opportunity would permit and yielded some interesting information. Also of value has been the observation of children while playing after seeing motion pictures.

It is perhaps needless to say that all of these different lines of inquiry taken together have yielded a wealth of material, only a portion of which is being used in the present report. Only that which seems most significant has been chosen. It should be remembered by the reader that the accounts of motion-picture experiences which are given in the report are only a small fraction of the instances which are on hand. They have been chosen as representative of types of experiences on each of which many instances are available.

[1] The delinquency areas used as bases of selection were those worked out for the city of Chicago by Mr. Clifford Shaw. See Shaw, *Delinquency Areas*, Chicago, 1929.

The general plan of procedure followed in the report has been to let the accounts of experience speak for themselves. Consequently they are used very liberally. The remarks of the author are limited mostly to interpretation.

CHAPTER II

IMPERSONATION—CHILDHOOD PLAY

THE most tangible influence of motion pictures on conduct is to be found in the field of overt or external behavior. While this form of influence is most easily discernible, it is not to be supposed that it is the most significant. We will begin our treatment with some consideration of this area of conduct, devoting ourselves to play impersonation by children and in the following chapter to imitation by adolescents.

Anyone who is familiar with the life of American children knows of the use of motion-picture themes in their play. Few kinds of conduct show a more striking influence of motion pictures. Most readers have had the familiar sight of children impersonating movie characters and carrying out movie themes in their games, as in playing "cowboys and Indians" and "cops and robbers." Domestic rôles in the case of girls are very common expressions of the play fostered by motion pictures. The most casual survey of the form and content of childhood play reveals motion pictures as a very important source. This is shown in the extent, the variety, and the vividness of such play.

We are presenting material on the use in childhood play of patterns of behavior taken from the movies without seeking particularly to ascertain the significance of this imitation. A knowledge of the function and psychological meaning of play is necessary to explain the effects of the imitation. Our purpose is merely to direct attention to the way in which motion-picture ideas and patterns are carried out in the behavior of children at play. The realization of this matter will help one to appreciate the extent to which motion pictures may be used as a source for more serious copying—a topic which is considered more directly in the next chapter, where imitation by adolescents is discussed.

Let us begin our sketch of the rôle of motion pictures in shaping the play of children by giving a few typical accounts chosen from the vast number of instances available.

TYPICAL INSTANCES OF MOVIE PLAY

Male, 20, Jewish, white, college junior.—Quite often I would band together with other youths of my age, and we would play "Cop and Robber" or "Cowboy and Indian" trying to imitate the antics of the actors we saw in the movies. We would arm ourselves with toy pistols and clubs and chase each other over streets and yards. We would climb fences and barns, imagining them to be hills and all other objects necessary to make a realistic scene. At times we would get a little girl to play with us and we would have her be the heroine. Then someone else would rescue her, as we had seen it done in the movies.

Female, 19, white, college sophomore.—We had a small hobby horse which was used by the hero and heroine alternately. As my cousin's backyard was large and contained a large number of trees, we soon learned to climb these with agility, with only one or two casualties resulting—a cracked arm and a sprained wrist. From these trees we would lasso the villain and his band as they rode by. We wore this plot almost threadbare and then began to use Indians as the villains. They were always cruel and painted terrifically—with mud. These cruel villains—usually about three—would hide behind a tree about six inches in diameter. This hid them so completely that no one could see them, especially the heroine who happened to be out walking. Then the villain would fall upon her and drag her to the Indian camp about three or four feet away. By that time, of course, the dashing hero would try to make the daring rescue. Sometimes he would succeed, but at other times he would be captured. He would then make the spectacular escape with the heroine in his arms and the wild Indians at his heels. This plot was used many times with but few variations. It provided such a great amount of action that it was always a favorite.

Male, 14, white, high-school sophomore.—After seeing such a bloodthirsty set of pictures (because there usually were double features on Saturday) I went outside; and if a bunch of playmates were around who had seen the pictures, we would make for an empty, vacant lot and re-act the parts. If alone, I would usually walk down the street looking at men and women with a half-open eye, thinking I was a detective or a tough cowboy. Then of a sudden I would imagine a stage holdup, and whipping my horse (which was usually my hip) I would run down the street as fast as I could go, firing imitation toy guns all the way.

As a rule, the play of girls reflects themes of beautification and domestic activity. Society pictures also yield many striking ideas and schemes for play. The dramatization of love themes likewise is frequent in play enaction among young girls.

Female, 20, white, college junior.—From these pictures I received some of my ideas of beauty. I had a great desire to have curls like Mary Pickford's and was forced to try to secure them secretly because my father forbade the curling of my hair. . . . I got some comfort out of being "Mary Pickford" in our games, and improved my appearance with the aid of shavings from new buildings near by. I was also fond of old-fashioned clothes which I had first seen in the movies. I always loved to dress up as the old-fashioned lady, and used everything available to make my skirts stick out like a hoop skirt.

Female, 16, white, high-school junior.—As a result of some of these "society" pictures I frequently saw myself the adored and spoiled darling of rich parents, popular in society and of course havings heaps of beaux. I would come home from one of these pictures and drape myself in a curtain for a train and put duster feathers in my hair. When I attempted to force my brothers to play my admiring men friends, they would laugh me to shame and I would go off to mother and cry.

Female, 20, white, college junior.—My friends and I used to get together and dramatize a movie we had seen recently. This was one of our favorite pastimes. How serious and sincere we were! I remember after we saw Rudolph Valentino in "The Sheik" we returned home, tied kimonas around our heads to give the effect of Arabian costumes and went through the entire play.

Female, 20, white, college sophomore.—That night I slept with my sister and at her request I related the story of the picture. In order to make the story an effective one, we acted out the scenes, I taking the part of the hero and my sister the heroine. I was indeed an ardent Romeo caressing and kissing my Juliet as often or perhaps oftener than the movie required.

Female, 19, white, college sophomore.—The first picture which stands out in my memory is "The Sheik" featuring Rudolph Valentino. I was at the impressionable and romantic age of 12 or 13 when I saw it, and I recall coming home that night and dreaming the entire picture over again; myself as the heroine being carried over the burning sands by an equally burning lover. I could feel myself being kissed in the way the Sheik had kissed the girl. I wanted to see it again, but that was forbidden; so as the next best thing my friend and I enacted the especially romantic scenes out under her mother's rugs, which made excellent tents even though they were hung over the line for cleaning purposes. She was Rudolph and I the beautiful captive, and we followed as well as we could remember the actions of the actors.

These instances probably will merely confirm observations made by many of the readers. They are not given as discoveries nor are they unique. Indeed, it is because they are instances of a common nature that they are of value for this discussion. They give us some understanding of how schemes of behavior portrayed in motion pictures may be taken and embodied in play. They suggest how the plot of a picture, as well as certain of its scenes, may catch the attention of the child, excite his impulses, stir him into action—even though it is mere fanciful play—and provide him with patterns of behavior which may serve as an outlet to his awakened wishes. Whether it be in the form of combat, or of the excited chase, or of parading in costume, or in the practicing of courtship or love, the play incited by motion pictures shows how a movie theme may command the conduct of the child. For the time being the child assumes a new rôle. All phases of his make-up—thoughts, intentions, interests, vocalizations and gestures—reflect the rôle which he is acting. Construed in this way the spread of the effect of the movie characterization seems extensive. Acting on the imagination, the desires, and the movements of the child, it would seem likely to leave some traces—but there is little to say on this point, as we shall see later. Here consideration is confined to the mere fact of imitation.

The inclusion of themes of costuming and love in the play of young girls and the use of notions of the "cowboy-Indian" type in the case of young boys are frequent. They are the most common of the patterns of motion-picture behavior to be incorporated into the play of children. However, there is a wide variety to the motion-picture themes which may enter into their play. The boy may play policeman, gangster, soldier, pirate, swordsman, aviator, "funny person," "bad guy," lawyer, rum-runner, college athlete, gorilla, hypnotist, and so forth; the girl may impersonate society lady, ardent lover, old lady, poor rich girl, orphan, mother, adventuress, cowgirl, dancer, radio singer, and other rôles given in the movies. There is a wide spread to the play experience arising from the witnessing of motion pictures.

VARIETY IN THEME

LET us give a series of instances to illustrate this point and to suggest, by the use of concrete experience, how motion pictures affect play impersonation. The first of the instances is a description given by a playground worker, showing a form of play which arose in response to a number of motion pictures which portrayed "rum-running."

The modern version of "Cops and Robbers" as manifested by the children of the present age is played in the following manner. The sandpile of the school yard serves as the ocean from which the whiskey is taken off boats docked there. Little boxes of sand represent the cases of liquor. Supposedly at night trucks drive up to the water front and load up and try to sneak past a police barricade. The driver, that is, the boy who sits and steers the coaster wagon, is considered the lieutenant in charge of the truck. Two other boys push the wagon and are on the lookout for men or guards.

The cops on the other hand are divided into squads (depending on the number of wagons available); the driver here also is a leader; he is called the squad chief; the two boys pushing this chief are known as detectives. The rest of the boys available for the game are the motorcycle cops; some ride their "bikes" while others merely run.

It seems to me that the most coveted rôle is that of a gang chief, but to a great extent the boys also prefer a job of driving on either side, and so there is an arrangement by which at each trip a different boy is a driver. In general, the boys prefer to be on the cop side for the tendency to be the aggressor is very strong. The cops are supposed to come out ahead with the thieves caught and many more of the gangsters killed than there are cops killed.

Female, 20, white, college junior.—"The Connecticut Yankee in King Arthur's Court"[1] I marked down as one of the most humorous of my childhood. The anachronisms were so vivid that I grasped them easily and thoroughly enjoyed it. Result: For weeks afterwards I and my playmates were royal knights and ladies and bowed and battled to our hearts' content.

Female, 19, white, college junior.—The feature pictures that I remember were long-drawn-out affairs. Only a few of them

[1] This refers to a presentation earlier than that appearing recently and featuring Will Rogers.

remain with me because of the way we played the parts later. "The Poison Letter" with Ethel Clayton, "The Woman's Secret" with Theda Bara, and Francis X. Bushman's "Relations" come to my mind as examples of the early movies. The day after I saw "The Poison Letter" I wrote weird notes to my friends using smears of catsup instead of blood as the heroine was supposed to have used. As I wrote these I sat with a shawl over my head just as Miss Clayton had in the movie.

Male, 21, white, college senior.—I can recall only one instance in which a movie influenced my actions greatly. This was just after I had seen the above-mentioned "Iron Man." The robot in this picture stalked about, swinging its arms alternately, and anyone upon whose head its steel fist descended was removed from action for quite a while. Seeing this caused me to walk about in a jerky imitation of the mechanical man. Any small child whom I encountered received a tap on the head. For some days the neighborhood children shunned me, and until I became tired of my assumed character I was not very popular!

Male, 17, white, high-school senior.—Later I imitated Norma Talmadge. She acted in a play as a thief, and threw daggers. After the show we went home and got some of our mothers' kitchen knives and filed them as daggers. We became quite skilled at the throwing and sticking of knives.

The final account is from a boys' worker who has had an opportunity to observe closely a group of boys in their play.

Another game is Spanish whip fighting. They saw Douglas Fairbanks in some picture where he fought a Spanish crook with a long whip. The boys use whips made out of rope fastened to short sticks for handles. This game and another about which I will write were played last summer. The boys armed themselves with wash-boiler tops for shields, and sticks for spears and played natives of Africa. This game was played in a prairie near by, which is full of high weeds and thus provided excellent African jungles. The boys got their idea for this game from an African serial which ran at the theater during the summer.

It is not necessary to add any other instances to show the wide variety in play patterned after motion pictures. It is sufficient to say that the influence of motion pictures upon the play of children is widespread.

EXTENT OF INFLUENCE ON PLAY

IT is difficult to determine exactly the extent of this influence. Some estimates, however, may be given. Of 200 small boys under twelve years of age who were asked if they played at things seen in the movies, 75 per cent answered in the affirmative. Of 70 ranging in age from 12 to 14 years, 60 per cent indicated that they played at what was seen in the movies. Among a group of boys between 14 and 16 years, 25 per cent admitted still engaging in play reflecting the influence of motion pictures. All these three groups consisted of boys living in one of the slum areas in Chicago.

Of 458 high-school students who wrote motion picture autobiographies, 61 per cent made definite mention of occasions when their childhood play was patterned after motion picture themes; 10 per cent declared that there was no such influence in their own experience; while 29 per cent made no reference either way. In a questionnaire submitted to 1200 grade school children in the sixth and seventh grades, over 50 per cent reported playing at movie themes either a great deal or occasionally. Whatever is the actual extent, one cannot ignore the fact that the play of children is affected considerably by motion pictures.

COMMON THEMES IN PLAY

IN the course of this study an effort was made to determine whether the kind of themes which children choose from motion pictures for their play are likely to vary in accordance with the social and economic background of the children. For instance, do boys living in city areas known for their high delinquency rates select more violent themes for play—gangster themes, robber themes, and rum-running themes? The evidence we have been able to secure shows an essential uniformity in the kinds of movie-inspired play among children regardless of their social status. The taking of the rôle of the gangster or the policeman or the cowboy or the robber seems to be just as frequent among children in areas of little or no delinquency as among the children living in the areas of high rates of delinquency. Essentially the same kind of uniformity is manifested in the play of girls of different areas. The difference in the themes of movie play between the sexes is much greater than between areas.

Particularly common to all groups of children regardless of social status is the fascination of combat and mystery themes. Indeed, most of the patterns of play taken from the movies, even though they vary a great deal in content, reflect these two interests, as the following accounts illustrate:

Male, 20, white, college sophomore.—We had all seen in the movie "War Peril," as I believe it was called, sharpshooters, hand-grenade throwers, tanks, etc. Since our equipment was limited to boxes for the sharpshooters' armor and pans for helmets, we didn't worry about the aviation corps or the heavy artillery. Our rifles were air rifles, which were cocked and shot without any lead bullets in them. Our bell-pistols were much more convenient for our type of warfare; and besides shooting at one another we threw rocks back and forth as hand grenades. This battle-royal kept up all afternoon till we were called in for dinner, neither side having been victorious. This opportunity of having trench warfare was so rare that we had persuaded our mothers that we didn't have to quit at 4:00 P.M. as usual, to get cleaned up. Well, the sewer was repaired the next morning and the "trenches" filled up so our war was over.

Male, 19, Jewish, white, college sophomore.—In my childhood it was common for one to imitate consciously heroes of the screen. For instance, I would climb the lone tree that was in the yard of the Catholic school near us and hang by one hand or hammer my chest shouting "Tarzan" and the like. Jumping over fences on a run as did the heroes of the screen was usual in my young life. Fighting with one another, and after conquering him, placing one foot on his chest and raising our arms to the sky as Tarzan did was also common.

A boy of 9 years.—One time after a show I was with my brother. I was chasing him and I was supposed to be the hero. He was a crook. I hid in some bushes and when he came along, I jumped out on him and pushed him in the hiding. Then I got on top of him and played like I shot him. I had fun after that. Every time my brother and I played like we were in a show and we were the people in the picture.

A boy of 10 years.—When I come home my brothers and I play cowboys like in the show. I sock my brother and his gang, and they chase me. I get a bunch of boys, and my brother gets his gang. We let them chase us. When they are tired we jump on them. Then we tie them up. After the game we run away and hide. My brother and his gang sit in the shed tied up. After we eat we let them go.

A boy of 12 years.—"The Four Musketeers" was going to play up at the Tiffan, and three other boys and I planned to go together. After the show we went home planning where we would make our swords and who would be the leader like Douglas Fairbanks was. We made swords for some other boys who were in our cub patrol. We held our meeting in a tent in our leader's yard. After an hour meeting we started to have sword fights to see who the leader would be. You would have to be able to fight every one there. One boy won over all of us, so we had to keep fighting until the four Musketeers were picked out. The rest was just part of the gang. We played for about a month and did not stop.

A boy of 12 years.—After seeing "Cimarron," which means wild and unruly, I was inspired by how fast he (Richard Dix) could draw a gun, which was true of frontier men in boom towns, where a man's business was his own. Most real "tough" characters would "burn" a man down at the first trace of an insult of any kind. One day after seeing this picture I was on my porch with a gun belt and holster around my waist and a toy cap revolver in the holster. The boy next door to me had a rifle which made a clicking sound. We agreed upon a gun-drawing match and he held the rifle in the crook of his arm, with the action lever back so it would make a sound; and I stood on my porch with the gun in the holster, with my hammer back, and my hand hovering near the gun butt. We went for our guns, and I beat him. We did this many times, and I won most of the matches. I also had a sombrero (my father's former hat).

A boy of 11 years.—The picture I saw was "The Dawn Patrol." After I came home, we played it. I pretended I was Richard Barthelmess. I pretended I was bombing the German ammunition dumps. Then I went over the airports and bombed the planes and killed the men. Then three German planes came after me. Von Richter, the best German aviator, came up too, and I shot him down and shot his pal also. But the other aviator came from the back and shot me.

A few instances are given showing the presence of mystery themes; the first is by a ten-year-old boy, and the other two by eight- and ten-year-old girls, respectively:

What I played after I came home from the movies is one play "Dracula." I pretended I was the vampire. I played especially good when I had to suck the blood out of the warden's daughter. The maniac who could change himself into a bug and crawl out of the prison bars called me his master. I also played well the part where I use my power, but fail to suck the doctor's blood. I loved to play the part where I disappear. I didn't like to have a big nail driven into my heart and make me lifeless, but it had to be done. I am still alive—thanks to God.

I like to be a Phantom and catch my sister. Then my sister screams. Then I put her in the fire and I play that she burns up and she doesn't come back alive any more. Then my sister is the Phantom, and she starts to put me in the fire, and she couldn't get me in, so another Phantom came in, and he got me in the fire and I was gone, and that was the end of me.

After I saw the "Gorilla" we went to Marjorie's playhouse. We played the show of the "Gorilla." Marjorie played the part of the gorilla, and the other girls played parts of the other people in the show. After a while we all get scared and hid our faces under things in the playhouse. I went home and couldn't think of anything except the Gorilla.

The predilection of children for the theme of combat and to a lesser extent for the theme of mystery is a problem not devoid of psychological significance. It may be the expression of certain nascent impulses, or it may reflect instead the dominant kind of themes ordinarily presented in motion pictures.

INTERPRETATION OF PLAY

OF greater and central importance is the effect on the child of impersonating a movie rôle or theme. To show that motion pictures influence the play of children is quite easy; to explain the significance of this play is very difficult. What is the residuary effect of such impersonation on attitude, interest, and thought? To make such an inquiry is to raise the larger problem as to the significance of play for the subsequent conduct and personalities of children. It is proper to essay a few remarks about this problem.

We may begin by calling attention to the absence in scientific thought of any adequate psychology of childhood play, particularly of that kind that takes the form of impersonation. The most familiar theory, and the only one to which we shall devote our remarks, is that of the German psychologist, Groos, who finding that play was common to many forms of animals was led to declare it to be essentially a preparation for the serious forms of adult behavior. Thus the play of the young kitten with the woolen ball is preparing its capacities and skill for pouncing on mice and other sources of food.

The effort to interpret the play under discussion by the theory of Groos does not yield much understanding or illumination. If we are to construe play, as would this theory, as a form of preparation for subsequent behavior, as a sort of incipient adult activity, then it would seem that much of motion-picture impersonation would be useless. It is true that in certain instances the rôles carried out in play may have a training value, as in the case of the young girl rehearsing love scenes, or practicing home life, or as in the experience of one boy who became successful in drama as a consequence, he believes, of his intensive movie play as a child.[1] Yet in the main the movie rôles taken by children are too confusing. Many of them are contradictory, such as between the "good guy" and the "bad guy," the detective and the gangster; many are of a weird and bizarre character, such as in the imitation of Dracula mentioned above; and many represent characters outside the range of modern experience, as in the case of medieval knights or primitive warriors. It is probably true in one sense that the taking of such rôles may develop a facility for the behavior which they represent. However, it is apparent that most of the rôles never have an opportunity to materialize in adult behavior.

Two phases of the effect of motion pictures in relation to the impersonation of rôles seem to stand out clearly in our materials: the earnestness of the child in play, and yet the ease with which he may detach himself from a rôle. The seriousness with which children engage in such play is apparent, yet very puzzling. As a rule, they show a keen

[1] See case in Appendix C, pages 223–233.

preoccupation with the rôle taken, marvelous attention to detail, ingenious accommodation of material to suit the plot, and above all a condition of heightened excitement. The living of the rôle seems quite genuine. Indeed, there are many instances in which the individual in the excitement of play loses control of himself and pays little attention to the consequences of his action. Behavior becomes impulsive and unreflective and on occasion distinctly harmful. This immersion in a rôle to the exclusion of ordinary thought of consequences can be illustrated in the following instances:

Male, 20, white, college sophomore.—One serial that I remember particularly was "The House of Hate," in which Pearl White was the heroine. This was one of the most exciting pictures that I ever remember seeing. It was a story about the antics of an insane man called the "Hooded Terror" who went about with a hood over his head, murdering people. After seeing one of these episodes we boys would come home and try to enact some of the parts. It was while we were playing like this one day that I nearly lost the sight of one eye. One of the other boys took the rôle of the "Terror" (who in the last episode that we had seen had gone around killing people by blowing poison darts through a pea shooter), and made some darts with needles, and proceeded to blow them at the rest of us; one of them hit me just to the right of my right eye, nearly making me lose the sight of it.

Male, 20, white, college junior.—Two peculiar events are still impressed upon my mind as directly resulting from the influence of the movies. Once we tied one of our members to an oak tree, and notwithstanding his frantic cries, proceeded with a boisterous war-dance about the victim. The struggling boy was almost strangled by the numerous coils of rope about his neck before his frenzied mother appeared to secure his release. At another time, I was compelled to walk home through the deep snow in my stocking feet because my playmates had chosen to forcibly remove my shoes and conceal them, in imitation of a humorous scene which they had witnessed at the theater on the same day.

Female, 15, white, high-school sophomore.—We used to act out the different movies we saw. I remember once we saw one that had robbers and policemen in it, and ever so long after that we played robbers. I always used to be the policeman; I guess the reason for that was because I was the tallest. One time we pretended we had a boy up to be shot. The boy that was to shoot had the gun, filled with peas, and he was supposed to direct them toward the boy's feet. The boy was nervous and instead of shooting at his feet shot at his head. The pea hit the boy's eye. The boy ran screaming home. He could not see out of the eye for several weeks after, and all of us that had been playing were sure scared that he would never be able to see again.

Male, 18, negro, high-school senior.—As a child I usually went to the show with my brother every Saturday afternoon, but now I usually go with my girl friend or chum. Once I went to see a cowboy picture and after returning home the little boy next door and I were playing with broomsticks calling them horses. I had a blank pistol, so I wanted to play Tom Mix. As the boy would run around me, I would run after him, so finally I decided I was close enough to shoot. The powder went in his skin; he hollered. Of course my mother heard it, and I was soundly spanked. This stopped me from going to wild west pictures for some time.

Such instances show the familiar trait of genuine seriousness in playing out motion-picture rôles and themes. Still this observation is to be set over against another; namely, the ease with which the rôle can be cast off. There need be no consistency in the rôles taken by children in play. At one moment the boy may be acting as a policeman, a few minutes later as a robber, and still later as a cowboy; and he may end up as an aviator. The ease with which children step from one rôle to another rôle is as interesting as it is apparent. It gives one the impression that, although the rôle taken is considered seriously, it seems to be worn lightly, like a cloak.

One may surmise from the genuine way in which the

child carries out the rôle in play that he acquires some feeling of its nature. The rôle becomes in some sense a part of intimate experience. The mode of life or the type of character which it represents becomes more familiar to him than it would to a disinterested observer, just because for the time being the rôle does gain possession of him. It is probably in giving to an individual a certain appreciation of familiarity with the character or rôle impersonated that impersonation is mainly important. The individual develops certain feelings which make the rôle understandable to him and forms images which cause him to interpret the rôle, or behavior similar to it, in certain fixed ways. In providing content for children's play, motion pictures may be regarded, then, as familiarizing the child with certain kinds of life, and in providing him with certain stereotyped conceptions of them.

Problem of Play

There remains the important problem as to the effect of childhood play on specific conduct. Thus, while it is clear that motion pictures exercise a significant influence on the pattern and content of play and in doing so, familiarize the child with certain forms of conduct, just what this signifies in the way of subsequent behavior cannot be declared at present. Does the taking of a rôle shape aspiration? Does it leave a deposit in the form of an attitude, disposition, or habit? Does it give a sanction to conduct which is at odds with customary standards? Does it alienate the child from the cultural milieu in which he lives? Does it stimulate unrest or make the child aware of the limited possibilities in his actual world? Does it make him look more sympathetically at tabooed characters and activities, and by assuming their rôles, to share their sentiments? [1] One would surmise that it would have some effects of these sorts, yet from the accounts of hundreds of high-school and university students who have passed through the stage of childhood play and who look back retrospectively, one can detect little in the nature of a deposit or carry-over of influence. The subjects recall their childhood play with warmth and pleasure, but express the belief that the play has been of little consequence on their subsequent attitudes and conduct, as far as they can judge. We have to conclude, then, with a problem. That motion pictures have a profound influence on children's play is incontestable. The significance of this influence, however, is uncertain. It depends on more knowledge than we now have of the effects of impersonation on attitude and character.

[1] Something of this effect is suggested in the following statement from the autobiography of a convict:
As soon as I got to be old enough to wander around a little without getting lost, my first thing I done was to get acquainted with the other neighborhood tots and we would all get our nickels together and go to see the thrilling western or crook pictures that happened to be shown in the neighborhood. It was a great thrill to see the guns in action in a big train robbery or cattle-rustling breakup. As soon as we got tired of looking straight up at pictures we would decide to go back to the neighborhood and start our evening game of "cops and robbers." It used to be hard for us kids to decide as to who would be the "coppers" because everyone wanted to be the bold robber they just saw in the moving pictures. As a small lad I did not have much use for a copper in crook plays, I always hoped the robber would get the best of the copper. I got a kind of grudge up when I saw the copper conquering the robber; I decided some day to grow up and show the coppers something, but I was only a child then. The boys always used to choose me for their chief robber, because I was the biggest and strongest, and if they wouldn't choose me as chief, I would punch a few of them and break up the game. I was always a very bad man for the kid coppers to catch and if they would corner me, I'd fight my way out. So you see motion pictures were responsible a little in bringing or starting me up in the racket.
For a further discussion of this point see the author's *Movies, Delinquency, and Crime*, Chapter III.

CHAPTER III

IMITATION BY ADOLESCENTS

In childhood play the element of make-believe is a conspicuous feature. This accounts in a measure for the difficulty we encounter in evaluating the significance of the impersonation of movie rôles by children. Our materials seem to show, however, that among older individuals there is a wide imitation of motion picture patterns which are seriously incorporated into conduct and so pass out of the realm of mere make-believe. In this chapter attention is directed to the most conspicuous forms of such imitation, which are grouped under the heads of Beautification, Mannerisms, and Technique. If one may think of the imitation of the patterns for play as characterizing childhood, one may think of the copying of make-up, mannerisms, and technique as a mark chiefly of adolescents. In contrasting the behavior of these two age groups in this respect, the essential difference is between impersonation and copying—meaning by the latter the actual utilization in the ordinary conduct of life of what is imitated.

BEAUTIFICATION AND DRESS

It is common knowledge that motion pictures provide patterns for dress and beautification. They serve many as one of the main sources of information on styles of clothing and make-up. Probably every reader knows of some friend or acquaintance who has selected some detail of dress or make-up from motion pictures. The importance of motion pictures in the presentation of models of dress has been recognized recently by the employment in one of the producing companies of a famous Parisian fashion expert. It is not necessary to give more than a few instances of the influence of motion pictures on dress and beautification. The following have been chosen at random:

Female, 19, Jewish, white, college sophomore.—I remember that I got my first striking illumination through the movies of the difference clothes may make in appearance. It was in Daddy Long-Legs where Mary Pickford paraded for five scenes, bare-legged, in dark brown cast-offs, pig-tailed, and freckle-faced, good, sweet, but hardly beautiful; and then in the final scene, after a visit from Daddy and a bath in milk, with the curls down, the gangly knees covered, the ankles silk-shod, in pink satin, pearl-studded dress, a re-born gorgeous queen she emerged, as striking as the caterpillar-butterfly transition. At home that night I tentatively hinted about putting my daily glass of milk to better use, wound my straight black hair in tortuous curl papers, draped myself in red gauze, and compared effects. Since then I have carefully studied, attempted, and compared the effects of these past mistresses of the art of dressing and make-up. They are always first with the latest, my most reliable guide to styles, colors, accessories, combinations, lines, and general effects. So varied are the types, it is simple to pick out the ones they most closely resemble, and thus learn to bring out my best points. I have a little two-piece sweater suit suggested by something I saw on Colleen Moore; Norma Talmadge was the inspiration for my dignified dinner dress; my next formal is going to be a reproduction of something that was bewitching on Nita Naldi; and I am wearing my hair with a view to getting the same entrancing effect that Greta Garbo gets with hers.

Female, 19, white, college junior.—I am always more interested in what the heroine wears than in what she does. Most dresses worn in movies are too striking or too elaborate for me to copy, but where there is shown a different collar, a pretty cuff, or a novel trimming it is certain to crop out in some dress.

Female, 16, white, high-school junior.—Most likely if it weren't for the movies we would wait a long time for styles to change. I copy all the collegiate styles from the movies. In the "Wild Party," starring Clara Bow, she wears a kind of sleeveless jumper dress which attracted my attention very much. Nothing could be done about it. My mother had to buy me one just like it.

Female, 16, white, high-school junior.—No, I don't think that I have ever imitated any stars in their manners. But I remember after having seen "Our Dancing Daughters" with Joan Crawford, I wanted a dress exactly like one she had worn in a certain scene. It was a very "flapper" type of dress, and I don't usually go in for that sort of thing.

Female, 19, white, college sophomore.—Just one other habit I will speak about which I adopted from the movies and that is the use of perfume on my ear lobes when I am going out (whether on a date or just a dinner engagement). This habit I acquired when I was about eleven years old; I do not know whether it is done generally or not, but I saw Norma Talmadge do it once and then her husband kissed her aside on her ear, and I thought, "Well, that is something new."

Frequently the tendency to copy types of dress and beautification seen on the screen appears in the semi-play activity of children. This type of behavior is shown in the following instances:

Female, 19, white, college freshman.—My interest became centered in hair dress—due to the fact that my hair was going through the growing stage. Many an hour have I spent trying to effect some style I had admired in the movies, so effectively, in fact, that I almost burned the cherished locks off and the shoulder bob curls seemed doomed for a while. This new way of dressing my hair "went over" fairly well with the family, but when I attempted to wear an ankle bracelet one evening, I learned that certain adornments in the "reel" world are not always appreciated in the real world.

Female, 19, Jewish, white, college sophomore.—Then came the fascinating production, "The Poor Little Rich Girl." I think I saw it three times, and as a result, let my hair grow and put it up in rags every night. I became an ardent Mary Pickford fan and hardly a picture of hers escaped me—"Pollyanna," "Rebecca of Sunnybrook Farm," and the rest.

The tabulation of instances of imitation of dress and mannerisms from the motion picture autobiographies of 458 high-school students shows that 62 per cent report having made such imitations, 16 per cent are not aware of having made any imitation, and 22 per cent do not give indications which permit one to judge either way. It is clear from these figures that motion pictures are an important source of ideas of dress and beautification for many young men and women.

Imitation of Mannerisms

The interest shown by adolescents in the gestures and mannerisms displayed on the screen is not less keen than it is in the dress of the actors. Many kinds of pictures, particularly those dealing with society drama, portray forms of polite life in a vivid fashion. In doing so, they provide models of conduct for individuals who aspire to such life. This is seen in the following instances:

Female, 15, white, high-school sophomore.—Then came my desire for romantic pictures. By this time I was allowed to go to the shows more often and was a bit older (14 years). I took a great interest in the "pretty girls." I noticed how they wore their hair and I especially watched their actions; by this I mean, when the setting would be in a café I would watch how the young ladies sat at the table, how they managed to carry on a conversation, and how they danced. These things had quite an influence upon me. I wanted to "fix my hair nice," and act nice in the presence of my masculine friends.

Male, 20, white, college sophomore.—The appearance of such handsome men as John Gilbert, Ben Lyon, Gilbert Roland, and the host of others, dressed in sport clothes, evening attire, formals, etc., has encouraged me to dress as best possible in order to make a similar appearance. One acquires positions such as standing, sitting, tipping one's hat, holding one's hat, offering one's arm to a lady, etc., from watching these men who do so upon the screen, and especially if they do it in a manner pleasing to your tastes.

Female, 19, white, college freshman.—When I discovered I should like to have this coquettish and coy look which all girls may have, I tried to do it in my room. And surprises! I could imitate Pola Negri's cool or fierce look, Vilma Banky's sweet but coquettish attitude. I learned the very way of taking my gentlemen friends to and from the door with that wistful smile, until it has become a part of me.

Female, 20, white, college sophomore.—When I see an actress who makes a good appearance by standing and sitting with a straight back, I try to do the same. Good posture in an actress influences me a lot, also a graceful way of sitting. I think one learns from the movies something in the best of ways of portraying one's charms. A graceful way of sitting (as I have mentioned) is one way to present a charming picture. One can set forth one's figure and limbs in a graceful and appealing manner. I believe that I try to sit gracefully when I want to make a good appearance, in imitation of much of what I have seen on the screen.

Something of the variety of items which may be copied is indicated in the excerpt from the account of a high-school girl:

Female, 15, white, high-school sophomore.—I will add that I picked up little trivial mannerisms. Some of these may seem foolish, but as this seems to be a sort of confession anyway, I'll confess; I figured that when I ever want anything real badly and am almost at the point of tears begging for it, I should clench my fists; that when I go out for the evening, drop earrings are more becoming than the screw earrings; that my hair behind my ears, like Greta Garbo, emphasizes the facial contour; that when I cry, I should not even attempt to wipe away the tears as they are so much more effective rolling downwards; and then there are hosts of other similar trivialities.

The following remarks represent the judgment of a college girl concerning the extent of imitation of mannerisms among her companions at high school:

Female, 20, white, college junior.—The discussing of movies at high school was an indoor sport. The girls and boys always talked of the pictures. They imitated the gestures and mannerisms of their favorite stars. They wiggled their eyebrows, moved their eyes in a certain way, pursed their lips to create an impression on each other. In this I was no better than the rest.

The accounts which have been given illustrate the copying of gestures and mannerisms by older girls and boys. Such copying, of course, extends down into childhood experiences. In fact, it is very difficult to draw a clean-cut line between the imitation of mannerisms in play and the later deliberate practicing of gestures in more serious conduct. The following instance shows borderline behavior representing incidentally conduct which one finds rather frequently in children.

Male, 20, white, college junior.—Yes, constantly I practiced Bill Hart's narrowing of the eyes, twitching of the face muscles. I was never able to reproduce it as Bill did. I tried, I persevered, I did everything I could—but never could I reproduce Bill's murderous, menacing look. I never decided where I would use it. After months of tortuous, vain sweating before the mirror—interrupted on different occasions by my mother or father, sister or brother—I gave it up. I didn't decide that Bill's look wasn't worth while. I finally concluded that I didn't have the stuff. It was Bill's alone.

As in this instance, so in the case of others, there is considerable practicing before a mirror, of mannerisms and poses seen in motion pictures.

Female, 19, white, college sophomore.—Naturally, I pictured myself in the place of my favorite actresses, and often would stand before a mirror and try to assume some graceful position characteristic of them that I admired and wanted to copy.

Female, 17, white, high-school junior.—If I was impressed by
the beauty of the heroine, I usually tried to imitate her facial
expression. I seldom failed to dramatize some scene that particularly appealed to me. This I did in front of my mirror when
I was alone in my room, and I enjoyed doing it very much.

Female, 19, Negro, high-school senior.—Oh, to possess what
Miss Bow has—that elusive little thing called "it!" After seeing
her picture by that name, I immediately went home to take stock
of my personal charms before my vanity mirror and after carefully surveying myself from all angles I turned away with a sigh,
thinking that I may as well want to be Mr. Chaney. I would be
just as successful.

The significance of the imitation of mannerisms and poses
by adolescent girls and boys comes in recognizing that at
this age they are usually being introduced to a realm of
life somewhat new and strange. Forms of conduct may
be imitated which promise to aid them in their adjustment,
and at the same time to satisfy aspirations to be popular,
"stunning," "proper," and sophisticated. Many motion
pictures depict the life of polite society and deal in a vivid
way with the conduct of young men and women. Selection of details for imitation is relatively easy for the interested observer. Viewed in this way, the mannerisms copied
from motion pictures serve as a control—that is, as an
instrument to adjustment or to the satisfaction of one's
desires.

TRYING OUT WHAT IS IMITATED

As one might expect from these remarks there is a great
deal of experimentation of the mannerisms or poses chosen
from motion pictures. Whether in mirror-posing, or in
association with one's companions, mannerisms are tried
out as a means of gauging their personal effectiveness.
Some are found to be successful and are taken on; much

of what is imitated seems to be rejected shortly. This is frequently the result of disapproval or censure by others who regard unfavorably the conduct shown by the one who has made the initial imitation. The experimental character of this imitation of mannerisms with the subsequent acceptance or rejection of different forms of behavior is brought out in the following abbreviated accounts:

Female, 15, white, high-school sophomore.—I have attempted to imitate the manners of several actresses, but I have never received any satisfactory results. I bobbed my hair when I was only eight years old, as a result of seeing someone in the movies doing likewise. I try to walk and move with ease and grace, but I find that it is a little difficult to act like others if I can't see how I look. I remember one movie star, Mabel Normand, who had large eyes, and from the admiring of them I gradually began to stare at others with wide eyes. My friends thought there was something wrong with my eyes because I did this, and perhaps I did acquire poor eyesight as a result. At other times I curled my hair, manicured my fingernails, and dressed like my favorite stars. Of course my attempts never brought any pleasing results, so I abandoned my imitations and became original. Sometimes I posed for hours at a time before my dressing table mirror, posing with my hands about my face, and moving my arms as gracefully as I could. In the movies, it always seems that the innocent, wide-eyed girls have the most suitors, and that shyness promotes respect and adoration on the part of the opposite sex. When I went to parties I tried to be a meek little maid, but it proved to be a failure in attracting sweethearts; only gay and vivid types are wanted by the modern generation.

Female, 20, white, college sophomore.—I'll admit I have watched Clara Bow to a great extent to see how she develops "It," and I'll also admit I've done my best to have "It" too. However, I'm certain it is nothing more than a pleasing or rather more than pleasing personality.

Female, 15, white, high-school freshman.—Once in a while I decide to wear sloppy socks like Sue Carol does. But my father does not approve of it. I only wish we could wear them to school, which I can't, of course. I simply adore Greta Garbo. She wears her clothes so sporty, and the way men fall for her. Boy! I'll bet every girl wishes she was the Greta Garbo type. I try to imitate her walk. She walks so easy, as if she had springs on her feet. But when I try to copy her walk, I am asked if my knees are weak. How insulting some people are!

The following is a more concrete account of an attempt to make use of a particular mannerism—this time, however, with ineffective results:

Female, 19, white, college sophomore.—About two years ago I saw a picture in which the heroine very coyly, when conversing with a young man, would close her eyes, slightly nod her head and smile. And when she closed her eyes, her eye-lashes were shown off to their best advantage. And so I decided that this was very "cute," and having always been vain about my eyes, I adopted the trick. It so happened that within about a week I attended a formal dance. During the evening I used my charms, but to my dismay they weren't appreciated; but rather criticized! After several closings of the eyes and noddings of the head, my friend asked me if I was tired and wished to start home. You are assured that I didn't continue my newly acquired trick. And my coquette career came to an early end.

AID TO ADJUSTMENT

INDIVIDUALS may retain certain mannerisms which have been found to be effective and which yield satisfactory adjustment to the mode of life which is encountered. Considering once more that the adolescent may be confronted by a type of life for which he is not prepared by training and experience, one can understand that by copying forms of conduct seen in the motion pictures he may adjust himself more easily. That these models may serve as aids to behavior and subsequently give the person control is suggested by the following instances:

Male, 21, white, college senior.—As I got into high school and into my sixteenth and seventeenth year I began to use the movies as a school of etiquette. I began to observe the table manners of the actors in the eating scenes. I watched for the proper way in which to conduct oneself at a night club, because I began to have ideas that way. The fact that the leading man's coat was single breasted or double breasted, the number of buttons on it, and the cut of its lapel all influenced me in the choice of my own suits.

Female, 19, white, college sophomore.—Movies first taught me that hands could be used so as to make them appear beautiful. A soft, relaxed pose, I learned, was the best; I began to notice carriage and bearing and to check up on myself and on others. Whenever I see a character with a nervous habit such as tapping of the table with a finger tip, rubbing the side of the cheek or swinging a leg, I hurriedly search myself lest I have any such habits.

Female, 19, white, college sophomore.—At present I am aware of two mannerisms which I have consciously adopted from the motion pictures or at least from actresses. The first is my manner of walking when I am wearing a formal evening dress; the second is the style of dressing my hair likewise for formal attire. I have consciously adopted these mannerisms for the simple reason that I think one must be cautious as to one's manner of walking and to becoming hair-dress. I think this either makes or mars a girl. The reason for my actually searching for an attractive gait and I might even say posing goes back to a dinner dance which I attended at high school some few years ago. I remember one young lady in particular (whom I will never forget); she was wearing a stunning evening gown. She had a pretty face and when she stood still she looked remarkably well. However, when she walked she just sort of sagged and flopped together; her shoulders rounded, her back looked hunched and her entire appearance was spoiled; no doubt her case was due to too high heels; at any rate she seemed to be laboring with her gait as if she were walking behind a plow. I noticed that each girl at the party had her own individual walk which proved either attractive or unattractive and I wondered what other people were thinking about me. Right there I decided I would adopt a definite walk and be more careful about standing straight; either

I would get my imitation from a screen star or from some story description. Immediately the movies proved helpful for I saw Gloria Swanson in "Fine Feathers" (or some title similar to that) and I have been trying to imitate her gait since then—carrying myself upright with a rather swagger effect and still acting as natural as possible. As you may well see, it is difficult to describe; but I might say, not as a matter of boldly bragging, many people have remarked that I carry myself very well in an evening dress; each one attributes the appearance to the manner of walking.

Female, 18, Negro, high-school senior.—Movies are the means by which a great many people obtain poise. This is especially true as far as girls are concerned. I am sure I haven't the poise of my movie idols, but I am trying to develop a more ladylike composure as I grow older. My father has caught me several times, as I stood before the mirror trying to tilt my head and hold my arms as the girls on the screen would do. He does not know that I am trying to create that sophisticated manner, which is essential for social success.

Male, 20, white, college sophomore.—When I first started going out with girls, I did not feel at home. I did not know how to conduct myself properly. After facing this situation for some time I attempted to conduct myself in a manner much like I had seen the young fellows do on the screen. That is, look comfortable, whether I was or not. I was very much surprised when it worked. Evidently I was not the only one in a very unpleasant position. Adopting an easy-going air brought me through many tight situations. I am very thankful that the movies gave me some education along certain lines of etiquette. Ways of address, conduct at the table, etc., have been incorporated into my conduct merely by seeing them in the movies.

This help furnished by motion pictures to the initiation of the novitiate is stated simply in the following excerpt from a life history of a country girl introduced into urban society:

Female, 24, white, college senior.—I soon detected a difference between my manners and those of the screen. Sometimes I shocked my people by trying out some new-fangled idea of etiquette. I remember while being chastised for my behavior on one occasion my sister spoke up and said, "Oh, she's just trying to act like that girl in the picture the other night." She had recognized my action. I may have shocked them, but on various occasions I shocked myself also. Sometimes before other boys and girls I'd try some of my stuff to show off, but imagine my chagrin when I had to fall back on my country manners, having come to a point where I did not know just what to do. Nevertheless, I gained sufficient knowledge to enable me to step from the one into the other easily when we left the country. But for real refinement the shy, modest manners I first knew were most becoming although little used today.

One girl writes in some detail about her successful use of an incidental mannerism selected from motion pictures. The account shows the rather careful attention paid by many to details of action as offering possibilities of subsequent employment.

Female, 19, white, college sophomore.—Then came the time when I became interested in men. I had heard older boys and girls talking about "technique" and the only way I could find out how to treat boys was through reading books and seeing movies. I had always known boys as playmates, but having reached my freshman year in high school they became no longer playmates but "dates." I didn't want it to be that way but it seemed inevitable. I was asked to parties and dances and friends' homes. The boys were older and sophisticated. I felt out of place. I noticed that older girls acted differently with boys than they did when with girls alone. I didn't know what to do.

I decided to try some of the mannerisms I had seen in the movies. I began acting quite reserved, and I memorized half-veiled compliments. I realized my "dates" liked it. I laid the foundation with movie material. Then I began to improvise.

Of course, I had a rival in the crowd. Every time she began to receive more attention from the boys than I, I would see a movie and pick up something new with which to regain their interest. I remember one disastrous occasion. She was taking the center of the stage, and I was peeved. I could think of nothing to do.

Then I remembered the afternoon before I had seen Nazimova smoke a cigarette, and I decided that would be my next move. The party was at a friend's home and I knew where her father's cigarettes were kept. I got one, lit it, and had no difficulty whatsoever in handling it quite nonchalantly. The boys were fascinated and the victory was mine.

Very frequently the imitation of mannerisms as well as of dress is not confined to the mere selection of this or that detail, but instead becomes part and parcel of the effort to emulate in its entirety the conduct of some favorite actress or actor. In such instances one seeks to act out a rôle in life—to mold one's own conduct in conformity to it. Psychologically this imitation is more deeply motivated and somewhat different from copying of separate mannerisms; and therefore it seems convenient to say a few words here on the matter. The character of this form of imitation is brought out in the following instance:

Female, 19, white, college sophomore.—When I became of high-school age I took a strong fancy to Norma Shearer. I went to see every one of her pictures. I wore my hair like hers, imitated her smile, and went into the seventh heaven of delight if told that I resembled her. Even though I am at an age now when I don't have crushes on movie stars, I still like Norma.

However, she goes on to remark:

I wouldn't be natural if I didn't like —— ————. She is really the modern gin-crazy type. But her eyes! They make her. If I could look like her, I'd give Norma Shearer the air.

The following humorous account reveals the same point in the case of a young boy:

Male, 16, white, high-school sophomore.—When Wesley Barry was in his height of popularity, it was my ambition to become an actor like Mr. Barry. I was going to try because I had the ideal make-up for him, having red hair and oh! so many freckles. Every movie that Mr. Barry played in I went to see. I soon got into the idea of walking around with my hands in my pockets, my hair not combed; and my hands, face, and clothes were very dirty. Another thing I tried to imitate was going barefoot. Many a toe I have stubbed which has caused me agony, and many a cut I received on the bottom of my feet; and oftentimes I would go barefoot when it was too cold for bare feet.

Experiences more typical of adolescent girls are shown in the following:

Female, 17, white, high-school senior.—I have tried in many ways to adopt the mannerisms of my favorite actress, Anita Page. My first realization of this was after I had seen her picture entitled "Our Dancing Daughters." This picture, as well as Anita Page, thrilled me as no other picture ever has or ever will. She didn't take the part of the good and innocent girl, but she was the cheat and the gold-digger. One would think the leading man could never "fall" for that type of girl, but he certainly did. Many a time I have tried to tilt my head as she did, and wear my hair in back of my ears, and even stood in front of the mirror going through the same actions she had done.

Female, 18, white, high-school senior.—At different times, or after each movie, I think there is a great tendency to try to act like the girl you have just seen. Clara Bow has been my ideal girl, and I have tried to imitate some of her mannerisms. The way she wears her hair (which is a rather hard thing to do, because she changes the style so often), how she rolls her eyes, her quick smile, and all her little actions. I have learned from the movies how to be a flirt, and I have found out that at parties and elsewhere the coquette is the one who enjoys herself the most.

Female, 17, white, high-school junior.—In the movies the girls were always beautiful and lady-like and so I tried to be too. When I was twelve years old I had already decided to join a "bathing beauty" contest when I was old enough. I'd pose for a long while some times before the big mirror trying to get "effects." The reason I was such a conceited person is because I had been told I resembled a movie actress and I tried to look like her as much as possible. She had a beautiful face and figure and I determined to be like her. At night in bed I would lie awake and day-dream about the big hit I would make if I were to go to California.

The remarks which have been made and illustrated concerning the experimental character of imitation apply also in the emulation of an actress or actor. A given rôle may "take" and be retained or else found to be unadvantageous and so be abandoned. Whatever the disposition, such instances show how people may copy mannerisms and schemes of behavior from motion pictures.

IMITATION OF LOVE TECHNIQUES

A third form of imitation of conduct portrayed in motion pictures may be termed "technique," in accordance with increasing use of this word in the vernacular. This term refers to a particular way of doing something; the form of behavior is regarded as a devise or instrument leading to the realization of a definite end. Probably the most interesting technique to adolescents shown in motion pictures is that of love.

It is an item of common knowledge that forms of love-making are presented with extreme vividness in motion pictures. Of course, love appears as the main theme in the majority of productions. General recognition of the great attention paid to the theme of love in motion pictures, and evidence showing extensive copying of love-technique dictate some consideration of this form of imitation. From the sample of 458 motion-picture autobiographies written by high-school students it has been found that in 33 per cent definite imitation from motion pictures of the ways of making love was present. In 28 per cent of the cases there is a definite denial of this kind of effect; whereas in 39 per cent information is lacking which permits one to judge either way. These figures err, if at all, on the side of conservatism because of the reluctance of many self-conscious adolescent boys and girls to admit copying such forms of behavior from motion pictures. It is safe to assume that the extent of such imitation is even greater than is shown by the figures mentioned.

The instances which are given as illustrative of this kind of influence of motion pictures are but a few of many and have been chosen to exhibit the different kinds of experiences written about by high-school and college students. While some of the descriptions may seem "sensational," they are presented merely to show a significant type of influence wielded by motion pictures on the conduct of young men and young women.

Early instances of the imitation of forms of love-making appear in the semi-play of girls or older children, and in the so-called "puppy-love" of early adolescents. In these instances, the behavior is still somewhat of a fanciful or play-like character, although it may easily become more serious. The following cases will illuminate the nature of this early use of love-making copied from the screen:

Male, 20, white, college sophomore.—Love stories and pictures never held much attraction for me at this time (age 12). I had a cousin, however, who was extremely fond of them. As she was one year older than I, and was much stronger and bigger, I had to do as she wished. She would make me go with her to see ————— ————— and ————— ————— in some of their silly love pictures; and then when we returned home, she made me make love to her as she had seen the other two do on the screen. I did not appreciate this at all. Whenever we boys would go to see a love picture and the hero kissed the heroine we would always make a lot of noise and smack our lips very loudly.

Female, 16, white, high-school junior.—I have one girl friend that I love a good deal. She and I have been kissing each other "hello" and "good-by" for some time. It is on her that I make use of the different ways of kissing that I see in the movies.

Male, 20, white, college sophomore.—After I entered high school I got to going out with girls and often took them to the movies. It was then that I became interested in passionate love scenes and deep, soulful pictures. After I had had one unsuccessful love I became aware of the basis for so many of the pictures. Often I would actually live the picture out. My favorite actors and actresses then changed to the type that was young and good-looking. In acting and talking to a girl I would often use the knowledge I gained from the screen and the actors. During my puppy loves this was especially true.

When the relations between girls and boys become more serious, as in the case of courtship, schemes of love-making are used more in accordance with their meaning in motion pictures. The following cases are a few examples of many autobiographical accounts showing this more serious use of "love-technique."

Male, 22, white, college sophomore.—By this time in my life I had begun to pay some attention to girls. I soon lost my enthusiasm over western pictures and developed a sudden appreciation of love pictures. I tried to dress after the fashion of the hero in these pictures. Of course, I had a girl that I called my sweetheart, and whom I wooed with all the technique of loving that I learned from my movie idols. Whenever I kissed her I tried to imitate the movie hero who had perhaps just rescued his girl from the villain.

Male, 18, white, high-school senior.—The first interest in love pictures came when I was about fourteen. This interest gradually developed as I grew older. I became more interested in girls, and began to love them. I sometimes practiced making love to my friends, after I had seen a love scene. I have seen plays of love and passion where children were not admitted, and from this I got ideas of how to make love to a girl.

Female, 14, Negro, high-school sophomore.—I learn how the movie stars kiss and make a dumb-dora out of boys they don't care for.

Male, 21, white, college senior.—The technique of making love to a girl received considerable of my attention, and it was directly through the movies that I learned to kiss a girl on her ears, neck, and cheeks, as well as on the mouth.

Female, 16, white, high-school junior.—When I saw "The Pagan" I fell harder than ever for Ramon Navarro. All my girl friends talk about is these wonderful love stories. When I see a picture like that it makes me like my steady boy friend all the more. All I have ever done is kiss him good night; and it happens that through the movies I have learned to close my eyes, and I use that "Deep Bend —— ——" pose.

Female, 17, white, high-school junior.—I have learned some technique. I have sometimes told the boy friend, "Well, here goes for —— ——," but otherwise I don't copy anyone.

Many of the writers tell in their autobiographies of observing their associates employing forms of love-technique which have been taken from motion pictures. Girls, particularly, mention incidents of such behavior in the case of their boy companions. Two instances of this sort are given here to illustrate the point.

Female, 15, white, high-school sophomore.—Many times I've been with my friends and have thought of how some actress talked, or kissed her lover. Many times fellows have tried new ways of loving on me which they have seen, such as: how —— —— holds and kisses the actress which he plays opposite, or something of that nature.

Female, 16, white, high-school junior.—I know a fellow who (every time I'm with him) wants to neck. He wants to practice, I guess, but I have a sneaking suspicion that he's got his method from the screen. It's so absolutely absurd. I get a kick out of watching him work up a passion—just like —— ——, but it doesn't mean a thing. Now, that fellow is absolutely getting an education from the films, but what good does it do him? It makes him appear silly. He's a nice fellow, though, but he has his "weakness."

From the accounts one judges that many boys and girls feel that they are expected to use such forms of conduct in their association with their companions; or else they anticipate such behavior in the case of their associates. Something of this sort is suggested by the two following cases:

Female, 15, white, high-school sophomore.—From watching love scenes in the movies I have noticed that when a girl is kissed she closes her eyes; this I found that I also unconsciously do. I guess it shows whether or not a girl is thrilled if she opens or closes her eyes. When with the opposite sex I am rather quiet and allow them to tell me what to do. When they go to make love, to kiss or hug, I put them off at first, but it always ends in them having their way. I guess I imitated this from the movies because I see it in almost every show I go to.

Female, 19, white, high-school sophomore.—When I had my first "puppy" love affair I was very much disillusioned in my Prince Charming because he merely pecked me when he kissed me. In fact, I was quite disgusted—I thought him bashful, and a fool for not knowing how to kiss after seeing so many movies.

Some of the girls call attention in their accounts to the frequency with which love practices are shown in motion pictures and express their judgment that it is natural for such practices to be copied by young men and women. Since these judgments arise out of personal experience, as is clearly seen in the accounts, they may be submitted as further evidence on the nature and extent of imitation of conduct shown in motion pictures. Several of these declarations follow:

Female, 16, white, high-school junior.—What movie does not offer pointers in the art of kissing? I do not think that it is surprising that the younger generation has such a fine technique. Movies have become so universal and apartments so small that the modern miss and her boy friend have to go to the movies so that the family may retire (the in-a-door bed is probably in the living room). A young couple sees the art of necking portrayed on the screen every week for a month or so, and is it any wonder they soon develop talent? I am not allowed to have dates at home, so I know how true this is.

Female, 15, white, high-school sophomore.—I have learned quite a bit about love-making from the movies. They have so many love scenes nowadays that it can't be helped. They sure know how to pose for a kiss, especially —— —— and —— ——, and also how to perform it.

Female, 16, white, high-school junior.—In some movies I think there is too much love-making which is sickening, but on a whole the love scenes are sure to be imitated. Especially the manner in which an actor holds and kisses an actress, how long, and the pose they both take. As for myself, I get—well, in slang I would say a big kick out of watching movies, and then when going to a party see the boy-friend trying to do the same thing or do as near like it as possible.

Female, 17, Jewish, white, high-school junior.—What I have learned about love-making in the movies I never have exhibited although many young girls think a way to attract boys is to wear tight clothes and keep their hair bushy with curls, as —— —— does.

Female, 17, white, high-school senior.—I think that a lovelier pair than —— and —— cannot be found. I think that they are divine in their love scenes. My boy friends try to act like —— does. It's funny to watch the way they try to kiss you and embrace you, and the expression they get on their faces, just like —— and other he-men in the movies.

The forms of "technique" which may be selected from motion pictures and appropriated for use may consist merely of small items, as in certain details of kissing, or in the use of one's eyes in attracting attention. They may also, however, include larger patterns of conduct covering, for instance, the full span of one's relation to the opposite sex. A rather detailed statement of the use of a "flirtation" pattern selected from motion pictures appears in the following account written by a high-school girl:

Female, 16, Negro, high-school sophomore.—I imagine from what I see in the movies that love-making is very interesting, and I imagine there is fun in it. Before I was old enough to realize what love-making was, I would just see a love picture and that was all. But now when I go to parties I go for a good time and not to see someone else have a good time. I always go with a girl friend and she is very flirty, and I keep up with her. We flirt and talk with the boys; then sometimes we leave one party and go to another one in a car with two boys. We go out for a good time and we have it. One night my girl friend and I went out and we said we were going to try —— —— method about "Love 'em and leave 'em." When we arrived at the party we were introduced to some very good-looking boys. They offered to take us car-riding. We accepted. While out, they began to ask us many questions about love and making love to us. We didn't resist and when we had gotten home, we made a date for the next evening and we never did see those boys again, and we kept doing this until we got tired. I wanted to see if that method would or could work for me and my pal.

THE MOVIES—A SOURCE OF INFORMATION ON LOVE BEHAVIOR

THE instances which have been given offer a picture of the variety in the selection and appropriation of techniques of love-making which are presented in motion pictures. They force upon one the realization that motion pictures provide, as many have termed it, "liberal education in the art of loving." Many boys and girls secure from motion pictures much of their information on forms of conduct incident to relations between the sexes. *A priori*, this is to be expected. Boys and girls whose interests are being attracted to love seek knowledge of items of conduct which may be involved. Motion pictures with their vivid display of love-techniques offer a means of gaining such knowledge. The possibilities of motion pictures in providing such instruction are suggested in the accounts already given, but are shown more fully in the following statements of experience:

Male, 19, white, college sophomore.—Not being much interested in flirting and vamping, I have not received from the movies any ways of flirting or vamping. And beyond the "collegiate" clothes I imitated from the screen, I have not learned any new or valuable ways to show my masculine charm (if any!). But I have learned a great deal about how to kiss and make love, a subject in which I am still so profoundly ignorant that it will take a great many more movie experiences before I will have become an expert in the art. But since my osculatory experiences must await the time when SHE says "yes," I haven't taken advantage of my movie education. Nevertheless, I am bubbling over with ideas along that line, and I don't think I'll have much difficulty, thanks to my movie education, in learning the technique of kissing.

Female, 20, white, college sophomore.—But movies are a liberal education in the art of making love. Every young person probably appreciates a love scene subjectively. I never learned any ways of flirting, because flirting is against the family code. I did learn something about the art of kissing, however; that the tableau looked far more graceful if the young lady put more weight on one foot than on the other; the effect was softer. It has been helpful, too, to see how two screen lovers manage their arms when they are embracing; there is a definite technique; one arm over, the other under.

Male, 20, white, college sophomore.—As I progressed in years I became interested in the girls about me at school and at play and had a sweetheart whom I admired from afar, for as yet I was so bashful I became tongue-tied in her presence. I recall how I wished that I could be as free and easy in their presence as Rudolph Valentino was, and I watched for his pictures with special interest for I thought that I might be able to assimilate some of his ability or technique, if you wish to call it that, and would be able to use it on my girl.

Female, 19, white, college sophomore.—The movies certainly teach a person to flirt or perfect one's self-developed powers of flirting. They have, in a way, taught me a little in the use of my eyes for different purposes—the demure, the childish, the quaint, the puzzled, the come-hither, or go-thither glances (and such that a girl in her youth makes use of); and they have all been strengthened by learning different uses for them.

Male, 19, Jewish, white, college sophomore.—I do admit that I have learned not a little "amateur" necking from such pictures as "Children of the Ritz." Whether I have applied my knowledge or not, I will not relate. Kissing, vamping, flirting, making love, etc., are a very valuable educational influence in the lives of the younger generation. Such techniques are very necessary, and I feel that here the movies are performing a real service.

In our discussion of mannerisms some attention was paid to the trying out of schemes of conduct which the subject attempts to approximate by deliberate copying. Such experimentation is also found, as one might expect, in the use of love-techniques. In view of the interest which pictures depicting love have for boys and girls who are, as many of them confess, unenlightened in this respect, it perhaps is to be expected that some "trying out" would be made of certain techniques. A case of whole-hearted experimentation along this line has been selected from the autobiography of a high-school senior, a girl aged eighteen:

White.—Most of my ideas of love have been formed by the movies. It seems on the screen that the wild girl or the one that pets gets the one she loves. I am now trying that method and am going to see how it will work. However, I find it pretty hard to kiss someone else besides the one I love. But the movie heroine does it, and so can I. The movies give one many ideas and I'm going to try this one. Time will tell.

As in the case of all experimentation there is here a process of rejection and appropriation. Individuals who "try out" love-techniques seen in motion pictures may suceed or may fail. To experience failure, frequently, is to discourage further imitations of motion pictures. Instances of unfortunate results, or of futility in using love-techniques, are given in the following series of experiences:

Male, 18, white, high-school senior.—Oh! for imitating a star I'm a card. Once I tried to imitate ——— ——— smart-alecness at a dance, by kissing the girl I was dancing with. She gave me a "sock" in the jaw. As I saw she didn't like it, I went to her and apologized to her. This convinced me that imitating a motion picture star does not work; I gave it up.

Male, 19, white, college sophomore.—When only fourteen years of age I fell in love with one of my classmates; and I can remember that after seeing Rudolph Valentino in "The Sheik of Araby," I would try to make love to my girl as he did to the heroine, but I guess I was a miserable failure.

Male, 20, white, college sophomore.—As to the art of kissing, the movies truly make of it an art supreme. Well, in spite of my attempts to duplicate such, I have not been an entire success.

Male, 17, white, high-school senior.—The movies were the first to give me the idea of kissing a girl. I tried it twice, but I failed to get the thrill out of it that was plainly evident when the hero kissed the heroine.

Male, 20, white, college junior.—Later Valentino. I studied his style. I realized that nature had done much less for me in the way of original equipment than she had for the gorgeous Rodolfo, but I felt that he had a certain technique that it would behoove me to emulate. I practiced with little success. My nostrils refused to dilate—some muscular incompetency that I couldn't remedy. My eyes were incapable of shooting sparks of fiery passion that would render the fair sex helpless. I made only one concrete trial. The young lady who was trial-horse for the attempt is still dubious about my mental stability. Worse yet, she made a report of the affair to her friends. The comments that came drifting back to me left no doubt in my mind about the futility of carrying on any longer. I gave up.

Male, 20, Jewish, white, college junior.—I say without hesitation or embarrassment that on more than one occasion I have attempted to imitate the John Gilbert-Greta Garbo methods of love-making and that while the fleeting glimpse of Gilbert technique has not been sufficient to teach me to become the world's greatest lover, I place the blame not on my inability to imitate what I have seen on the screen, but on somebody else's inability to imitate Greta Garbo's receptive qualities. But then we're still both going to movies.

It is probable that most forms of love conduct copied from motion pictures prove unsatisfactory in use, and so are abandoned, or else merely entertained in imagination. A number of the writers of the motion-picture life histories speak, however, of the successful employment of schemes selected from motion pictures. A few illustrations may be cited:

Male, 18, white, high-school senior.—I think what benefited me the most from the movies was manners. I think that most of my manners I learned at the movies. It has shown me other parts of the world, which I don't expect to see. I have learned how to make love and kiss a girl, and the most peculiar part is that it works.

Female, 19, Jewish, white, college sophomore.—To-day I have no ideal—it is rather ideas that the heroines give me now. I am especially interested in those closest to my own possibilities, in all points about them, but especially with the more perfect actresses (I pick them by their acting now), in their carriage, conduct, and particularly love-making technique—I find this much more suggestive and effective than I could possibly find any book by, say, Elinor Glyn on How to Hold Your Man.

Female, 19, white, college sophomore.—Although I have never adopted any ways of flirting, I do not mean that I have never tried out the technique of the stars. Once I decided to try out a type of eye work that I had admired in a movie. It worked so well that I have not dared to use it since.

Female, 19, white, college sophomore.—Now here's a real confession! Ever since I saw Joan Crawford use her eyes to flirt with people, I caught that trick and use it to good advantage.

Finally, we have accounts which show how individuals may appreciate the aid which motion pictures may give in this respect, indicating, incidentally, that what was copied has proved of value in adjusting oneself to different situations:

Female, 17, white, high-school senior.—I have learned how to flirt, and how to "handle 'em." I have also learned different ways of kissing, and what to say when made love to. I have had all kinds of chances to use what I've learned from moving pictures, and I've taken advantage of them. If it hadn't been for what I've learned from the movies and seen what the actresses did in such cases, it would go hard with me at times.

Male, 22, white, college junior.—As I look back over my experiences, it occurs to me that in this matter of the technique of love-making I have been more influenced by the movies than by any other factor. My ideas about love I received from books, but my "method," to put it rather crudely, I got from the movies. Incidentally I am not sure whether this influence has been wholesome or otherwise. Without it I might have become an unbearable prude; with it I was encouraged into indiscretions which I have later come to regret. On the whole, I think it was an evil; but, as with most evils, it was not unmixed with elements of good.

Several of the last accounts suggest the use of ideas, gained from motion pictures, as aids to adjustment in critical situations. In so far as motion pictures portray types of life which are likely to be encountered in the experience of a young man and woman, they may suggest ways of successfully meeting situations peculiar to this life. The formal relations between young men and women, the methods of attracting attention, courtship, and even more intimate relations are likely to be novel and unfamiliar situations to many. Motion pictures may furnish knowledge of how to act in such situations.

CONCLUSION

FROM the discussion of childhood play and adolescent imitation it appears that there is a considerable amount of copying of forms of conduct shown in motion pictures. Our consideration has been devoted to those forms of such imitation that are most widely current and outstanding in the written accounts of the experiences of boys and girls, young men and young women. The discussion is not meant to convey the impression that selections from motion pictures are confined to patterns of play, mannerisms, gestures, and forms of conduct in relation to the opposite sex. There are undeniably many other details in motion pictures which are chosen by the spectators. Material objects such as household furnishings, forms of interior decoration, schemes of architecture, patterns of business behavior and other items are subject to imitation, as is shown by casual and scattered references in the motion-picture autobiographies. Such instances merely strengthen one's appreciation of the extent to which motion pictures are influential in the matter of imitation. As has already been remarked, in this discussion attention has been given mainly to those forms of copying which appear outstanding and salient in the accounts.

It is extremely difficult, of course, to ascertain the extent of this imitation with exactness. Yet the evidence is quite conclusive in indicating that the degree is by no means small, if we may take the subjects of this report as somewhat representative of the general population in the age groups considered.

The explanation of why young people imitate forms of conduct presented in motion pictures does not seem to be an abstruse problem. It is much too simple, of course, to assume that because a detail of action or of a situation is shown it will therefore be automatically imitated. The psychology of imitation is somewhat more complicated. Its nature, however, seems to be reasonably clear; in the judgment of the writer it might be summed up in the statement that if an individual sees some form of conduct which promises to aid the realization of one of his aims, it is likely to be chosen. Thus, the young boy interested in play is quite likely to select as a theme the daring combativeness of a Wild West picture. The high-school girl who is interested in making herself beautiful and popular may be expected to select details of beautification and conduct which may be effective to the fulfillment of such interests. The young man who has become concerned with the courtship of girls is quite likely to choose types of behavior that he regards as helpful in such courtship. The delinquent boy who witnesses some clever manner of burglarizing might be counted on having some disposition to use it if it offers possibilities of serving his own interests. The appearance of imitation in such instances does not seem to raise any problems of a serious theoretical character.

It is of course true that motion pictures do not present patterns as mere skeletal forms of behavior—mere instruments devoid of feeling. Ordinarily such details of action are clothed in romantic form, presented in appealing fashion, and followed usually by successful consequences. Their possibilities, in other words, are more vividly brought out and to this extent they are likely to invite imitation. In general, as long as motion pictures present in intimate detail and with a romantic garb, forms of conduct that arrest the attention of the perceiver and promise some success in the realization of his own interests, it is to be expected that there will be a great deal of copying from motion pictures.

It should be remembered that there is a considerable amount of deliberate effort and trial and error procedure in this process of imitation. Sufficient mention and illustration of this tendency have been given above so that here a mere reminder will suffice. Much, perhaps most, of what is selected for imitation is rejected in the process; much is confined to limited use in separate situations and on special occasions. Yet much is taken over and is incorporated into conduct. Occasionally success in experimentation may open up a new rôle so that one comes to exploit the possibilities of a new line of conduct contingent on the effective use of what has already been imitated. In this way the influence of the movies may be cumulative.

We have consciously refrained from placing any judgment on the value or harmful consequences of what is imitated from motion pictures by youths, since the interest of this study has been merely to show that such imitation goes on and to give some idea of its character.

CHAPTER IV
DAY–DREAMING AND FANTASY

In the past chapter we sought to present some idea of the influence of motion pictures on conduct by considering overt or external forms of behavior. The play of children and the copying of forms of appearance, mannerisms, and techniques of action, while not lacking in subjective significance, chiefly represent activity outwardly expressed. As we begin to move into inner areas of experience where we may detect the action of motion pictures, our attention is arrested by day-dreaming and fantasy. Here the touch of motion pictures is shown in the most incontestable fashion.

Obviously not all people, even though they be romantically inclined adolescents, are led to day-dreaming by the witnessing of motion pictures. Yet it is distinctly clear, from our materials, that, while exceptions are many, individuals—chiefly adolescents—are incited to fantasy by motion pictures. In 66 per cent of the 458 motion-picture autobiographies written by high-school students there is distinct evidence and mention of day-dreaming as a result of motion pictures. Denial, sometimes emphatic, of such influence is made in 10 per cent of the cases. In the remaining 24 per cent of the documents no information is given on this type of experience. While many of the documents which are blank in this respect may be judged on the basis of their contents to imply experiences of day-dreaming occasioned by motion pictures, the evidence is not convincing enough to permit us to classify such documents with those which show conclusively motion-picture day-dreaming.

If we take the figures, then, cautiously in their most conservative form, a picture is presented to us of two-thirds of the writers expressly pointing to motion pictures as an influence in some way or other on their fantasy life.

Indications of such influence are quite perceptible also in the case of children. Indeed, it becomes exceedingly difficult to draw the line between the impersonation of rôles in children's overt play and such impersonation in their imagination. In one sense, day-dreaming appears to be generic with play; it is seemingly but the internal playing of rôles. Childhood play which takes the form of impersonation has a noticeably fanciful character and readily merges into distinct fantasy. The boy may be not merely playing cowboy, policeman, gangster, aviator, but he may imagine himself performing the deeds of these respective characters. The girl may just as easily picture herself, in her imagination, as the much sought-after heroine as to act out this theme in play.

This proximate character of play and day-dreaming is suggested in the following descriptions of childhood experiences:

Female, 20, white, college sophomore.—I saw "Pollyanna," "Mrs. Wiggs of the Cabbage Patch," and others. For days after I had seen them, I acted just as they had done. I wanted mother to dye my hair and curl it as Pollyanna's was. I even wanted to be struck by an automobile so that I could enjoy the experiences of being a heroine like Pollyanna. But no matter how much I looked I never did see a child who needed saving, nor did any automobile come near enough to hit me; it seemed that I never had any luck whatsoever. And then of course I was a "glad girl" around the house for a little while. Everything made me glad and I told the rest of the family that they too should be glad about everything until finally they grew so tired of this that they politely but very firmly suggested that if these actions were repeated something that might not make me glad would result.

Female, 21, white, college senior.—The first type of picture that captured my fancy was the "wild west" type in which William Hart played such an important part. How I envied and admired those heroines who could at one moment do some exceedingly daring feat and at the next faint very lady-like and delicately. To me they were all that a young lady could or should be. How often I wasted time day-dreaming, picturing myself as the heroine of these wonderful pictures. I could just imagine myself doing things just as marvelous as they did, and I tried to imitate their mannerisms in everyday life, much to the great amusement of my brother, who was just old enough to have graduated from this class of motion pictures.

Male, 20, white, Jewish, college junior.—For a long time I had diligently read the Tarzan books, and now I was to see one enacted before my very eyes. With bated breath I watched Korak jump from tree to tree. His rescue of Meriam from the villainous Arabs took my breath away. I at once fell in love with Meriam. She was plump and dark-skinned. She had dark hair and sparkling black eyes. How I loved her! For hours at night I lay awake thinking of her. I would have liked to live in the jungles, strong, carefree, laughing at death, with Meriam at my side.

Male, 21, white, Jewish, college sophomore.—While I sat in school I used to dream about the hero of the picture, visualizing that some day I would play the part in real life by rescuing one of the pretty little girls in my class on whom I had a "crush." I used to continually love to scrap, picturing myself as one of the fighters in a picture I had seen.

Such instances of childhood fantasy appear frequently and point to this form of behavior as an additional way in which motion pictures play upon the lives of children. Those who have been accustomed to regard childhood as characterized chiefly by a life of action would be impressed by the extent to which fantasy appears as part of childhood experience as revealed by motion-picture autobiographies. In the questionnaire submitted to 1200 of Chicago's school children in the sixth and seventh grades, over 50 per cent acknowledge being influenced in their day-dreaming by motion pictures. This form of imaginative activity is bound up so closely with the play activities of children, however, that it will not be given further attention.

The influence of motion pictures upon day-dreaming becomes most conspicuous in the case of adolescents—high-school and college boys and girls. It is to the experiences of this group that we now turn. In these higher age groups day-dreaming tends to appear unaccompanied by overt play activities and to become an important and relatively independent phase of life, indulged in, frequently, with deliberation for the satisfaction it offers.

As an aid to understanding the relation of motion pictures to fantasy a few accounts of experiences chosen from the written autobiographies may be cited. These instances will exhibit, incidentally, the variety of the content of day-dreaming incited by motion pictures.

Female, 20, white, college junior.—I think it was during early adolescence that the movies had its greatest effect on me. I spent the time just before I slipped off to sleep in planning and dreaming about the pictures I should play in, my clothes, my admirers and suitors, my cars, my jewels, and even the home I should have, which was to be the most magnificent structure in all Beverly Hills. I had a name picked for this house and for myself—very ornate, fanciful and ridiculous names, which I thought quite beautiful and lovely. I was a bit hazy as to how I should accomplish all this and just when I was to start for Hollywood. I felt quite comfortable about it all coming true, however, and put off my departure somewhere in the future—when I was sixteen or seventeen, say. I never told anyone about my brilliant future, but I felt quite superior, all to myself, over other girls who were not to have such a glorious career as I was to have. Then one day I confided in my best friend and was distinctly surprised to hear that her future was to parallel mine, and that she too was going to be a star of the first magnitude.

Female, 20, white, college sophomore.—Day-dreaming was my chief pastime and I can trace it back to being aroused and stimulated by motion pictures. I'd picture myself the wife of a star, living in Hollywood and all my friends envying me my handsome husband. But no one ever took him away from me; he was always faithful to me.

Female, 19, white, college sophomore.—Just as these pictures have influenced my thoughts, they have influenced my dreams, if I may be permitted to draw a distinction between the two. The collegiate movies played an important part in my dreams. From them I gained an enthusiasm to come to college, to enter into all the "pranks," and social life. I dreamed of being one of the most collegiate, the girl to be the football captain's friend. Just as I have feasted on the thoughts of school I have dwelt hardily in the days of the settling of the west. Many times I have crossed the desolate desert wastes, encountered the Indians, loved some hero of the trail. After having seen a movie of pioneer days I am very unreconciled to the fact that I live to-day instead of the romantic days of fifty years ago. But to offset this poignant and useless longing I have dreamed of going to war. I stated previously that through the movies I have become aware of the awfulness, the futility of it, etc. But as this side has been impressed upon me, there has been awakened in me at the same time the desire to go to the "front" during the next war. The excitement—shall I say glamour?—of the war has always appealed to me from the screen. Often I have pictured myself as a truck driver, nurse, HEROINE!

Female, 24, white, college senior.—The pictures I saw became the chief source of subject matter for day-dreams. I would lie awake for hours after going to bed, day-dreaming. After seeing an especially good show I have gone off to bed especially early to get those dreams started. Sometimes they lasted a long time, especially for one who has had to go to bed by ten. The striking of the clock downstairs often warned me of the late hour, and I would reluctantly turn to thoughts of sleep. Other times I fell to sleep in the midst of my dreaming. If a picture had been set in Alaska, I'd hop off to Alaska and ride over the snows and have thrilling experiences based on those of the picture, and, of course, colored by my active imagination. The more unusual the picture, the better I liked it.

Female, 24, white, college senior.—During my high-school period I particularly liked pictures in which the setting was a millionaire's estate or some such elaborate place. After seeing a picture of this type, I would imagine myself living such a life of ease as the society girl I had seen. My day-dreams would be concerned with lavish wardrobes, beautiful homes, servants, imported automobiles, yachts, and countless handsome suitors.

Female, 16, white, high-school junior.—The day-dreams were many. A tall, dark, greasy-haired handsome man and me, tall, light, thin, pretty attractive girl. A large estate in the woods with everything that one could wish for. Then again it might be just a small, cozy, white cottage on the side of the sea where two could be very happy. Sometimes I dreamed of beautiful clothes that the "poor working girls" in the movies wore. I think that my day-dreams were aroused by movies. Not only the few that I saw, but also those that my friends told me about.

Male, 20, white, college junior.—As for day-dreaming about movies, I have done this quite a bit. At present I cannot recall the exact movies, but I remember that it was the adventure pictures which usually started me on this line. I believe it was shows of things that I had never seen in real life, as of the South Seas, or the lumber camps of the northwest which affected me so. I would often imagine myself in either of these two situations and it was quite true.

Male, 19, white, college sophomore.—I became exceedingly fond of plays dealing with the adventures of "lounge-lizzards" and "gold-diggers." Gay ballroom scenes and fashionable mansion sets held a mighty "kick" for me. I pictured myself dressed in a Tuxedo, seated in some ultra-exclusive club, sipping a cocktail. Or I would be stepping out of a luxuriously appointed machine with some society queen richly attired at my side. I would enter a fashionable night club whereupon the manager would rush over and direct the seating arrangements with many obsequious bows and smirks. An entire staff of *garçons* would be at my beck and call, bringing to my table the choicest foods and the rarest wines. After an epicurean feast I would depart for my private box at the Opera.

The weaving of fantasy around motion-picture themes and the patterning of the former after the latter seem to be clearly indicated in the instances which have been given. The accounts should serve to present some understanding of how motion pictures may act upon the day-dreaming of young men and women. The influence of scenes of adventure, travel, gay life, fine clothes, wealth, luxury, success, heroism, and so forth, is quite pronounced. Yet, apparently, the chief theme emerging in the day-dreaming of adolescents is that of love. The romantic and entrancing love depicted in motion pictures represents to many an inaccessible type of experience. Hence the motion picture provides them with vicarious enjoyment. This frequently takes the form of the boy or girl imagining himself or herself either playing opposite, or being in the company of, some movie favorite under specially conceived circumstances.

The sample of 458 documents from high-school students was subjected to tabulation on this point. With respect to the item, "Has the individual imagined himself playing opposite the actor or actress in love pictures?", it was found that this was true in the case of 30 per cent of the motion-picture autobiographies, denied in 17 per cent; whereas in 53 per cent no references appeared on the matter. Without attempting to interpret its significance it is pertinent to remark that evidence of this form of day-dreaming appeared twice as frequently in the cases of girls as in the cases of boys. Following are a few typical accounts:

Male, 17, white, high-school junior. ——— ——— is my suppressed desire in the movies. I used to day-dream of —— by the hours. She has had several love letters from me. Though

I have never had any answers from them as yet. I wrote these letters as a dare.

Female, 21, white, college senior.—The greatest effect the movies had on me can be found in my day-dreams—that period between wakefulness and sleep. As for day-dreaming, Tom Meighan has caused the most. I really believed in my day-dreams of him, that he was the man for me. This was when I was around 19 years old. Day-dreams for me are as far from real life as is possible. The love scenes in motion pictures have always played a great part in my day-dreams. The characters in the pictures never came before my eyes, but the picture suggested some original scene; the rest I worked out myself.

Female, 21, white, college senior.—As a young high-school student, I attended the movies largely for the love scenes. Although I never admitted it to my best friend, the most enjoyable part of the entire picture was inevitably the final embrace and fade-out. I always put myself in the place of the heroine. If the hero was some man by whom I should enjoy being kissed (as he invariably was), my evening was a success, and I went home in an elated, dreamy frame of mind, my heart beating rather fast and my usually pale cheeks brilliantly flushed. I used to look in the mirror somewhat admiringly and try to imagine Wallace Reid or John Barrymore or Richard Barthelmess kissing that face. It seems ridiculous if not disgusting now, but until my Senior year this was the closest I came to Romance.

Female, 20, white, college junior.—Movies have definitely formed part of my day-dreams. Every girl, I think, must have the mental image of a man to idealize and build dreams about. Before she finds an actual person, she draws an imaginary figure. In any event that was what occurred in my case. And my imaginary man was made up mostly of movie stars. At one time it was even the height of my ambition to marry Dick Barthelmess. I spent much Latin-grammar time thinking up ways of becoming acquainted with my various heroes. Sometimes, though not often, I identified myself with the heroine of a picture I had seen. The rôle of the fragile, persecuted woman never appealed to me; it was always as the queen, the Joan of Arc, the woman who had power that I saw myself. These day-dreams took up pretty much time, especially during my second year at high school, when I was in a strange environment; but I was always inwardly ashamed of them and I do not believe that they ever carried over into action of any sort. I have never even sent for autographed pictures.

Female, 15, Negro, high-school freshman.—I fell in love with Gilbert Rolland. I would imagine I was the leading lady in the pictures he played in. I used to sit and day-dream. One day I would marry Gilbert Rolland and we would have a lovely time until I went out with, maybe, Ramon Navarro and Gilbert would catch me kissing Ramon. Then there would be a law-suit and my picture would be in the paper. I would win the law-suit and marry Ramon Navarro. I would keep on until I had married and divorced all of my movie actors.

Male, 15, white, high-school sophomore.—My interest in girls sure was awakened by the motion pictures. I remember one hearty fall I took for Clara Bow. Boy, did I fall hard, but, oh well, what is the use. Many times I pictured myself playing the part of her most ardent lover. To come to her rescue, and carry her from the roof of a burning building, or out of the path of a stampede of a wild herd. Many times I came to my senses in the midst of a hero act, much to my sorrow, as mother called me to go to the store or to perform some chore around the house.

While witnessing a picture one not infrequently projects oneself into the rôle of the hero or heroine. Such imaginative identification, as we shall see particularly in the discussion on "Emotional Possession," may assume a character different from mere day-dreaming, although some element of fantasy is always present. A few accounts of this imaginative identification will illustrate further how love pictures may act on day-dreaming.

Female, 18, white, Jewish, high-school senior.—I think I first became interested in love pictures when I saw Conrad Nagel in "Three Weeks." He made love in a way that sent thrills down my back, and when he put his arms about the heroine, I closed my eyes *almost* shut and saw *me* in his arms.

Female, 16, white, high-school junior.—As for day-dreaming, I suppose every girl does that! I know I did, and still do. I like to day-dream about my favorite male actors and I always picture myself the heroine when I attend a theater. I just make-believe I'm the heroine and the hero is making love to me. As for being thrilled by love scenes, oh goodness! I can picture John Gilbert and Greta Garbo rehearsing a love scene right now, but in my mind it isn't Greta Garbo, it's me!

Female, 18, Negro, high-school junior.—In "The Pagan" I imagined I was Dorothy Jordan. I think she is beautiful. But Ramon Navarro is so different from the rest of the movie actors. He is so boyish. I imagined I was on the island with him and could almost see myself running hand-in-hand with him along the island, eating coconuts. During the whole picture I sat there as if I was in a dream. At the end I drew a long breath and came back to earth again.

In the following instance we seem to have a postponement of the day-dreaming until the girl is by herself:

Female, 17, white, high-school junior.—When I witness love pictures I do not show my feelings until I leave the theater. I either practice on my family or even the boy friends. It is usually a ——— ——— scene that makes my temperature rise. They are the ideal love-makers. I usually converse about these pictures with someone, but not seriously. When I am alone I go over them. Sometimes they seem a bit exaggerated, yet so real! I picture myself the recipient of Gilbert's kisses. Folded in his arms I could forget all my school worries.

The reader who grasps the spirit of these accounts can probably realize the immense popularity of certain outstanding motion picture stars known for their appeal and skill in love scenes. One immediately recalls Rudolph Valentino who impressed himself on the minds of girls as no other movie character seems to have done. It happens that he was a very vivid image in the minds of many high-school and college girls from whom motion-picture experiences have been secured. A few instances of the way in which his image was woven into the texture of day-dreaming of such girls are given, chiefly—let it be borne in mind—to further reveal the rôle played by love themes in the life of fantasy.

Female, 20, white, college junior.—Whenever I saw desert pictures, I thought it would be thrilling to live in a tent like the Arab and travel from place to place. I thought it would be wonderful to be captured by some strong, brave Arab and be held prisoner amidst that barren, dry land. These pictures impressed me so much that I used to dream about them at night. I loved the beautiful scenery both in the day and at night. I hoped that some day I would be able to visit the desert land and ride a camel. Rudolph Valentino and Vilma Banky were my favorite desert stars. I always thought of Rudolph Valentino as a typical desert hero and Vilma Banky as a beautiful angel of the desert.

Female, 19, white, college sophomore.—Rudolph Valentino was quite my ideal when I was at this age. My mother did not approve of my going to see these pictures, but what did a little thing like that matter to me? His pictures, more than any of the others, I believe, carried me over into a fancy-life. His leading ladies I always resented. I repeatedly tossed them aside and put myself in their places. After seeing "The Sheik" I was in a daze for a week.

Female, 18, white, high-school senior.—When I saw "The Sheik," for a long time afterwards I couldn't think of anything grander than that of being on a desert and being kidnapped by an Arab that was as handsome as the late Rudy.

Female, 16, Negro, high-school junior.—I fell in love with Rudolph Valentino and Warner Baxter. Rudy was such a perfect lover and he kissed divinely. I could imagine myself being in his leading woman's place when he prostrated her with a kiss, and I even thrilled at the thought.

Female, 19, white, college sophomore.—Vivid in my memory is the image of Rudy Valentino as the Sheik. His passionate love-making stirred me as I was never stirred before. For many days I pictured myself as his desert companion in the most entrancing scenes that my imagination could build.

Female, 19, white, college junior.—The first picture which stands out in my memory is "The Sheik," featuring Rudolph Valentino. I was at the impressionable and romantic age of 12 or 13, when I saw it. I recall coming home that night and dreaming the entire picture over again; myself as the heroine, being carried over the burning sands by an equally burning lover. I could feel myself being kissed in the way the Sheik had kissed the girl. I wanted to see it again but it was forbidden.

Female, 19, white, college sophomore.—After seeing such a picture as the "Sheik" I go home to day-dream about being carried off by a tall, dark, handsome sheik to a beautiful place out in the desert, a thousand miles from no-man's-land, where all one has to do is to clap one's hands and a servant will appear to bring anything one's heart desires. Such a dream goes "blooey" when someone says that sheiks are usually horrid, ugly, bearded old men, dirty and ill-smelling. But how can one imagine them as anything but a "Rudolph Valentino"?

Some publicists and editorial writers have expressed their amazement at the overwhelming popular interest displayed in Valentino at the time of his death, particularly in contrast to the slight attention given to the death of former President Eliot of Harvard University, which occurred at the same time. If American girls and women were affected to the extent to which many of the high-school and college girls who have contributed to this study seem to have been, there is little occasion for bewilderment over the incident.

From such accounts as those which have been given and from casual reflections on the content of day-dreaming one would be led to expect that fantasy is largely monopolized by kinds of experiences which are tabooed by the moral standards of community life. While it appears inexpedient to mention in this document the full extent of this type of fantasy incited by motion pictures, a few milder, but representative, incidents can be given to emphasize the point.

Female, 18, white, high-school senior.—I have had many day-dreams resulting from moving pictures. Sometimes they were inspired by the actors themselves, and at other times it was by the acting. I have dreamed of having wonderful adventures, some of which were impossible, and of falling into the hands of villains, then being rescued by some dashing young Romeo. I have also dreamed of being a beautiful but haughty and pampered daughter of some rich man, and of going out and making "whoopee" with crowds of worshiping young men at my feet; and of doing things I'd never really do in actual life. I have had dreams of practically every phase of life, worked out in every imaginable way. I've had all sorts of young men as lovers. From an American to an Egyptian, and back.

Female, 17, white, high-school senior.—I have fallen in love with the movie heroes, but the time was short, because I thought it would be no use to think of such an event that could not happen; I mean of seeing the beloved in person. I imagined myself caressing the heroes with great passion and kissing them so they would stay osculated forever. I never wrote love letters but I practiced love scenes either with myself or the girl friends. We sometimes think we could beat Greta Garbo, but I doubt it.

Male, 19, white, Jewish, college sophomore.—When I went to the movies and witnessed a flirtation scene where petting dominated, I was emotionally stirred. Often before I would fall asleep, while lying in bed, I would live through the part of the man under such conditions and I derived pleasure from it.

Male, 19, white, Jewish, college sophomore.—Later, about the age of seventeen and eighteen I became interested in sex pictures, pictures expressing variations on the love theme. The pictures of youth, the escapades of young people of the opposite sex appealed to me. The wild, gay life of theatrical women was a delightful theme upon which to dream.

Female, 16, white, high-school sophomore.—Of course, if I was to tell mother or anybody the things I think of right after a picture of passion and excitement, they would think I was a sort of maniac.

In the light of the above it can scarcely be doubted that motion pictures affect the day-dreams and fantasies of boys and girls of different ages in providing content for day-dreams on the one hand, and, on the other, in stimulating them through the dramatic depiction of scenes which stir one's impulses. Motion pictures unquestionably have proven to be a great incitant to fantasy.

It is difficult, however, to interpret the meaning of this day-dreaming in the life of the individual. As in the case of childhood play, we are presented with a vivid picture of the touch of movies yet are unable, in a large measure, to indicate its effect on the general conduct of the individual. This admission is inevitable in the light of our meager knowledge of the rôle of day-dreaming in life. In general, the interpretations of day-dreaming, which in the judgment of the author are quite unverified, take two expressions. It has been contended by some that day-dreaming has an expressive or cathartic effect. In this sense, it has been regarded as a palliative to hardship, a sort of softener of life, a means of infusing joy and romantic experience into the routine of life in a dull world. Through fantasy, some declare, one can satisfy vicariously certain impulses which, if overtly expressed in everyday life, would cause trouble and which, if repressed, would cause personal strain and disturbances. In this sense day-dreaming has been regarded as a means of maintaining wholesome life in a world of antagonism and frustration.

Other theorists on fantasy have called attention, however, to its introversive character. They regard day-dreaming as a turning inward of action and correspondingly of a deadening of the incentive and capacity for outward action. In this sense day-dreaming becomes a method of escape, a sign of failure to meet one's problems externally, and of an unwillingness to work out one's frustrated impulses into some form of social adjustment.

These are conventional theories, which are far from proved. The reader may apply them to the day-dreaming incited by motion pictures and derive whatever benefit they seem to yield in the way of interpretation.

In forming a judgment one should not forget that indulgence in day-dreaming may stimulate impulses and whet appetites. To this extent, the content of day-dreaming may pass over into patterns of thought, intention, and desire, and accordingly encourage overt forms of conduct, or at least become closely linked up with such forms.

The evidence on motion picture fantasy presented in this chapter has not been evaluated, in view of the absence of an acceptable interpretation of the effect of day-dreams on conduct. That motion pictures stimulate day-dreaming among large numbers of young men and women may be stated as an inescapable conclusion. If it be true that the content of day-dreaming represents what people would like to do, and would do if conditions made it possible, then the study of day-dreams offers us an indication of what the movies would do in the way of overt behavior if external conditions were such as to allow for the actual expression of impulses.

CHAPTER V

EMOTIONAL POSSESSION: FEAR AND TERROR

STUDENTS of conduct are familiar with a type of experience (which, for want of another term, we may label "Emotional Possession") in the course of which, through having his emotions aroused, the individual loses self-control. Some of our most interesting motion-picture data are of this sort. Emotional possession refers to experiences wherein impulses which are ordinarily restrained are strongly stimulated. In this heightened emotional state the individual suffers some loss of ordinary control over his feelings, his thoughts, and his actions. Such a condition results usually from an intense preoccupation with a theme—in this case, that of a picture. The individual identifies himself so thoroughly with the plot or loses himself so much in the picture that he is carried away from the usual trend of conduct. His mind becomes fixed on certain imagery, and impulses usually latent or kept under restraint gain expression or seriously threaten to gain such expression. This emotional condition may get such a strong grip on the individual that even his efforts to rid himself of it by reasoning with himself may prove of little avail. The state is usually short-lived—yet while it is experienced impulse is released and self-control reduced. These abstract remarks will be made clear in the consideration of the following series of findings. The discussion will be concerned with such experiences induced by the movies as fright, sorrow, love, and excitement. Each of them will be treated briefly in a separate chapter.

The experiencing of fright, horror, or agony as a result of witnessing certain kinds of motion pictures seems common from the accounts of children, high-school, and college students. The experience is most conspicuous in the case of children, although it is not infrequently shared by those of greater age. Its manifestations vary from the shielding of eyes at crucial scenes during the showing of the pictures, to nightmares and terrifying dreams, including sometimes experiences of distinct shock, almost of neurotic proportions.

Pictures with highly dramatic scenes of mystery and agony such as "The Phantom of the Opera," "Dr. Jekyll and Mr. Hyde," and "The Gorilla" are chiefly conducive to these kinds of experiences—although scenes from pictures not of a particularly horrifying character may occasion them, depending upon the sensitivity of the observer.

It is not infrequent for a young child to experience some kind of hysteria when introduced to his first motion picture. It is rather interesting that in many of the motion-picture autobiographies the earliest incident as well as the first memory is frequently that of fright occasioned by a motion picture. Let us give a few cases of this character to serve as an introduction to the treatment of fright as a form of emotional possession.

Female, 19, white, college sophomore.—My very earliest recollection of a movie is vague in a way and yet one part is very vivid. I do not even know where I saw my first movie, but it was in some very small theater in Englewood. I do not know who the heroine was, but I do remember that at the most dramatic part she was bound, laid on a pile of sticks and burned. At this point, I became hysterical and had to be taken from the theater. I never knew if the unfortunate girl was rescued or burned to death, but I never forgot the smoke and flames curling around her slender body. This little episode characterizes to a great extent my reactions to my early movies. I never could be convinced that the actors were not really suffering the horrible tortures depicted in many films and my sympathy knew no bounds.

Female, 15, white, high-school sophomore.—When I first started going to the movies, I was actually afraid of them. After every picture that I saw, I had horrible nightmares about it. I think that I was about five years old when I saw my first movie, and this fear didn't leave me until I was almost eight.

Female, 20, white, college sophomore.—I was taken to see my first movie at the age of about five or six; I was horror-stricken and mother and dad were requested to leave. I remember as though it was only yesterday how my intense fright had its effects. For several nights I had troubled dreams about that horrible Chinaman, and as a result I refused to sleep alone. Sometimes I would cry so loud in my sleep that mother had to wake me and sit for hours comforting me. This taught my parents a lesson and they never took me to see another movie for a long, long time.

Male, 21, white, college junior.—My first experience with scenes of suffering came when I was less than five years of age. A Negro slave cowered before his master, who was reaching for his whip. This alone was enough to make me burst out into a series of screams which drew the spectators' attention from the picture. When the whip actually touched the slave's back I redoubled my efforts, and as the man fell to the ground unconscious I ran out into the aisle and had to be taken home!

EXTENT OF FRIGHT

CHILDREN who are easily frightened by a picture merely because it is strange lose this susceptibility in the course of a short time. It is in a little older group ranging from the age of eight upwards that one finds more genuine instances of fright, depending more upon the nature of the picture than upon the strangeness of the situation. The number of children who admit such experiences, or of older people who recall them, is quite large. As part of this study inquiry was made on this point of 237 school children in the fourth, fifth, sixth, and seventh grades, in one of the Chicago public grade schools. In answer to the question "Were you ever frightened or horrified by any motion picture or scene in any motion picture?", 222 or 93 per cent answered "Yes"; 15 or 7 per cent replied "No." In the 458 high-school autobiographies there are definite accounts of being frightened in 61 per cent. In 17 per cent of these documents there is a denial of this kind of experience; while in the remaining 22 per cent of the autobiographies there is no information on the point. It may perhaps be surmised that the smaller percentage of acknowledgment of such experiences of fright in the case of the high-school students indicates some failure to recall such experiences. Both sets of figures are quite convincing in showing the high percentage of individuals who have been frightened by the witnessing of motion pictures seriously enough to make some acknowledgment of the fact.

It is perhaps of interest to mention that of the 222 grade-school children admitting experiences of fright, 48, or 21 per cent, spoke of having hidden their face at some time or other while witnessing motion pictures. This tendency to shut out the horror or agony of the picture by covering one's eyes or turning away one's gaze can be frequently observed in the behavior of children at the picture show when certain kinds of movies are being displayed. This behavior further suggests the extent to which motion pictures may occasion horror in children.

Following are given a series of accounts which will help one to appreciate what has just been said concerning the character and extent of fright induced by motion pictures.

Female, 20, white, college junior.—Now, I enjoy mysteries immensely, but they affected me unfavorably as a child and still do. After seeing a few people murdered by unknown men who sprang up from nowhere, after seeing a girl accidentally tap the wall only to have a dead body fall out in front of her, I am a nervous wreck. As I said before, I enjoy the play while it is going on, but when I get home I jump at the slightest noise and imagine all sorts of things are going to happen. After the "Phantom of the Opera," I had terrible nightmares. After "The Cat and the Canary," I was afraid to sleep alone. Just recently I saw "The Canary Murder Case," and as I walked home through the dark night, I cannot say I felt perfectly at ease.

Female, 18, Negro, high-school senior.—I went to a movie once by myself and I had the most terrible experience I have ever witnessed. The picture was of a rich girl who had many jewels and much money; she lived in a house with her father until she died; then the house was supposed to be haunted. One night some girls were on a picnic and passed the house. Someone spoke of its being haunted and dared anyone to go back, but since there were so many of them, they decided they were not afraid. They went back. When they got in the house and were going upstairs, the door through which they had come slammed shut. The next thing that happened was terrible. There was a scream that almost took the roof off; then the figure of a young girl with staring wide eyes and matted hair all dipped in blood appeared before them screaming as she went. Up the stairs she ran leaving the girls unable to move. I was frightened for a year or more. All of my dreams were of the girl with the bloody hair. I was afraid to go in a dark room alone for fear the door would close suddenly.

Female, 19, white, college sophomore.—The first picture that left an impression of horror with me was one in which a fiendish man, living alone in the country, would lower a mirror across the near-by highway. Thus any travelers would see the reflection of the auto's headlights coming towards them, and so to avoid a collision would swerve into the ditch. Then the fiendish person would take them to his home and torture them. This scene so affected me that I believe I shall never forget it. For nights I saw the expression of devilish delight that came over his face when some particularly young person was hurt.

Female, 21, white, college senior.—One of the most horrible pictures I have ever seen was that in which a surgeon transfers the brain of a dying lunatic to the skull of an ape. The ape then reacts to the ideas that were those of the lunatic; he killed several people before they were able to capture him. Since then it seems that next to rats and mice, monkeys and apes are the most disgusting.

Female, 20, white, college sophomore.—I liked anything, just so long as it was exciting. A certain amount of horror pleased me, but I remember one picture which I saw that scared me so much that I couldn't sleep at night, and I would put my head under the covers to protect myself from the image construed by my imagination. In this movie a horrible, hairy ape, with a habit of breaking into people's houses, came in through a window and ran off with the heroine. After seeing this picture, I was afraid to go into a dark room at night because an ape might be just coming in through a window and carry me off. I was a nervous child anyway, and in the course of an exciting movie like this, I would bite the finger nails on both hands, until my fingers would bleed.

Male, 20, white, Jewish, college sophomore.—I sincerely believe that during those high-school days photoplays made little impression on what I thought or how I acted. But on one occasion I saw a movie which has always stayed fresh in my memory; I look back on it with horror. The theme of the picture was about a convict who was hung, and upon his hanging his brains were transferred to a gorilla. The result was that the gorilla escaped and with the human brains was possessed with the desire to kill all those who had a hand in the conviction of the criminal. The entire city was thrown into an uproar, for every few days the newspapers would come out with the news that the judge or the opposing lawyer or some juryman had his back broken in two by the gorilla. The whole episode was gruesome and blood-tingling and something that I remember distinctly this day, even though I saw the movie some seven years ago.

EXPRESSIONS OF FRIGHT

ONE might be inclined to think that the state of fear induced by the picture in children and youths lasts just as long as the picture is witnessed and then disappears after the individual leaves the theater. Very frequently, however, this is not the case. The feeling of fright may continue for some time and show its presence in a number of ways. The most conspicuous of its expressions is in the form of nightmares and terrifying dreams. The recognition that mysterious or fear-inspiring pictures may lead to terrifying dreams helps one to appreciate this power over emotions. Let us continue with some experiences of this sort.

Male, 21, white, college junior.—Another time a serial with the famous Houdini shocked me very much. In it there was an iron man which would break through all sorts of traps, kill people, and cause terror to every one in the picture. Many a night I dreamed that the iron man had me in his grasp or was trampling all over me.

Female, 19, white, Jewish, college sophomore.—I was perhaps eight years old before I saw a picture which left any definite impression on me. It had to do with the Devil, and the main part was played, I believe, by William S. Hart. My understanding was such that I grasped only the horrible side of the story. That picture caused me many a nightmare, and I loathe William S. Hart to this day.

Female, 19, white, college sophomore.—The picture was supposed to take place in the Andes mountains in South America, and the plot was concerned with a feud between two mountaineer families, each of which inflicted all sorts of torture on the other family whenever a chance arose. It was these terrible punishments, so strikingly portrayed, that left such an impression on my mind. As I look back now it seems foolish for me to have been so frightened, but I was young and impressionable, and then, too, the whole theme of the picture was the dreariness, the horror, and the futility of a life such as the characters lived. The picture frightened me so that I wouldn't sit through it to the end, but I got up and walked out into the lobby and waited there for my parents. For days the picture haunted me, and I couldn't stop thinking about the suffering of the people in the picture. It was too realistic for anyone as young as I to see. For two or three weeks I was still so frightened that I wouldn't be left alone. I was afraid to stay by myself, and I wanted to have someone with me all the time.

Male, 20, white, college sophomore.—The most horrible experience I had in my life was occasioned in this manner. I had seen a picture in which a Chinese parade was featured, and included in this parade there were a number of enlarged demons, monsters, etc. That night I had one of the few nightmares of my life and by far the worst. I awakened in abject terror, and sleeping alone I ran to my mother's bedroom. On the way I had to pass the basement door, and through it I perceived an endless procession of these monsters marching. The door was closed, but they came right through and headed for me; needless to say, I made all haste to mother's side. When you realize that I was at least partially awake when this occurred, the force of the nightmare is apparent.

Female, 20, white, college sophomore.—It happened that I went to see a mystery play one night, in the course of which were several blood-curdling scenes,—one of a girl locked in a room where she saw long, bony fingers creeping over the back of a chair, and who found behind the chair a man who died as she bent over him;—one of a dim room with a pile of rags in the corner, and as I looked the rags moved, crawled forward and became a person, an odious, horribly maimed, hideously bound creature which sent cold chills running over me. I was horrified. That night I dreamed of those horrid scenes, and was so frightened that I dared not pull the spread higher. The next night was not so bad, and gradually the memory faded; so I again became a movie enthusiast. Yet, there was an effect, and as I think of the scene which frightened me so, a half horror creeps upon me.

Female, 19, white, college sophomore.—The horror-pictures and serials used to frighten me when I was a child. I remember one picture in particular—I cannot even recollect the name of it— but it was a newspaper story and concerned several mysterious killings which, it came out later, were committed by a huge orang-utan which had been given the brain of a man in an experiment by a doctor—one of the men killed by the animal. I remember distinctly the scene which frightened me so. The ape was standing in an open window leering at his next victim who was lying in bed, a helpless invalid, rendered even more helpless by fear and horror. Of course, a newspaper reporter, the hero in the story, came in to his rescue just in time and shot the ape, but by that time I had been so thoroughly frightened that I could not sleep that night. Every time I closed my eyes, I could see this ape standing in the window and as the foot of my bed was only a few feet away from an open window, unprotected by even screens, I soon decided to spend the rest of the night in my mother's bed with her. I remember being so paralyzed with fear that I could scarcely get out of bed, but once my feet touched the floor I ran as fast as I possibly could to my mother and spent not only that night but the next one, also, with her. I do not believe I cried, but I became speechless, powerless, rigid, staring wide-eyed into the dark, and the fright did not leave me for several days.

The accounts which have been given are rather impressive in showing the experiences of fright which may be occasioned by certain kinds of motion pictures. Some further light upon this item is given by the findings in the cases of a class of 47 children whose ages ranged from seven to nine years, and of another class of 41 children with ages from nine to twelve years. Both classes of children were questioned about any experiences of fear or fright recently induced by motion pictures. Only accounts of actual experiences as related by the children were used in compilation of results. The movie objects which produced fear in the youngest class were: spooks, ghosts, phantoms, devils, gorillas, bears, tigers, bandits, "bad men," grabbing hands and claws, fighting, shooting, falling or hanging from high places, drowning, wrecks, collisions, fire, and floods. Expressions of their emotions during the witnessing of such pictures were: getting nervous, biting finger nails, pulling hair, crunching teeth, twisting caps, grabbing one's neighbor, feeling shivery, hiding eyes until the scene changed, looking away, screaming, jumping out of seat, and getting under the seat. Expression of the emotional behavior on the way home as mentioned by the children were: running home, being frightened by shadows, avoiding dark streets, holding on to mother, sister, or brother. Expressions at home were: staying close to mother, looking in back of one's chair, afraid to go to bed, looking under the bed, closing window, begging for a light to be left burning, hiding head under covers, seeing devils dancing in the dark, wanting to sleep with someone, bad dreams, calling out in sleep, and walking in sleep.

Expressions of emotion at the theater in the class of older boys and girls were: screaming, jumping out of seats, holding seats, falling out of seats, biting finger nails, gritting teeth, hiding face in hands or cap, and holding people in the adjoining seats. Approximately one-fifth of the boys and girls in the class spoke of having great fear on the way home after having seen some frightening picture; some ran, others took short cuts to get home quickly, others hesitated at alley crossings; some were afraid of open spaces. One boy was afraid that a trapdoor would open up in the pavement and swallow him; and a girl claimed that the sidewalk lifted up in back of her as she hurried home. Approximately one-third of the children in this class mentioned having bad dreams following upon the experience, including shock, nightmares, keeping one's head under the blankets, asking to sleep with mother or father, crying out in sleep and falling out of bed.

DURATION OF FRIGHT

SUCH instances and expressions of fright induced by the witnessing of certain kinds of motion pictures are ordinarily short-lived. The individual regains control of his thoughts and feelings with the passage of time, sometimes by the next day, sometimes in the course of the next few days. It is probably because of the transitoriness of the fright that this kind of behavior has never impressed people as much of a problem. But while it is true that the fear or fright induced by motion pictures is generally short-lived, still in certain individuals it may become fixed and last for a long time. Instances of this duration of the emotional experience follow:

Male, 19, white, college sophomore.—When I was ten years old I experienced a great shock in connection with a motion picture that affected my behavior for years, and still has a subconscious influence over me. One afternoon I went to see the first reels of a new serial mystery movie. The incidents in this play opened with the discovery by a certain young man of certain secret processes whereby he was able to endow a mysterious inhuman machine with life. He kept this machine in a mummy case. On the eve of his wedding, when the bride and the guests were all assembled waiting for his appearance, he is seated before his desk in a dark room with only a desk lamp burning, when suddenly this horrible, powerful, inhuman hand reaches across the area of light, seizes him by the throat, and strangles him to death. That scene frightened me as nothing ever has before or since. I went home in a perfect paroxysm of fear. For many months after that I was afraid to enter a dark room or even to sit in a lighted one at night without someone else with me. For many years I had a strange distrust of the dark or of being alone at any time, and still at times I feel the same uneasy lack of confidence returning on me when I am alone at night, although I realize that it is extremely silly. Strangely enough, it was never the thought of something natural that frightened me, such as a man, a burglar, for instance, but it was the fear of something supernatural, something entirely outside the physical field. For the same reason I have never yet been able to feel comfortable among the mummies in a museum, and I instinctively look upon them with revulsion and disgust.

Female, 20, white, college sophomore.—When I recall the first movie that made an impression upon me, I am filled with horror. I do not remember how old I was when I saw it, but I know that

I was quite young. Posters outside of the theater attracted me to the movie. I insisted upon going to see that particular one. I can still see the pictures on that poster. I went that time with my mother and one or two other people. The picture had as a setting an insane asylum. The heroine was a nurse. The ghostly-featured crazy woman tried to stab the heroine to death while she slept one night. Another time she crept in behind her in an effort to stab her in the back. A fierce struggle followed this attempt, after which the heroine was just barely rescued. In the end the asylum caught on fire. The hero dashed in to save his sweetheart, and came out with the clawing, cringing, insane woman. At that time, I had many nightmares as a result. Since then I have recalled these scenes many times very vividly. I have always had a horror for crazy people.

Female, 18, white, high-school sophomore.—As I write, clear pictures of a certain movie I saw come to my mind. These pictures stayed in my mind and troubled me for two years after I had seen them; they haunted my dreams. Many nights I remember lying awake in bed, clinging to my sister, who slept with me, while I tried to shut out horrible pictures that would not be shut out. After such a description as this, one would think it was a really horrible picture; but it was not. It was, however, one that I should not have seen. It was a picture of a young man who had married a beautiful girl, who had become insane. The girl was taken care of by a woman, who was very careful to see that she was never free to do any harm. One day, years later, he fell in love with another girl and was going to marry her. He did not tell her, however, about his first wife. After the ceremony the young man took his bride to her new home. They spent a happy evening together and then the bride went up to her room. She carefully arranged her beautiful wedding gown over a chair and crept into bed. Then a terrible thing happened. The keeper of the insane woman fell asleep and the lunatic stole her keys and freed herself. The picture of her in her rags with hair hanging down her back, almost crawling down the stairway, snatching the wall with her unkept nails, was very hideous. When she reached the bride's room, clawed at her door, and finally entered and stood looking wickedly at the sleeping bride,

I could stand it no longer and finally buried my head in my lap. As far as I can remember, this is the only picture that troubled me this way.

Female, 19, white, college sophomore.—One picture stands out in my memory at this time, and one actor. The picture is Viola Dana in "The Cossacks." That again was a tragedy. It was a horrible picture. It left an indelible impression upon my mind, for not only weeks but months. When I wanted to go to sleep at night, I would again see those Cossacks slaughtering the peasantry, or the heroine's sister thrown out of the window of a twelve-story hotel building. Gee, when I think of it now, I feel tremors of horror and aversion.

Female, 17, Negro, high-school senior.—The first picture to produce upon me the feeling of fear was "Earth Bound." It was a story of an unfaithful husband who was murdered by his best friend. Through the whole story his spirit lingered. As I watched this visible shadow stride the halls, passing through doors, and reaching out in pity to his young daughter and wife, my nerves became shattered. The spell of its effect remained upon me for a period of a year or more. The sight of a dark hall or room horrified me.

Male, 19, white, college sophomore.—One picture, "Dr. Jekyll and Mr. Hyde," gave me quite a severe fright. I saw it when I could not have been more than eleven years old, and I can still remember the fear I had of the dark alleys and shadows when walking home from the theater with my aunt. I think the evil character in the play worked at night in dark places. For some weeks and months later I had a fear of dark shadows at night when I was alone. I ran quickly past dark alleys and I avoided poorly lighted sections of the street. I never took short cuts through the prairies when by myself for fear that some lurking danger beset me. In short, the effect of that movie was to make me afraid of the dark and of all unseen passages. It was more than two or three years before I fully outgrew this fear.

Because of such a similar type of experience the writer of the following account built up a definite aversion to the attendance at motion pictures.

Female, 26, white, college senior.—The picture was Dante's "Inferno," and I am quite certain that there never was a picture less suitable for any child of that age to see. It showed weird and horrible monsters, and people being tortured in every possible manner. At the end of half an hour I was thoroughly miserable and begged to be taken out, but my mother bade me keep quiet and stop looking at it if I didn't like it. I writhed in my seat during the remainder of the picture and was in tears and nearly a nervous wreck when we finally left. For weeks I dreamed of the atrocious creatures and the terrible tortures I had seen. I was afraid to go to bed and was frightened by the dark, although I would never tell anyone. During the next few years my mother offered many inducements to get me into the movies, but I always held my ground, vowing to myself that nothing in the world could ever make me. Two or three times, when I was a little older, she even commanded me, and although I hated myself for it, I defied her and said, "I will not," for I still could not forget that horrible picture. I won out, too, but I knew that my mother was very angry, because I always obeyed her when she told me I must do anything. She finally realized that she could not make me go, so she stopped mentioning it to me, and I gradually became a little less hostile.

EFFECT OF SPECIFIC PICTURES

SUCH instances draw one's attention to the importance of considering a problem which has been rather conspicuously ignored. While it perhaps is to be admitted that the fixation of such experiences of fright presupposes occasionally a very sensitive disposition on the part of the individual, still it also points to the excruciating character of what may be presented in motion pictures. Motion-picture producers and censors seem to have ignored this aspect of experience. The influence of certain specific pictures in inducing the kinds of reactions described has been very great. Such pictures as the "Phantom of the Opera," "Dr. Jekyll and Mr. Hyde," "The Gorilla," "The Cat

Creeps," "The Lost World," have particularly occasioned terror and fright. The influence of "The Phantom of the Opera" can be gauged from the following run of instances:

Male, 19, white, college sophomore.—For several nights I was very uneasy, scared to go into dark rooms or to be alone in the house after having seen the "Phantom of the Opera." As I recall it, and realize I am in the house alone, I feel the cold chills promenading up my spine. When that ugly face, which was disclosed to the audience after much suspense and excitement, becomes a visual image and you are alone in a large, very quiet house, there is a tendency to scream or run (but I guess I better finish this paper first). I remember "screeching" in the show when that horrible face was shown.

Female, 18, Negro, high-school senior.—The picture, "The Phantom of the Opera," was the most horrible, the most gruesome and horrifying picture I have ever seen. This scene, for instance, I consider the worse. The phantom had captured the girl and the next morning the girl discovered that he wore a mask and slipping up behind him, she jerked the mask from his face. But oh, what a face he turned on her! Eyes staring from great deep sockets, no lips, just ugly picket-like tusks for teeth, and a white pasty-like complexion—this was the ghastly thing that stared forth from the screen.

Female, 15, white, high-school sophomore.—"The Phantom of the Opera," with Lon Chaney as the phantom, frightened me more than any other motion picture I have seen. He was made up as the most horrible creature with long teeth, glaring eyes, and a bald head. When he was unmasked by the heroine, I gasped and almost screamed. Although I tried to draw my eyes away from his terrible face, I couldn't; his ugliness was so fascinating. The entire picture was so weird and fantastic that the shivers ran up and down my back. For a long time after that, I dared not go near dark places, particularly the cellar. I did not let anyone else know I was frightened for fear they would call me silly.

Female, 14, white, high-school sophomore.—Yes, I have been frightened by a scene from "The Phantom of the Opera." This one was when the phantom pulled the mask from his face. I gave a little inward cry, for I was so frightened that I couldn't scream. The boys and girls around me were screaming and hiding their faces. The girl that went with me got under her seat. I couldn't move for two or three minutes. I can't explain my feeling; it was a mysterious sensation, and my blood became cooler.

Female, 16, white, high-school sophomore.—I was severely frightened when I saw Lon Chaney in "The Phantom of the Opera." I went home and could not sleep that night, and many nights after that. I would wake up in my sleep and scream from fright.

Female, 17, Negro, high-school senior.—I witnessed one of my most terrible experiences when I saw "The Phantom of the Opera." I will never forget the chill and fear that played tag up and down my spine as the singer approached the figure of the phantom playing the organ. I can see her now moving slowly toward that ugly, inhuman thing. My heart seems to stand still as she snatches the grotesque mask from his face, and his face stands bare. No wonder she fainted. I came near it myself. Every time I think of that scene, I shudder. It is needless to say that for weeks after I was afraid to enter a dark room.

These accounts suffice for an understanding of what can be done by a picture which is consciously designed around the themes of mystery and fear. Of course, most of the experiences of fright in young children result from these specific kinds of pictures, yet it would be a mistake to assume that they are confined to them. Pictures which seek in no sense to play upon the impulses aroused by such scenes may contain an incident here and there which actually induces fear in the child. A college girl writes:

Female, 20, white, college sophomore.—Another unfortunate picture, "Little Lord Fauntleroy," meant only to be a delightful movie for children, left a deep impression: The little girl heroine was delirious for several days and imagined she was wandering through a strange land where she met a horrible creature who chased her; I will never forget the huge snake which crawled at her. After seeing that picture I had nightmares in which I was being chased by horrible things; usually I woke up so terrified that my father had to come in and quiet me. I doubt whether the producers realized how such a picture would stimulate the imagination of growing children.

The inability on the part of well-intentioned people to visualize just how the child's mind and feelings may be disturbed by gruesome and frightening pictures is shown by the recommendations occasionally made to children to see pictures of the type represented by the following instance:

> *Female, 20, white, college sophomore.*—The next stage does not stand out so very well in my mind. I think they were mainly horrible, mysterious types. One that sticks in my mind, and to a certain extent in my dreams, was "Dr. Jekyll and Mr. Hyde." We were urged at school to go to see the picture. If I ever have contact with children I will certainly keep them from seeing any such plays. For weeks I would wake up scared so that I could hardly move because I had had a dream about some phase of the play.

The chief objective of this discussion is not that, however, of seeking to assess the value or harm of showing such kinds of pictures to children. It is difficult perhaps to evaluate motion pictures in this respect. While, as we have seen, many informants declare that the witnessing of a terrifying picture has left some permanent effect on them, in the main the effect was temporary. The fact, moreover, that people, including children, have a distinct desire for such kinds of pictures is reflected both by box-office receipts and by personal acknowledgments. It may even be found that children display some avid liking for pictures which frighten them. On one occasion the writer spoke to a class of boys and girls of the third grade. Out of the class of 44 students 38 gave instances of being frightened, on occasion severely, by certain motion pictures. Yet in response to the further question as to whether or not they like to be frightened by motion pictures, 31 out of the 38 replied that they did.

FRIGHT AS A FORM OF EMOTIONAL POSSESSION

WHAT these experiences do show is that ordinary control over one's feelings and perceptions may be lost on certain occasions. Individuals in the state of fright induced by the witnessing of a motion picture see non-existent things and take special precautions for safety that ordinarily would be ignored. Indeed, many of them realize the absurdity of their ideas and their conduct, yet find it impossible to control either their impulses or their feelings. The very effort taken by the child or youth to explain to himself that what he saw was only a picture and that it is foolish for him to feel afraid points to the condition of emotional possession. It is this overpowering by an impulse or feeling, this arrest of reflective judgment, and the subsequent loss of control that loom up as the most important aspect of this experience of fright.

We follow with some instances which bring out more vividly this point:

Male, 20, white, college sophomore.—"While the City Sleeps," "London After Midnight," both starring Lon Chaney, "Chicago," "Cat and the Canary," and "Shadows of the Night" are mystery and gang war pictures that I have seen and well remember. The shooting in them never frightens me at the time because I always say to myself that it is just a movie and nobody was really hurt in making it, and that blanks are always used in the guns. Nevertheless, when walking home down some dark street, I notice myself walking as far from the buildings and as far from the big trees and bushes as I can get. Sometimes I clench my fists for fear someone will jump out and hold me up.

Female, 19, white, college sophomore.—About four years ago (I was then fifteen) I saw "The Lost World"—a movie portraying the prehistoric animals which were supposed to have been rediscovered still living in the African jungles. An American sportsman and his wife believed they could still find dinosaurs of enormous size. Consequently they went on this expedition. As this picture goes on, we see them hunting and searching everywhere for this great reptile at one time seen by a native. Tracks are discovered and finally they come upon the dinosaur which is about seventy feet long, with an ugly, scaly body and a nauseous, slimy neck upon which is perched a little wriggling, pointed head. By this time I was ready to creep; I had to cover my eyes to prevent dizziness; I felt as if all of my insides had turned around; it was not exactly a sick feeling, but terribly creepy and slimy. My companion saw my reaction and suggested leaving the theater, but I was determined not to let my emotions get the best of me. As the story goes the hunters succeed in trapping the beast and in getting him crated for the homeward journey. Meanwhile news has reached London that this rare species had been discovered and masses crowd the wharf to await its arrival. A special raft-like ship was built and the trip goes well until about ten miles from port. Then the dinosaur succeeds in breaking loose and plunges into the sea. He hits some bridge and breaks it to pieces; upon reaching the port he smashed things right and left with his huge tail, tears upon the city, waves down office buildings, crushing and eating people on the street. A panic follows; people get down on their knees to pray; everyone thinks the world is coming to an end. I think the picture ends with the dinosaur's plunging into the ocean, never to be found again and leaving the city in a turmoil about its return. "The Lost World" was probably the most terrifying picture I ever saw, and it certainly left me with a bad imprint for a few days. After I got home I knew that I could not sleep; therefore I sat in the living room and decided to read a book; only the reading lamp was burning and I still insist that I saw all sorts of huge, strange shadows on the wall. Every little noise made me jump.

Finally I dozed off and suddenly began to kick and struggle as if I were trying to get away from being crushed; my entire night was spent in that manner and the next day I could not concentrate on my work at school. I knew perfectly well that it was all imagination but try as I might I could not get that picture out of my mind. Even now as I write about it I shudder and feel the tension of my nerves.

Female, 20, white, college sophomore.—I saw many pictures which almost scared me out of a year's growth, but the one that had the greatest effect, so far as I can remember, was "Dr. Jekyl and Mr. Hyde." When I saw the awful Mr. Hyde creeping and cringing around, I wanted to yell. In one spot, when Mr. Hyde was hiding behind a door and was about to spring upon a girl, I actually shut my eyes. I *could not* look. It was awful, then. It probably would seem awful to me to-day too. This terror inspired by the film version of Stevenson's story remained with me for several weeks. It was real, as no other movie-inspired terror ever lasted that long with me. I hated to go into dark rooms alone. I always had a terrifying vision of this ugly, misshapen thing meeting me in the dark. If I couldn't find a light I wouldn't enter the room. This may sound absurd, but it is true. Finally, I started the old trick of whistling to keep up my courage. It worked more or less successfully, but by the time I had mastered the trick the effects of "Dr. Jekyll and Mr. Hyde" had worn off to a great degree.

Female, 15, white, high-school sophomore.—About four months ago I saw Douglas Fairbanks in "The Gaucho." In the picture was a hideous man who had some kind of a "black death" disease. His face was covered with a veil and he was bent and stooped. He blinked like a monkey and he looked like one, only worse. Altogether, he presented the most horrible sight I have ever seen. For months I imagined this man to be hiding in the dark, behind a door. I tried to dispel this crazy idea by calling myself silly, but it didn't work. I don't like to write about it now because if I recall the picture too vividly my imaginings may begin again. Once I even dreamed he was chasing me. What a nightmare! For a few nights after I saw the picture, I kept a light in my room, much to the disgust of my mother.

These instances added to those given above should suffice to establish the point that motion pictures may play very vividly upon a given emotion of the individual; his impulses may be so aroused and his imagery so fixed that for a period of time he is transported out of his normal conduct and is completely subjugated by his impulses.

CHAPTER VI

EMOTIONAL POSSESSION: SORROW AND PATHOS

ESSENTIALLY the same psychological characteristics which have been specified in the last chapter in the discussion of fright are shown in the intense sadness or pathos induced by certain kinds of motion pictures. Under the stimulus of some particularly sorrowful picture or scene, an individual may be moved to tears. He is held in the grip of the dramatic scene, feelings of sadness and impulses to weep surge up within him, and ordinary control diminishes. In many individuals, as we shall see, strenuous efforts to subdue such feelings may come to naught in the situation.

Anyone with a merely casual acquaintance with the movies will probably recall some picture which was particularly effective in arousing intense feelings of grief and impulses to weep. "Over the Hill" and "The Singing Fool" are two outstanding examples of pictures of this kind. Of those who witnessed these pictures probably few, particularly those of tender age, did not experience some tendency to feel sad or to weep. It is not only such special pictures, however, which may induce those effects. The extent to which motion pictures induce such experiences is probably much greater than one would ordinarily think.

EXTENT OF SORROW

IN checking through the group of 458 life histories of high-school students it was found that 64 per cent spoke definitely of such experiences, 19 per cent denied such experiences, while the remaining 17 per cent of the documents contained no information on the point. Among the 293 who described having such experiences as a result of seeing certain motion pictures, there were about twice as many girls as boys. Following are a few instances chosen at random which mirror these experiences:

Female, 20, white, college junior.—The first picture that I ever cried at was " Uncle Tom's Cabin," with Marguerite Clarke playing the part of little Eva. I didn't want to cry and tried my best to fight against my emotions, but it was of no use, the tears rolled down just the same. I read the story of "Wings" and in spite of myself I cried over it. When I saw the movie I tried to tell myself that I wouldn't cry as I had already read the book and could have myself steeled against any display of sorrow. It all went well until one of the last scenes and I found myself crying. Most any picture with a touch of pathos to it has me using my handkerchief a great deal.

Female, 19, white, college sophomore.—Crying at a movie is my second nature. As soon as an event occurs which is the least bit sad my throat chokes up and very often I shed tears; I have never sobbed or made boisterous noises, thank goodness, for crying is a chief source of embarrassment with me; if I can get by with silent sorrow I feel all right. One of the saddest pictures I ever saw was Hardy's novel "Tess of D'Urbervilles" dramatized on the screen. I took that so hard and lived through Tess' part so real that I was embarrassed to go out on the street with my eyes all red and swollen. For that reason I do not enjoy a sad picture; it usually makes me miserable. Likewise "Way Down East," "Ramona," and "The Hunchback of Notre Dame" afforded me heartaches. I do not merely cry, but it seems I actually feel the pain as acutely as the actor himself. "Sorrel and Son" affected me so strangely that I cried over it the next day. Try as I might to control my tears I cannot, and I certainly do not find pleasure in crying.

Female, 14, white, high-school sophomore.—I often cry at picture shows whenever there is a sad scene or someone in the picture is crying. In "The Singing Fool," I cried when Sonny Boy was taken away from "The Singing Fool," when his mother took him to Paris. Also, I cried when Sonny Boy died and when the "Singing Fool" sang the last verse to that famous song in his performance after Sonny Boy had died.

Female, 16, white, high-school junior.—Cry? I should say I do. Even now. A week or two ago I saw "Coquette." I thought I'd have to sob aloud, it was so terribly sad. Too sad, in fact. When I was young, about ten, they ran that "Over the Hill" or some such name. I felt so mournful over that and sobbed so loudly that everyone turned and looked at me. I was embarrassed for being so emotional.

Male, 18, white, high-school senior.—It seems that I very seldom cry at pictures. The only picture that I cried at was a play called "Over the Hill," starring Mary Carr. This picture would make anybody cry, even if you are a brute who can't cry or an easy-going chap who cries at almost nothing.

Female, 20, white, Jewish, college sophomore.—Yes, I have cried at movies, in fact, I still do, much to my own disgust. The "weepiest" picture I saw as a child was "Over the Hill," with Mary Carr. I had two handkerchiefs drying on my lap, while I used the third. It was one of those "mother-neglected-by-children" pictures, and people were sniffling all through the theater. I just cried buckets-full. The pictures in which Pauline Frederick, Norma Talmadge, Lillian Gish played usually made me cry—incidentally, they were my favorite actresses. Of the more recent pictures I remember having cried at "The Way of All Flesh" (Emil Jannings), "Father and Son" (H. B. Warner), "Cyrano De Bergerac," and especially "Singing Fool" (Al Jolson).

Female, 19, white, college sophomore.—Have I ever cried at motion pictures? And how! Most sad pictures can get a few tears at least out of my eyes. Just the other day I saw Mary Pickford in "Coquette." Anyone who enjoys crying at pictures should see that picture. Another picture at which I "swam out" was Al Jolson's "Singing Fool." Likewise, the "Big Parade" at which I cried more the second time I saw it than the first. Pictures of soldiers marching usually bring tears to my eyes.

But, nevertheless, I really don't like to cry at movies. I'd rather sit and watch a sad picture and not cry, but I just can't help it. I guess I'm too tenderhearted.

Attention should be called to the many pictures, often of a melodramatic nature, that induce tears by merely portraying touching or sentimental themes. There is, of course, a wide range of susceptibility to this kind of experience. Certain individuals are easily led to weeping by scenes which would have little effect on others. An instance of one who has such a ready disposition to cry follows:

Female, 14, white, high-school sophomore.—I hardly ever go to a show without crying in some part of it. A short time ago I saw "Mother Machree" and I cried most all the way through the picture when other people had no idea of crying. To me it was sad and I couldn't restrain my tears. I don't like to cry because when you do and other people are not crying you appear conspicuous and this is not a pleasant feeling. The picture is good, even though one may cry while seeing it. For example, the picture called "Mother Machree" is very sad, but I consider it a very good picture in spite of that fact.

In the case of other individuals some particular kind of scene or picture which is intimately linked to their personal career is required to induce this emotional expression. This is illustrated in the following case of a girl whose parents became separated through divorce:

Female, 20, white, Jewish-Gentile, college sophomore.—I have already said in the course of this autobiography that early in my youth my family was broken up. My father and mother separated and finally became divorced; and my sister and I were given into the care of my mother by the court ruling. It is this factor in my life which figures in my emotional reactions. It is almost impossible for me to feel no desire to cry, when I see a movie in which the break-up of a home is featured or where the results of such a break are the subject of the play. It is just this which makes me like Emil Jannings' pictures, and which makes me cry at them, as I do not at others' pictures; for such is his ability to portray family scenes that they "hit home." And, too, it is my overwhelming love for my sister which was a factor in my crying over "Beau Geste." I would point out here that the only time I am really moved to cry in seeing a movie, is when it harks back to some personal feeling or experience of these two aspects of my life; my love for my sister, and the divorce which has severed my family and which has had results too many and too hard.

Difficulty of Control

As in the experience of fright, the individual who has his sympathy and sorrow aroused may experience great difficulty in controlling himself. Many, particularly girls, admit that their efforts to check their tears either prove futile or cause them to cry all the more. Others try to inhibit their feelings by telling themselves, "Oh, this is just a picture." These very efforts at inhibition bespeak further the impressive hold which such scenes and pictures acquire over the emotional state of the individual.

Difficulty in controlling the crying induced by motion pictures is spoken of by 39 per cent of the 458 writers of the high-school documents being used as a sample for tabulation purposes. Twenty-two per cent of the writers deny having any difficulty in controlling this feeling, whereas nothing is said on this point in 39 per cent of the documents. Here again one discovers an interesting sex difference. Fifty per cent of the girls who have written documents admit this difficulty of controlling their crying, whereas this admission is made by only 26 per cent of the boys. Again, only 12 per cent of the girls declare that they have no difficulty in checking this emotion, whereas 34 per cent of the boys declare that they are able to control their feeling. There is no information on this point of control in 38 per cent of the girls and in 40 per cent of the boys.

Following are a few accounts chosen at random indicating this inability to control oneself when experiencing sadness or in a state of tears:

Female, 14, white, high-school sophomore.—The picture "Wings" made me cry because there was much suffering. I love to cry. I always think it is a good picture if it can make me cry. I have found it hard to control my emotions and never think it as just a picture. Sometimes I try to check my emotions and moods, but to no advantage.

Male, 19, white, Jewish, college sophomore.—At this period of my life I found some unexplainable comfort and enjoyment in crying and suffering over the sad part of a picture. I remember how I wished to offer the poor old lady my help as she was left alone by her children in the movie, "Over the Hill." After seeing a show of this nature I felt rather downcast because I considered myself a *man* capable of controlling my emotions and this sort of picture made me feel so weak and small.

Female, 16, white, high-school junior.—Yes, I find it hard to control my feelings. For example, I couldn't have stopped my tears during the "Singing Fool" if I had wanted to, which I suppose I didn't. One can't enjoy a movie if one hasn't any feelings or heart.

Female, 14, white, high-school sophomore.—I don't find it so hard to control my emotions aroused by moving pictures, but if I once start crying it's hard for me to stop. Yes, I explain away the situation by saying, "Oh, well, it's only a picture," and I tell myself not to be such a baby.

Female, 18, Negro, high-school senior.—"The Noose" was the saddest picture I ever witnessed. I tried not to cry, but the tears rolled down my cheeks and I sobbed in my handkerchief audibly, for my companion chided me for being such a soft heart. I always considered people who cried at movies "great weaklings" and I was thoroughly disgusted with myself.

Female, 14, white, high-school sophomore.—Sometimes, no matter how hard I try, I cannot control my emotions. Sometimes when a picture is not even considered sad, I cannot keep from crying. I think it is embarrassing to cry at picture shows, but I can't help it. Before and after I see a picture I say "Well, there is nothing to it; it is only a picture." But during the performance I can think of nothing but the picture and all my good resolutions go to waste.

Female, 20, Gentile-Jewish, college sophomore.—Ordinarily, when I do attend a movie, I go with a young man; and it would be the last thing which I would do to let him know that I am crying. My one thought when I feel like crying at some movie which I am attending with one of the male sex, is that I must by no means ever display a semblance of tears! I have made myself miserable at times by adhering to this thought; it is not easy to keep from crying when one sees before him the same type of experience which he has been through and knows to be damnable. But each time I have fought within myself to keep the tears back; and I do not remember any time when I have ever showed that I was crying.

Ordinarily this loss of control over one's feelings is short-lived. The individual may stop his weeping with the passage of the scene or after leaving the theater. Sometimes the feeling of sadness may persist for a few hours or perhaps even for a few days. Ordinarily its effect is quite transient.

RESOLUTIONS TO "BE GOOD"

IT is of importance to observe that while under the influence of these feelings the individual may make resolutions "to be good." This is a very interesting experience—somewhat similar in nature to the "crisis" experience in religious conversion. With his awakened feelings of sorrow and grief the individual may become quite self-conscious and raise questions about himself, his relation to others, and his career. He may experience self-pity or self-blame, feelings of guilt, chagrin, remorse, and regret. And in this mixed mood of compassion and repentance he may vow to be good, resolve to help others or decide on a new form of life.

Ordinarily these resolutions disappear with the mood, or as one's memory of the given motion picture grows dim. A typical instance of this experience is contained in the following account written by a university girl:

> *Female, 19, white, college sophomore.*—I must have been about thirteen when I saw "The Old Nest." I wept copiously and resolved never to leave my family to such a sad old age. Of course, the resolution took wings at the first opportunity to go somewhere.

However, as in the case of certain of the experiences of fright spoken of before, an individual may show a permanent effect resulting from a particularly sad picture. In his state of heightened emotion some definite reorganization of his thoughts and feelings may occur and be perpetuated in the form of an enduring sentiment or intention. Discussion of this kind of experience will be made later; here, however, is an instance which illuminates the point:

> *Female, 19, Hungarian parents, college sophomore.*—As soon as I heard mentioned the fact that this autobiography was to be written, I thought of the one picture which really made a lasting impression on me. This, of course, was "Over the Hill" with Mary Carr. I saw it with my mother, and during the picture I cried profusely and promised mother that Mrs. Carr's fate would never be her own as long as I was alive to do my share. I don't believe the effects of that picture will ever wear off.

This point of discussion may be concluded by calling attention again to the peculiar and interesting emotional condition which may be induced by motion pictures—a state in which impulses surge forward and the ordinary run of thought and feeling is disturbed. The individual usually will either do what his impulses prompt him to or will experience strong pressure in this direction. Even though the state be, usually, transient, it is a distinct example of emotional possession and of an accompanying loss of ordinary self-control.

CHAPTER VII

EMOTIONAL POSSESSION: LOVE AND PASSION

THE same psychological effects which we have been considering appear in reaction to romantic and passionate love pictures, particularly when experienced by adolescents. From our accounts it would seem that this is the most vivid form of emotional possession. Under the stimulus of some effectively presented love scene a girl or boy may feel a definite urge for a similar type of experience. The observer may be so absorbed in the glamor of the scene as to be swept by the passion portrayed therein. In such instances one detects again the surging upward of impulse, the relaxing of ordinary inhibitions, the readiness to yield to importunities for love experience—and so a readiness to participate in conduct before which one might otherwise hesitate.

REACTIONS TO ROMANTIC LOVE

THIS experience may be, and frequently is, of a mild character. The boy or girl may experience merely a certain thrill and sentimental feeling which carries no further than to imagine oneself in the situation shown in the picture or else to arouse a wish for a similar kind of experience; or it may lead to timid love advances, as in the squeezing of hands by youthful lovers. This milder form of being "carried away" by love pictures is illustrated in the following accounts:

Male, 21, white, college junior.—At this time (age 15) also, I occasionally saw pictures in company with girls, but for the most part I was more conscious of the fact that I was sitting next to a girl than I was as to what was taking place on the screen. One incident, though, I never will forget. I happened to meet a girl I was particularly partial to on her way to the show one afternoon and I went along with her. What the movie was I can't remember, but it was a slow moving affair with plenty of idyllic love scenes in it. We were sitting off to the side in a more or less deserted portion of the theater, and under the influence of the hero's amour I slipped my arm about her waist and left it there with her permission the rest of the picture. Such a long interval separated the next time that I went to a movie with her, however, that when we did go again I was afraid to repeat the experiment.

Male, 20, white, college sophomore.—In my sophomore year at high school I fell deeply in love with a wonderful girl. Nothing else mattered, this was the girl of my dreams! I can see her now—laughing and chatting as we walk home from school, her books under my left arm, and my right entwined around her arm, and sometimes around her waist. Perfect lovers; we lived in each other's eyes. Our favorite pastime was that of going to the movies. We picked love-scenes to see. Sitting in the theater we would hold hands—you know—as all lovers do, and cast shy looks at each other. When our eyes met—what rapture—what complete understanding. How I wish I could see those eyes again. As the picture progressed, I delighted in placing myself in the position of the hero, and my sweetheart in the rôle of the heroine. When incidents happened on the screen which corresponded with incidents which we had experienced, we would squeeze each other's hand, and my sweetheart would snuggle up closer to my shoulder.

Female, 16, white, high-school senior.—Now I am interested in exciting pictures that will stir my pulse. I love handsome men and beautiful women in pictures. It makes the picture more interesting. Whenever I look at these good-looking men on the screen, I just sigh! and wish they would take me in their arms and kiss me like they do those pretty women. My ambition is to some day go to Hollywood.

Male, 20, white, college sophomore.—A few years ago I had a slight case of that youthful malady called "puppy love" and I recall the interest I manifested in the love scenes of pictures in the movies. I was eager to see such pictures as would teach me better and more effective methods of love-making and I often wished that the object of my devotion and admiration at the particular time could acquire the same feeling as the movies stirred within me.

Female, 16, white, high-school sophomore.—I have been thrilled by love scenes at times. On seeing these scenes I would depart from them very joyful and ready to love some handsome fellow.

Female, 15, white, high-school sophomore.—I have been greatly thrilled with love scenes. I always wonder how I would feel if somebody would kiss and hug me as they do in the movies. When I went to the show the other night with my boy friend whom I like very much, a funny feeling came over me as the bride and groom were being married and I wished that he would have kissed me. Yes, many ideas of my love have been formed by movies.

Female, 17, white, high-school junior.—Yes, the movies do change my moods. Sometimes, when I feel sort of blue, and I go to see Clara Bow or some other actress I feel like flirting with everybody when I get out of the theater. I usually feel that way until the next morning, if the picture made an impression on me.

The following account comes from the autobiography of a college girl of nineteen:

In the gloom of the Fox Theater, I sat with my gang, and I gasped in pleasurable anticipation as the tense moment approached. The hero placed his hands about the heroine's divinely small waist and pulled her half-fiercely toward him. Her beautiful lips parted slightly; he looked into her heavenly eyes with infinite adoration—and their kiss was perfect. My response was inevitable. My hand clutched Vera's; we thrilled in ecstasy.

Short-lived—this bliss which passed all understanding. From behind, where a group of boys sat there came a rude burst of laughter, of smacks and kisses. A furious wave of anger engulfed me. How revolting and vulgar they were! I wanted to knock their heads together, to destroy them, to tramp upon them— for they had hurt my sensitive soul without a thought. They had ruined the sacred beauty of that moment with their vulgarity. I had experienced that moment because I had put myself in the heroine's place; I had felt the sweeping silk of her garment against me; I had been as beautiful as she, in surroundings as glamorous; and the hero had been replaced by a certain boy a few rows away who, I felt, was watching me at that moment. It was a personal insult to me that they had laughed. I turned, haughty scorn in my glance, to look at those insufferable creatures,—and I caught his eye. He smiled—a warmth suffused me, in that moment I knew—

The minutes hurried by. There came the close-up, the flare of lights, the noise of stamping crowds, anxious to gain the exit. I walked in a dream, feeling a spell and a magic touch upon me. I had scarcely left my friends at the corner when the well-known lines of his roadster loomed before me, and the headlights cut gaudy streaks across the pavement. Came the creaking of brakes, a subdued question, my mute assent, the opening of the car-door, and the purr of the engine as we slid into the mystery of a vaguely fragrant night.

I had known it all along, from the moment I had seen that perfect embrace in the movies; I had felt that this would happen. He had parked in lover's lane, his arms were about me, persuading. To my bewildered mind there came two thoughts; one, "Mama said, 'Don't kiss the boys'"; the other, "What harm can it be? It is beautiful." So I struggled no longer; and I learned the charm which before I had only dreamed of.

Female, 19, white, Jewish, college sophomore.—After a fashion, such scenes have made me receptive to love-making. My desire is to be swept off my feet—to use a trite expression—by the man I shall love, if I ever do fall in love. I do think that this desire is in a great measure due to the movies.

Female, 19, white, college sophomore.—John Barrymore is a favorite actor of mine in whatever type of picture he plays; and in love pictures, how he can love, and make one want some!

In addition to impressing us with the way in which love pictures may induce strong yearnings for amorous experience, these accounts also point to the extent to which youths may gain love satisfaction through witnessing such pictures. There is ample indication that many high-school girls seek in such pictures a romantic love thrill, even though its setting be imaginative or vicarious. The repetition and accumulation of such experiences, it is fit to add, seem quite important in stimulating, nurturing, and organizing love impulses and amorous feelings, thereby imparting an effect to the mind which exceeds the influence which one detects in the experiences which have been given. Since our materials do little more than point to this more permanent fashioning of impulses and thought we merely direct the reader's attention to the point.

Some indication of the probable extent of the milder susceptibility to the appeal of romantic love scenes and pictures is given in the following figures. The 458 high-school documents serving as a sample were checked to see the number of writers speaking of having been thrilled or stirred by love pictures. It was found that experiences of this sort were given in 55 per cent of the documents, denials of such experiences in 24 per cent, and no information in 21 per cent. Sixty-seven per cent of the girls who wrote documents mentioned being thrilled or stirred by love pictures; whereas this experience was stated by only 41 per cent of the boys.

REACTIONS TO PASSIONATE LOVE

THE extent of the more vivid and more extreme forms of emotional possession resulting from the witnessing of passionate love scenes is suggested by the following figures. Out of 458 high-school documents, 134 or 30 per cent showed either admission or evidence that the writer had been made more receptive to love by love pictures. In 24 per cent of the documents there was a denial of having been made more receptive to love by the witnessing of love pictures; and in 46 per cent of the documents nothing is contained to permit one to make a judgment on the point. There is no difference between the proportion of boys and girls who write of being made more receptive to love.

Typical illustrations of the deeper stirring of impulses occasioned by the witnessing of love pictures are given here at some length:

Female, 16, white, high-school sophomore.—When I see a love picture or love scene, my heart beats faster, my stomach seems to roll, and I have a sensation of being deeply moved and thrilled. When I am with a boy and there is a passionate love scene, each of us can tell that the other one is thrilled by it and unconsciously his arm goes up or his hand clasps mine. Seeing such scenes has made me more receptive to love-making; before I didn't like it and thought it silly, but the movies have changed my ideas.

Male, 17, white, high-school senior.—My type of movie, as I grew in age, grew to be the romantic type. Each time I would hear of one of those movies with a romantic title, I would go to see it. These types of movies developed something in me that I sometimes like and sometimes dislike; that is, a craving for companionship of girls. I have been in that stage constantly since. By viewing one of those intense love pictures, I get a certain burning sensation within to perform those things which I see done on the screen, and I must admit that in so doing I get a great deal of pleasure. Many times I have seen actors kiss in a certain pose, and at my earliest convenience I would do as I had seen them do. This has, as I said, given me pleasure, and in some cases it has also given me the opposite, heartaches. At present I am overwhelmed with part of both. I suppose this stage comes in every one's life, but because of mine coming so young, I attribute it to my viewing that type of movie that portrays those scenes that are so intense in their dealings with love.

Female, 19, white, college sophomore. ———— and ————
are another famous pair of screen lovers. They go in for sensational love scenes, and much sex stuff. I must admit that one of
these scenes does thrill me and leave me with a rather goose-
fleshy feeling.

Female, 20, white, college junior.—The next year after finals,
I went with a group of girls to see ———— and ———— in
————. I have never seen an entire audience so wrought up
as that one. We vicariously enjoyed with ———— the thrill
of every flash of ————'s eyes.

Female, 18, Negro, high-school senior.—I remember the picture
"Resurrection," taken from the story by Tolstoy, of a wronged
Russian peasant girl. Its sensuousness played havoc upon my
emotions.

Female, 16, white, high-school sophomore.—I've been thrilled
and deeply stirred by love pictures and love scenes. Usually
when I see them, it seems that I'm a looker-on and one of the
lovers at the same time. I don't know how to describe it. I
know love pictures have made me more receptive to love-making
because I always thought it rather silly until these pictures,
where there is always so much love and everything turns out all
right in the end, and I kiss and pet much more than I would
otherwise.

Female, 17, white, high-school junior.—When I watch love
scenes I become very pensive and thoughtful. I am quiet and
imagine myself going through the same scenes with someone. I
hope to be in love with my dream-man some day. I am very
lovable and cuddly after such pictures. I certainly am thrilled
and hope some day to meet the man who will treat me as such.
Felt stirred? And how! Sometimes I am receptive and want to
be left alone with my thoughts. Coming home from the show I
have said, "Please don't put your arm around me. Be a good
boy." And all the while I was wishing he were like the overpowering, intoxicating lover of the screen who would take me in
his arms and crush me to him.

Female, 17, white, high-school junior.—When I see certain love
scenes I burn up and so does my boy friend. We both get the

same feeling (he has never told me, but I can read it on his face and in his actions). I have been thrilled loads of times, but when you ask to describe them, it's almost impossible. Words can't express the feeling.

Female, 16, white, high-school junior.—Love scenes always stir my emotions, and I sit enthralled through the picture. If I am with a girl friend, I make remarks: "Isn't that cute?" "Gee, I wish he was kissing me," and things of that vein. If I am with a boy friend, we sometimes hold hands or cast rather significant glances at each other. —— —— passion and —— —— impetuous love-making have urged me to act similarly on occasions when I have been out with a boy.

Female, 18, Scottish parentage, high-school junior.—I have always been very emotional over love scenes or anything like a love scene. I usually clench my fists, or if sitting next to anyone whom I know very well I will squeeze their hand. Sometimes if a scene is very "mushy" the cold chills run up and down my back. When I see such pictures I often feel that I would like to have someone make violent love to me.

Female, 19, white, college sophomore.—I didn't care for love and sex pictures until I was about sixteen. I never imagined myself in love with a movie actor, but there was one I surely loved to see. He disgusts me now and his love scenes are nauseating to me. John Gilbert in "His Hour," "Three Weeks," "The Wife of the Centaur," and "Flesh and the Devil." This last picture seemed to appeal to me, for I saw it twice and I would have gone the third time but I didn't have the money. The love scenes were so amorous and during them I throbbed all over. I will have to admit that I wanted someone so bad to make love to me that way. I didn't go with any boy then, steady; but I went away from the picture craving love. I thought him a perfect lover. Their long-drawn-out kisses thrilled me beyond words, but now he is disgusting to me.

Female, 18, Negro, high-school senior.—Valentino had no more ardent admirer than I. At the time of his advent upon the screen the feeling of sex consciousness was just awakening in me and Valentino stimulated it to the fever point. I can recall no instance, before or since, where I have given my money more cheerfully than I did when a picture of Valentino's was showing at the local movie house. I often imagined myself the object of his amorous love-making. I yearned with all my heart for someone to come and sweep me off my feet by his passion. But no one came.

Female, 22, white, college senior.—I have been thrilled many, many times by passionate love scenes and I have greatly admired passionate lovers. I can feel the thrill all over again when I remember some scenes; such as the love scenes from "Seventh Heaven," John Gilbert's "Flesh and the Devil," and Ronald Colman's "Two Lovers," etc. I have, instead of imagining myself playing opposite the male star of the picture, often imagined myself in the part with my own particular man opposite me as the hero. Love scenes have stirred me and they have stimulated my desire for loving and perhaps, in fact I'm sure, if my sweetheart had been there at the time I saw the picture or if it had been possible to be alone with him immediately afterward I should have been more receptive to love-making than at other times. But I have seldom gone to the movies with my boy friend and on the occasions when I have, we have been surrounded by the busy city afterwards, which is not conducive to love-making. I have time after time determined, while at a love picture, that I might as well experience some of the love scenes in real life and would be sure that the next time the opportunity offered I would take advantage of it. But by the next time the remembrance of the picture would have faded and invariably at the last second I would repulse all attempts at petting.

Female, 19, white, college sophomore.—Seeing passionate love pictures made me want to go out and try it but I was always disappointed. I used to feel very romantic but never very much aroused sexually. I never felt like going out to a party after seeing a romantic picture; I used to be quite willing to be made love to. We used to go out in cars and park and I always started out thinking that it might develop into a grand passion, but after being kissed once or twice, I wouldn't let them any more, for it was very disappointing and not at all romantic. "The Sheik" just about wrecked my life; "Three Weeks" and "The Merry Widow" were also rather important at that time. I used to dream of lying on a couch with roses all around me and violins playing behind screens.

Female, 22, white, college senior.—Some of the passionate love pictures which are terribly slushy disgust me, but the ones that appeal to my romantic sense make me passionate. Some of the outstanding love pictures I have seen are "Camille" and "Smilin' Through." The picture that affected me mostly was "Male and Female." It is the story of a very wealthy family who have a perfect butler. They are marooned on a desert island and the butler shows his superiority over the other people by meeting the situation and protecting the lives of his employers. He becomes chief of the small community. The daughter of these people falls in love with him and they become merely male and female. The tremendous male force of the man was what got me. Norma Talmadge was my favorite as a screen lover, she possessed such a wistful love appeal. The love-making in the pictures sets up a fantasy-love scene in which I am the heroine. It decidedly makes me want to be kissed and fondled. Going out with boys after a romantic love picture I would let them kiss me.

Female, 18, white, high-school senior.—As far as I can remember, I've never had a real hot date immediately after seeing a passionate picture. Perhaps it's just as well that I didn't, for my sake anyway.

Female, 15, white, high-school sophomore.—After seeing a love picture I think sometimes I would like to be the heroine, but I soon resume my natural life without any special desire for parties, etc. Although if I have a crush on a fellow at the time it makes me want to get him more.

That the impulses aroused by the witnessing of such love pictures and scenes tend to carry over into conduct is shown by the remarks of boys and girls that they observe such effects in the case of their companions.

Male, 20, white, college junior.—If there is ever any harm done by picture shows, I am willing to confess that it is the passionate love show that does it. I can notice it very plainly on many girls whom I have dated to shows of this type. I have noticed, however, that the ones it affects are those who have a strong tendency to be that kind anyway. I have also noticed its effect on myself and especially if the girl is inclined to "help make the party."

Male, 16, Negro, high-school freshman.—Many times I have gone to see a love picture. Sometimes I would find myself dreaming that I was the player and not one of the fans. I used to imagine I was an actor playing an important part in a love picture. I'd dream of making love to some beautiful girl like Greta Garbo, Clara Bow, and others. I used to fall in love with them. Sometimes I would think of them so much until I'd go home and dream about them. I remember taking my girl to the movies to see a love play. The pastime was very, very good. While sitting in the show I had my arm around my girl. She enjoyed the show better than I did. I could feel her tremble sometimes when certain things occurred in the play. I'd do the same thing. When we left the show we were in a daze. We talked of that picture for two or three weeks. We would make love to each other like the actors in the show did. I really think that show helped me to win her love. We often talk of that same picture.

Female, 19, Negro, high-school senior.—About love-making from the movies I learned a good deal, although I wasn't brave enough to attempt to imitate the love-making of Greta Garbo and others on my boy friends. Sometimes after we had seen a Greta Garbo movie, my boy friend would become so romantic that I had to send him home.

Male, 19, white, Jewish, college sophomore.—Movies affect my emotions rather than my actions. At the present time I have often noticed that when I come out of a love picture I have a tendency to want to kiss and fondle any young lady that happens to be with me. I have often been successful in attentions that at other times would have been taboo. The other night I escorted a girl to a movie who is usually very strict about such matters as kissing. In fact, I do not think that she ever allows herself to be kissed. Upon coming out of the movie and getting in the car (automobile) I noticed that she moved over very close to me and cuddled up to me laying her head on my shoulder. Remembering this paper that I had to write I tried to kiss her.

She was a little hesitant but finally permitted me to kiss her once. Immediately she realized what she had done and from then on stayed over on her side of the seat. I told her of this paper and she admitted that the only time that she has a hard time in restraining herself from kissing is when she attends either the movies or the legitimate shows.

Use of Passionate Love Pictures to Induce Caressing

It is of interest to note that some young men deliberately employ passionate motion pictures as a means of inducing a greater attitude of receptiveness on the part of their girl companions. Such behavior points further to the fact that the influence of motion pictures in arousing impulses and feelings and lessening ordinary self-control is being recognized and sometimes utilized.

Male, 18, white, college sophomore.—During my last two years of high school, I did a lot of dating. That is, I had a date about once a week. My program or plan of campaign was, first, a movie, then a dance, then a slow drive home. When I first started taking girls out to the movies, I was impressed with the enormous number of fellows that put their arms around their date in the show and I became aware that heads already close got closer when love scenes were introduced. I tried the things I saw and was pleased with the results. A good love story was more inspiring on a date than a picture in which love was not the important element, and the girls seemed to enjoy themselves more under these circumstances. I didn't get a kick out of what appeared on the screen, but I did like the effect a love scene had on my dates. In "reel life" a boy usually does not go with a girl a long time before he kisses her. The average high-school dating girl, it seems, follows this suggestion. The love scenes produce an emotional harmony that leads in some cases to kissing and necking. Mystery pictures help to produce desirable effects.

Male, 21, white, college junior.—A good movie plays upon the emotions of all of us, but many people are moved by any sort of movie. It has been my experience that nine people out of ten are so played upon in their emotions by a movie as to find themselves in a particularly sensitive and weakened mood in relation to that emotion which the movie most stressed. Let me make myself clear. For instance, after seeing a movie stressing the pathetic case of a white-haired and sweet-faced mother sent to the poorhouse by the cruel neglect of her children, most people react tenderly to their own mother in their thoughts. A movie featuring the torture of a noble white man by fiendish Chinamen works people up against the Chinese. And so a highly charged sex movie puts many girls in an emotional state that weakens, let us say, resistance. I took a girl friend of mine to a racy sex movie. It had the usual lingerie scenes, complications, etc. That night when I took her home she was, in the vernacular, quite warm. The next time I dated her, she wanted to see some gruesome thing with Lon Chaney in it. That night she certainly was not responsive to the same degree as the first, yet I knew her better. It merely means that her emotions weren't aroused in the same way by the second picture as by the first. It is perfectly logical that they can be controlled more or less, and therefore with most girls I generally pick the movies we attend with that point in mind. Remember, it is more or less a physical and natural phenomenon, and nine times out of ten with intelligent interpretation the girl's emotional state can be regulated and used to what may be either advantage or disadvantage.

These accounts reveal, again, a picture of emotional dominance—the effect to which we have referred as emotional possession. The details of this state (emotional possession) seem to stand out clearly. The individual "immerses" himself in the theme of the love picture, "loses himself" in the sweep of the drama. The scenes seem to play upon, "feed," and encourage the expression of impulses which are ordinarily latent or else restrained. Images become vivid and appetite whetted.

The impulses further may express themselves in desires for such passionate or romantic love experiences and in a greater readiness to such conduct. The emotional possession and the accompanying relaxation of ordinary restraint is, of course, usually transient. However, the repetition of this experience through the witnessing of a series of passionate love pictures may have a cumulative effect on the individual.

It should be recognized, also, that in this state, as in the instances of fright and sorrow, there may be occasions when one's experience tends to become relatively prolonged or chronic. In a state of emotional possession impulses, motives, and thoughts are likely to lose their fixed form and become malleable instead. There may emerge from this "molten state" a new stable organization directed towards a different line of conduct. The individual, as a result of witnessing a particularly emotional picture, may come to a decision to have certain kinds of experiences and to live a kind of life different from his prior career. It is perhaps of some social significance to observe that the impulses which are brought into play in witnessing passionate love pictures or scenes are those which our conventions and standards seek in some measure to check. In this sense, without attempting to evaluate the matter, it seems that emotional possession induced by passionate love pictures represents an attack on the mores of our contemporary life. It is probable that motion pictures exercise this indirect influence upon other phases of our conventional, social, and moral order.

CHAPTER VIII

EMOTIONAL POSSESSION: THRILL AND EXCITEMENT

MANY people have witnessed the excitement shown by children while watching certain kinds of pictures. This is another form of emotional possession which we wish to consider because of its prominence in motion-picture experience. Usually the child when seeing a picture which is exciting to him becomes quite animated and is likely to vent his feelings in shouting or in vigorous physical movement. Anyone who has witnessed the behavior of children at a small neighborhood theater during the children's matinée needs not to be told about this form of excitement. Particularly, during the showing of the so-called serial or chapter pictures one gets undisguised expressions of intense emotions, requiring no refined instruments for their detection. The shouting of the children when the opening scene of the serial is flashed upon the screen, their groans when the heroine or hero is in extreme danger, the din of their shouts when either is freed—these are familiar observations. The heightened feeling of children under such circumstances equals in intensity if not in loudness of expression the collective excitement displayed at "pep meetings" or football games.

THE "SERIAL" AND EXCITEMENT

IT is important to consider the excitement induced in children by motion pictures. A typical description of this kind of conduct shown by children while witnessing thrilling or exciting pictures is given in the following account. A trained investigator accompanied a little sister and two nephews (Dick and Roy) over a period of weeks to the weekly installment of serial pictures. Some typical illustrations of his careful observations are given. Speaking of the closing parts of the serial "Pirates of Panama" he writes:

> The minute the name of the serial was flashed on the screen a terrific storm of shouting and whistling filled the theater. Each time the madman nearly hurled the hero over the cliff groans could be heard, and I noticed that my sister and Dick seemed to be holding their breath, and then sighing in relief when the hero survived. Roy again was quiet. When the hero threw the madman over the cliff the theater was filled with ear-piercing noise. The children seemed to pay little attention to the scenes which did not contain the danger element. They talked about the fights while the happy-ending love scenes were on the screen.

Speaking of the first episode of "The King of the Congo" he says:

> Whenever the gorilla appeared on the scene or anyone was in danger of attack by ferocious animals, my sister hid her face and refused to watch the picture. I looked around and saw several other girls and small boys doing this also. Strangely enough Roy showed no hesitancy about watching these scenes and rather enjoyed them. Dick seemed merely excited, but not either afraid or pleased. The atmosphere seemed tense and the children in general seemed to express their emotions either by groaning when the hero was in danger, or shouting "Yay" and whistling when he miraculously escaped from it.

Speaking of a scene in the second episode of this serial he writes:

> When the elephant, which was a pet of the heroine, broke out the bars of a window the children clapped their hands and shouted "YEA." They also did this when the elephant lifted the hero and heroine up so they could climb through the window.

My sister shuddered when the gorilla approached the heroine after she had fainted. I noticed three little boys of about four years of age turn around and look back while this was on the screen, and I heard one of them ask an older companion if the girl was all right yet. In this scene the girl was saved by the crooks and here the children cheered for the crooks.

In response to an exciting scene in a subsequent episode, he says:

In the opening scene my sister acted as she had previously done and hid from the sight of the gorilla choking the hero. When I told her that he was safe she clapped her hands and laughed as the girl fired a couple of shots at the fleeing gorilla. Roy did not hide from the scene as he used to, and when I questioned him about the gorilla he said that he knew someone would save the hero. This seemed strange to me because he was affected by the rest of the suspense scenes. Dick was excited over the scene as were most all of the children, but his reactions were rather of the jumping up and down type than hiding from it.

Speaking of one of the later episodes he says:

The children cheered as the hero escaped from the gang of crooks and then when he read the note from the heroine they groaned, and Dick turned to me and said "Gee, he's one of those crooks" (referring to Mr. Smith). Again cheers broke loose when the hero was running to the temple. I did not see anyone turn away from the picture when the gorilla was chasing the heroine, and I attribute this to the fact that the heroine was making some effort to get away this time and was not standing helpless or fainting as she had previously done. The other scene to which the children reacted was the fight on the edge of the lion pit. As would be expected they clapped and cheered when the hero was on top and remained silent while the crook was winning. As they fell off the edge Roy said, "I'll bet it ends here," and Dick said "Sure." They seem to be able to see through the serials to a certain extent yet they enjoy them and go back for more.

These observations are substantiated not only by what the casual observer may witness in the behavior of children at a serial but also in the accounts which older boys and girls write in recalling their own childhood experiences. Here are some typical accounts:

Male, 20, white, college sophomore.—All during the week I waited eagerly for Friday night. Groups of us boys would get together to talk over and attempt to guess how the hero or heroine would escape that disaster which seemed inevitable at the end of the last episode. Although we knew quite well he would escape, we could not and did not wish to believe that there was no danger. It was the thrill we wanted and it was the thrill we got when a group of cowboys tore down the mountain-side at a "break-neck" speed hot in pursuit of a few desperadoes. In the show we (always a bunch of boys) shouted and clapped, wholly absorbed by the daring acts, narrow escapes, and intrigues of the villain or hero.

Male, 20, white, college sophomore.—Perhaps the earliest type of motion picture I can remember is the serial. This old type of thriller, usually consisting of ten parts, was shown every Saturday at the neighborhood theater. All the children of the district used to attend and then followed one glorious week during which each scene of the episode was enacted out in our backyards. We had grand times playing "lion men" and Tarzans. During the showing of the picture itself we used to be worked up to a terrific high state of emotion, yelling at the hero when danger was near, hissing at the villain, and heaving sighs of relief when the danger was past. The serial was nearly the sole object for going to the movies for me and for most of the children in the good old days when I was seven or eight years old.

Male, 19, white, college sophomore.—Did you ever visit a Saturday afternoon show and feel like cursing or beating the little shouting and screaming ruffians who raised the roof off the theater every time the picture became exciting? Well, I was once one of those little ruffians. The actors were fairly living on the screen before me, and like the rest of the children in the show I could not control my emotions.

It is interesting to notice that the thrilling serial picture has a peculiar relation to the excitement of the child. Contrary to the usual motion picture which finishes with a rounding out of the plot, the serial installment stops abruptly at a high level of suspense. Instead of leading the excited feelings of the child to a state of quiescence or satisfaction, the serial ends at the point where they are keyed up to the highest pitch. The result is to put the youthful spectator under the spell of suspense, sometimes of frenzy or panic, which persists for a week, only to be renewed at the next installment.[1] Just what permanent effects come from this persisting expectancy or keyed-up state of the mind cannot be declared with any certainty from our materials—although there is no question but that the effects are important, even though obscure. Some of the less ultimate effects on the mind are obvious, such as the preoccupation of the child with the precarious situation in which his favorites have been left at the end of an installment; his anxiety over their safety; his curiosity and reflection as to how they will escape; his excited conversation during the week with his companions on how the escape will occur—in short, the difficulty he has in freeing his mind from the thoughts of the picture. Our interest here, however, is not in the effects on the mind, however intriguing and important they are, but in the immediate expressions of the excitement aroused by the "thrillers."

EXPRESSION OF EXCITEMENT

THE excitement experienced by the children usually takes two expressions, that of enthusiasm and that of an-

[1] It is humorous or pathetic—depending on one's point of view—to discover that at the performance when the concluding installment of a serial is given there is usually introduced the first episode of a new serial. The child must not have a let-down in suspense!

guish, depending upon the nature of the scenes witnessed. When the favorite characters, such as the heroine or the "good guy," escape from danger or triumph in combat there is usually an outburst of cheering, of clapping, of whistling, a jumping up and down in one's seat, a throwing of caps and other objects into the air, and occasionally a scuffling with one's companions. When the heroine or hero is in danger, when the "bad guy" or bad character is about to inflict injury on them, one sees the other kind of expression in children. The clutching of the seat, the wringing of caps or handkerchiefs, the uttering of groans, the biting of finger nails and of lips, the covering of one's eyes so as not to see the picture—all of these are not infrequent during the scenes of intense suspense.[1] Illustrations of this kind of inhibited excitement appear in the following accounts:

Female, 21, white, college junior.—One Saturday afternoon when I was about twelve years old, my brother took me to the show. I don't recall the name of the feature picture, in which Pearl White was the heroine. The serial which was continued from the previous Saturday commenced with a scene in which the heroine was being strangled by the villain who had sneaky, narrow eyes. That was sufficient in itself. I refused to see the remainder of the picture and asked my brother to leave. He, however, was a serial fan and paid little if any attention to my request. Since I didn't choose to sacrifice my share of the remaining candy, I buried my head in my hands and asked my brother to inform me when it would be over; but at the most tense moments when the audience would shout with approval or disapproval and stamp their feet on the floor, I would remove my hands from over my eyes and glance at the screen for only a second, and then resume my former position.

[1] It is of some interest to notice that the distance between suspense and horror is short. Where there is possibility of escape there is suspense; where the hero or heroine are in danger and *cannot* escape there is likely to be agony or terror. Children have been subject to needless torture by the failure to recognize this simple point in constructing the plot and scenes of the "thrillers."

Female, 20, white, Jewish-Gentile, college sophomore.—I remember coming home from each installment of the serial "thriller" very much excited and with my nails all bitten off. I always look back on this movie experience with regret and sorrow that it ever took place, for I can never forget how frantic I used to get watching this picture in all its horror. It was ever my promise that when I went the next Sunday afternoon I would remain perfectly calm; but this never happened—I was an impulsive, nervous child beyond whose power it was to view it all unmoved.

The writer asked 232 children in the fourth, fifth, and sixth grades of two of the public schools in Chicago, "Do you ever bite your finger nails while excited, cover your eyes, or hide your face while at a show?" Of the 232 children, 65 per cent spoke of experiences at the movies in which they had done this. The remaining 35 per cent were unable to recall instances of such behavior. Ninety-seven, or 64 per cent, of the 150 who responded in the affirmative spoke of biting their nails during the witnessing of exciting pictures. Seventy-five, or 50 per cent, gave instances of covering their eyes or hiding their faces; some, of course, spoke of doing both of these actions.

These accounts and figures yield us the familiar picture of emotional transportation and the accompanying difficulty of ordinary control. To witness children at close range during exciting pictures and to speak to them subsequently about their behavior convinces one that they are laboring under the same kind of emotional possession of which we have previously been speaking. The child is carried away by the excitement. Many, as in the case of the girl whose account is given above, resolve not to get excited, not to wring their garments or bite their finger nails, yet during the intense scenes they are unable to resist the impulse. It is true, of course, that part of the impetus to the excitement is communicated by the conduct

of other children quite as much as from what is seen in
the picture. The overpowering influence of emotional possession and the consequent loss of self-restraint are, however, very evident.

The ways in which the excitement aroused by motion
pictures may carry over into conduct are varied. One vigorous expression is in the form of conversation. To see
and to listen to the talk of children as they come out of the
theater impresses one strongly as to the intensity of their feelings. Another manifestation is the excited playing or reënac-
tion of what has just been witnessed; still further, scuffling,
pushing, and similar forms of vigorous physical activity.
The children act "wild," so to speak. These and other forms
of conduct reflect the excitement which children may experience from witnessing certain kinds of motion pictures.

BRAVADO AND TOUGHNESS

It is quite common for the children after witnessing a
thrilling movie to feel adventuresome, brave, daring, and
even "tough." In response to the questionnaire distributed to 1200 grade-school children in Chicago, approximately 30 per cent declared that they "wanted to do something brave and daring" after seeing an exciting movie.
About 8 per cent declared that they wanted to act "tough
and fight some one." In the case of the first of these two
items, there is little difference in the proportion of boys
and girls; in the case of the second the boys are about
eight times as frequent as the girls. It is interesting to notice, incidentally, that this feeling of being "tough" and
the readiness to fight as a result of witnessing exciting movies is much more common among the boys from areas of
high delinquency than in the case of those from other com-
munities in Chicago. About 14 per cent of the grade-school

boys from schools in the former spoke of having this feeling as opposed to approximately 4 per cent of the boys in the latter.

Following are a few interview accounts as given by boys living in an area of high delinquency who speak of this "tough" and pugnacious feeling resulting from the witnessing of exciting pictures:

The tough guy in de "Hole in the Wall" made me feel tough. I tried to act like de tough guy in dis picture. He was husky and he was supposed to be a gangster and he hid in a fortune-telling place. He used to take people into this place when he had it in for dem and he would kill dem. When I go outside I tried to act just like he was. I saw a guy pickin on some kids and I told him to cut it out. He got tough and socked me and we had it out.

De "Big House" made me feel like I was a tough guy. I felt just like Machine Gun Butch. I felt just like he was in de picture, like I could take a guy and knock him down.

When I see an exciting picture I jump up and down. I feel just like supposing I'd do someting brave and daring like dat.

When I see an exciting picture I get all nervoused up. I don't know what to do den. Sometimes I feel big and tough and if a guy comes up to me I bang! punch him in de nose witout even askin him what he wants.

When I see an exciting picture I sometimes feel scared and shivery. Sometimes I feel big and tough after I've seen a movie. Bob Steel always makes me feel brave.

We went to a show on Madison Street and we saw a crook picture, when we got outside we turned up our coat collars and acted tough like we were stickin up guys.

I felt like a big shot, like I was ten times as strong and tough as I really am.

As in the case of the other kinds of emotion which we have considered, usually the feelings of excitement in children are short-lived. While he is in the mood of excitement the boy, however, may be ready to do things from which normally he would shrink or which he would ordinarily

hesitate to do; sometimes acts which assume the proportion of delinquency. Discussion of this point is reserved
for the volume *Movies, Delinquency, and Crime.*

Here it suffices to again draw the reader's attention to
the incitement of impulse, the sweep of feeling, and the
readiness to yield to impulses—the features which we have
seen in the case of fright and sorrow and passionate love.

CONCLUDING REMARKS ON EMOTIONAL POSSESSION

WE may think of the cases given in the last four chapters
as so many witnesses on the stand. They testify to the
power of motion pictures in arousing states of emotion
which some individuals experience difficulty in resisting.
By skillful and dramatic presentation which grasps the attention of the observer and plays upon his impulses, motion pictures seem able to lessen reflective judgment and
ordinary self-control, to stir impulses and facilitate their
expression. This is most pronounced, of course, in the case of
spectators who are already disposed to act along certain lines.
The nervous child, the romantically inclined young girl, the
young man "hair-triggered" on sex, the excitable boy, the
boy who wants to be daring and "tough," persons with a
bad or a sad conscience—all these, as the instances suggest,
in witnessing pictures which play upon their respective
tendencies are particularly likely to yield to incited impulse.

The psychological characteristics of emotional possession, as we may infer them from the accounts given, are
essentially a stirring up of feeling, a release of impulse, and
a fixation of imagery. The individual is so preoccupied
with the picture that its imagery becomes his own. The
impulses, which correspond to the images, are called into
play and encouraged, and the individual seems swept by
intense feelings. The main ways in which emotional pos-

session expresses itself seem also to be clear from the instances which we have given. There are easily discerned physical expressions such as the shouting, jumping, and excited movement occasioned by the witnessing of "thrillers"; such as the shrinking and avoidance in the case of fright; such as the weeping in the case of sadness; such as the sighing and breathing and fondling in the case of romantic or passionate love. Emotional possession may also show its presence in the field of perception. In states of fright the individual perceives strange objects—the slight noise, the flicker of the light, the crossing shadow are magnified by his perception far beyond their real significance. In sadness and love one's world takes on a new hue. A more interesting expression of emotional possession is in the readiness to act; the readiness to flee, to hide, to seek protection in the case of fright; to be good, to be compassionate, to be kind in the case of sorrow; to be daring and to act "tough," to move around in the case of excitement; and to enter into touch relations in the case of love.

To have induced emotional possession is a mark of the effectiveness of dramatic art. This is precisely what the dramatist endeavors to achieve—to grip the observer and to gain control over him so that he becomes malleable to the touch of what is presented. This is probably also what the movie-goer seeks: a picture which has a "kick" to it, one that literally jolts him out of himself, one that figuratively pierces his shell, dissolves his existing feelings and attitudes, and sets his impulses and imagery in a new direction. The more an individual is disposed along a certain direction the easier he succumbs to the drama moving in that direction.

Usually this state of emotional possession, when it is aroused by motion pictures, is transient or short-lived. The old state usually reappears, feelings and attitudes usually crystallize

again in the old mold, and awakened impulse and vivid
imagery usually lose their keenness.   This return is probably
never complete—although in the majority of the accounts of
emotional possession which have been found in this study there
is no information to show that the return is not complete.

Even though emotional possession be usually transient, and to that extent perhaps not ordinarily significant
in the life of the individual, it may under certain circumstances be crucial in one's career. While under its influence
the individual may be quite likely to experience temptation along the lines of awakened impulse, and because of
relaxed self-control to succumb to such temptations.

If the situation is such that incited impulse cannot be
easily translated into overt conduct, or if the individual
with the aid of his standards can check such overt expression, the impulses are likely to work themselves out in the
field of day-dreams or fantasy. Since some attention has
already been given in this study to this area of influence,
no further reference need be made here.

Finally, we should not fail to see, despite the usual transitoriness of emotional possession, that occasionally it may
leave some enduring effect upon the individual.   The instances which we have given in the case of fright and
sorrow will be recalled.   Individuals may be affected by
an intense emotional experience for some time, and the
memory of it may tend to arouse something of the earlier
feeling.   Also, under the stress of the emotional condition
the individual may form an abiding resolution or decision.
He may, as in the case of some people who witnessed "Beau
Geste" or "Over the Hill," adopt some enduring intention
to follow and to resolve on a new line of conduct. We shall
have occasion to deal later with some of these more lasting
influences which arise in states of emotional possession.

CHAPTER IX

EMOTIONAL DETACHMENT

OPPOSED to the condition of emotional possession stands an opposite state which may be called emotional detachment. In emotional possession one is, so to speak, at the mercy of the picture; in emotional detachment one immunizes himself to its grip. Consequently emotional detachment becomes a method of control over one's reactions. One who approaches the picture in this latter state discounts its character and resists its emotional appeal; whereas in emotional possession one has surrendered himself to the movement of the theme and to the appeal of the scenes.

As we have seen, emotional possession prevails when the individual comes to identify himself closely with the picture and so to lose himself in it. A few further instances of this aspect of emotional possession are being given to serve as a background to the treatment of emotional detachment.

Male, 20, white, Jewish, college sophomore.—A scene of agony which I don't seem to be able to forget is from "Moby Dick," in which Lionel Barrymore starred. In one of the scenes, Barrymore's leg is amputated, and his face is shown during the operation. I think I suffered as much as he did. I remember that I dug my nails into my hands until they almost bled. I am very impressionable, and I felt as if I was experiencing the same pain that Lionel Barrymore was supposed to be enduring. I went through the same experience in the "Flying Fleet" when a group of men were marooned on a raft and dying of hunger and thirst. My throat became dry and I almost felt as if I could stand it no longer unless I had a drink.

Male, 20, white, college sophomore.—Scenes of agony always made me shudder and want to shut my eyes. Scenes of blood-letting especially made me feel weak all over. I usually shut my eye to such scenes. When I did watch them, however, the effect on me was almost as bad as that on the victim. I recall one scene where a man had hot irons plunged into his eyes. I shut mine, of course, but even then I felt that my own eyesight was in danger.

Female, 21, white, college junior.—War pictures have played on my emotions; I distinctly recall seeing "Wings" last year. It was so realistic that I completely forgot that I was seeing only a picture, and I myself went through every experience in the picture. I became so oblivious of my surroundings that I shouted out in a time of distress, and I finally became so hysterical that my escort took me out. The rest of the day I was in a hysterical condition and that night I dreamt about airplanes and war; it took me several days to recover my equilibrium and now I hesitate before I consent to see pictures of such a caliber.

Male, 19, white, college sophomore.—Pictures of war, where Americans are in action, or better, marching along, with the theater organ playing "The Stars and Stripes Forever," always inspire me with a strong feeling of loyalty and pride towards my country. Scenes of that nature make my pulse race and I seem to have a queer shivering feeling of joy, much the same as I experienced when the news of Lindbergh's successful flight reached America. My throat tightens and tears almost come to my eyes, and I want to talk about it with someone. After I see one of the pictures I have described, I walk down the street with my shoulders squared and a smile on my face, and I like to take off my hat and let the breeze blow my hair about.

As opposed to the kind of experience revealed in these accounts, emotional detachment is marked by preserving distance, by maintaining a certain critical and reflective attitude. The individual either does not identify himself with the characters of the picture or else keeps this identification under control. The character of this experience is stated somewhat abstractly in the following remarks written by a college student about his earlier contact with motion pictures:

Male, 19, white, college sophomore.—When I became a senior in high school movies began to have an entirely new significance for me. They became sources of mere entertainment. I frequently went to them in the company of a few friends, not to see the show at all, but to pass the time away, and to be in the company of my friends. It was a totally different experience from my previous movie contacts, for when I was younger it had always been necessary to identify myself with the characters and the story. It was my inability to do this that had caused my subsequent loss of interest, and now I found myself able to enjoy a picture while maintaining a detached attitude toward it.

Emotional detachment is attained by building up certain attitudes which serve to fortify the individual against captivation by the picture. The attitudes which usually yield this emotional detachment are cynicism, scorn, analysis, indifference, superiority, or sophistication. The last two seem to be most common. They do not mean necessarily that interest is lost in the type of picture to which they are directed, but merely that the emotional or sentimental features are subject to a judgment which lessens their appeal.

The attitude of discounting a picture seems to arise from any one of three sources: first, through instruction, or the gaining of knowledge or experience which makes one feel somewhat superior to the kind of behavior depicted in the film; second, through response to the attitudes of one's group when such attitudes depreciate a certain type of picture or belittle a certain naïve reaction to a picture; or third, disillusionment which causes one to question the reality of what is being displayed. Some brief attention will be given to each of these three sources of emotional detachment.

Following are two accounts which indicate the change in

attitude brought about by instruction by one's parents. In these instances the individual comes to adopt a different perspective on certain forms of motion pictures; his new interpretation gives him a control over the emotional appeal of the pictures. The first of these accounts is of a girl who writes of some of her earlier experiences with motion pictures.

Female, 20, white, college junior.—However, I received one of the greatest disappointments of my young life, I believe, when I went to a movie that ended sadly. I cannot remember what it was, but it surely revolutionized my ideas. I had always believed that no matter how badly things seemed, everything would turn out happily in the end. Some people had a long period of difficulties, and others were more fortunate, but both at some time would finally obtain their desires and would "live happily ever after." I used to call that belief my philosophy (I liked the word), and comforted my playmates at every opportunity by telling them they just hadn't reached the turning point yet. I had quite a group of followers who were the same friends with whom I went to the movies. I could always refer to the movies to confirm my beliefs until that fatal day. They asked for explanations and I couldn't give any. I was almost heartbroken and finally went to mother and told her all about it. She didn't laugh. I often wondered why. She talked to me for a long time and told me I must not take movies too seriously. They only showed a few experiences of lives of imaginary people, both pleasant and unpleasant. She told me I could pity people who must live as some did who were represented in the movies and at the same time by contrast appreciate my own opportunities. It was during this talk too that she impressed upon my mind that to obtain money was not the main aim in life, another idea I had gathered from movies. There were two parallel points she stressed, happiness for myself and happiness for others. I shall always remember that talk.

The other account, which is similar in nature, is of a college boy. It is in the form of a brief description of one of his earlier attitudes.

Male, 20, white, college sophomore.—It was very common for me to be in extreme sympathy with sad scenes and this mood often continued after the show was over. It was through this serious and sympathetic attitude that my parents soon realized that I was receiving a bad impression from the movies and that I was worrying too much. Rather than see me perturbed by these post-movie moods they impressed upon me the untruth and unreality of the movie and thus corrected my former impressions. This change took place at the age of ten.

As one may imagine from the two instances which have been given, an individual by increased knowledge of a certain area of life may be in a position to markedly discount pictures dealing with such a field. An instance of this is in the following account written by a college girl with reference to so-called propaganda pictures:

Female, 19, white, Jewish, college sophomore.—Where I have knowledge of the situation, as for instance that of the Russian Revolution, I resent the sentimental distortion of the facts for the furthering of the plot, the caricature of the types of characters and their actions. With that as a basis I try to prevent myself from accepting situations and countries as presented in the movies, as a basis for opinions. And one of the greatest faults I have to find with them lies in this fact—what a strong force they are for molding the minds of the majority in the hands of a group of propagandists.

She also spoke of her suspicion of pictures of gay luxury which formerly had caused her feelings of dissatisfaction with her own mode of life:

A few years back the gay luxuriousness and wantonness of the lives of the daughters of the rich made a strong appeal and led to a vague dissatisfaction with the present and shaped my ideal for the future. Now, however, it is with evident skepticism, a trifle amusement and disdain, and occasionally a little sympathy or understanding with the better type of plot and actor, that I watch these shadow caricatures.

Another instance of this detachment is given in the account of a college girl. Her reëvaluation of mystery plays gives her an immunity to the emotional hold of such pictures.

Female, 19, white, college sophomore.—Breath-taking mystery plays provided not a little recreation, especially when a whole crowd of girls went together. I would be delighted to watch the effect the play had on my neighbors—the squeals of delight from one girl, the labored breathing of another who had let herself go and was living the rôle of the heroine. I delighted in the knowledge that I sat aloof, a "looker-on." No worries or fear for me—of course, it would all come out all right! Hadn't I discovered that all along?

Of the same nature is the following experience written by a college boy. His gaining of a certain kind of knowledge leads him to interpret differently a type of picture which formerly made a great appeal to him.

Male, 20, white, college sophomore.—During my early high-school life I developed a liking for the love scenes. I could not seem to get my fill of love pictures. This desire lasted through my first year of college. I suppose the existence of this period was analagous to a desire for association with the opposite sex. During my second year in college I became aware of the fact that the love scenes were more or less unreal. The natural is always better than the artificial. I saw that love didn't work like movie love. Then I wanted pictures devoid of this passion, being replaced by experiences of true life. My desire for the latter form was increased by a love experience of my own, giving me a new conception of love, leading me to have disgust for the vulgarity I had often seen displayed on the screen.

Apparently the chief source of emotional detachment lies in the effort to respond to the attitude of one's group. If one's companions or associates look askance at a certain kind of picture, make depreciating remarks about it, ridicule its character and term one's interest in it as childish, one's attitude is likely to change by adopting the attitude of the group towards the picture. One tends to withdraw oneself from its hold. It is apparent that through this sort of experience one comes to change and outlive one's former interest in a certain kind of picture. Thus, the upper-grade schoolboy or the young high-school boy may come to regard Western pictures and serials as distinctively juvenile; the college girl hearing remarks of ridicule made about the silliness or absurdity of love pictures may assume an attitude of sophistication towards them; and the growing delinquent boy in hearing his older companions refer to gangster pictures as "kid-stuff" becomes somewhat detached and "hard boiled" about them. Group conversation tends to define and set the individual's attitude. Of course, this may work both ways. The conversation may operate to stimulate one's responsiveness to a certain kind of picture; but also, as we have suggested, it may work to so revise an individual's attitude that he no longer experiences emotional thrill from a given kind of picture.

It is of interest also to notice how one's attitude may change as a result of disillusionment about the reality of a picture, or about its presentation. It very frequently happens that some knowledge concerning the technique of production, such as the use of artificial backgrounds, tricks of the camera, the "shooting" of consecutive scenes at different times, will come as a surprise to a youthful movie-goer and cause him to depreciate a picture. Again, information about the private lives of motion picture stars and their relations to one another may strip pictures of much of their glamor. Something of this disillusionment with the subsequent change in attitude is suggested by the following account:

Carlie Fisher on drugs

Female, 20, white, college sophomore.—The first film plot which ever made an impression on me was "Reaching for the Moon," which starred Douglas Fairbanks. This film had the usual exciting Douglas Fairbanks episodes, but it ended with the disclosure that they had all been a dream. Hitherto I had watched movies with an absorbing interest and entered unreservedly into the life portrayed, but after that I began to think about the reality of them, and began to question their validity. At first I was afraid that it all might be a dream again, and then I just began to think about the true life relationships. I began to compare the movies with life as I knew it. I began to be skeptical about many phases of movies. For the first time I realized that the effects presented were gained by technique and not by actual daring. I became curious about, and interested in, the methods by which various scenes were produced and I found out about "doubles" and artificial scenery and queer photography.

As a result of the impersonal attitude I began to have toward the movies, I felt sorry for the men who had to play the villain's part, while before I had sincerely hated them. My ambition to be a motion-picture actress was chilled considerably when I discovered that the action was not filmed consecutively. One of the charms of that profession, as I had formerly conceived it, was the living of those exciting and lovely stories which always turned out so well if one were the hero or the heroine. Having to separate the scenes would spoil it all.

Usually, the development of emotional detachment in the case of those who have been previously subject to emotional possession moves from a state of naïveté to one of sophistication. The transition, in general, is gradual. It is possible to trace it very nicely in the change in interest on the part of children with respect to "thrillers." The same kind of transition is exhibited in the change of attitude on the part of young men and women towards love pictures, and in the change of interest in crime pictures in the case of older delinquents. We may illustrate the process in the case of the interest of children in serial and Wild West pictures.

A study was made by the writer of the motion-picture interests of a class of fourth-grade children, a class of sixth-grade children, and a class of eighth-grade children in a public grade school in Chicago. Through the questioning of the children and from short accounts written by them it was possible to get a very interesting picture of the change in attitude towards serial pictures.

The fourth-graders showed in the most undisguised fashion a great interest in serial pictures, particularly in the case of one entitled "The King of the Congo" which was being shown at the time in the neighborhood theater. The fourth-graders were very communicative, spoke with pronounced interest and enthusiasm about the picture, and unanimously admitted that they liked it because it was "spooky," exciting, and mysterious. This expression of enthusiasm for the picture was spontaneous, with no accompanying signs of self-consciousness.

A very different type of behavior was shown by the sixth-graders. Here the children were very reluctant to talk about the picture. When drawn out, many of them admitted liking the serial yet they seemed to feel ashamed at the admission. A number declared that the picture and serials in general were "childish"; it was very interesting to notice that quite a few who declared that they liked the serial sought to explain their liking on the basis of its educational value, since the picture showed many wild animals. In general, the sixth-graders sought to convince the investigator of their disdain for what they considered childish things. Their conduct and attitude, however, was distinctly one of affected sophistication. These children were caught between two sets of forces; on the one hand, without doubt most of them continued to enjoy serial pictures; on the other hand, they were aware of the attitude of the older boys and girls that such pictures were childish. Their self-consciousness and inconsistency in attitude reflected quite clearly the presence of this conflict.

In the case of the eighth-graders the conduct was again quite different. Here the expressions of disapproval, dislike, and disgust of serials were rather spontaneous and straightforward. Such remarks as these came from them: "They are usually the lower class of literature"; "They are always ending with the villain hanging by a thread or some impossible thing"; "They are too silly"; "The hero is too great and never is beaten"; "I know they are trash"; "I realize that the pictures are only made and not real"; "They are the bunk"; "Only kids see them"; "They are all right for the punks." The indignant and decidedly emphatic denials which came in subsequent questioning when the investigator consciously sought to accuse the children of affecting an attitude, showed that it was instead quite genuine. Here, then, in the case of the eighth-graders one discovers a feeling of scorn and indifference towards a kind of picture which formerly had been quite entrancing to them.

The same process of forming protective attitudes by the substitution of sophistication for previous naïveté takes place in the other two lines of interest spoken of: the change of attitude towards love pictures in the case of older adolescents and the attitudes towards crime pictures in the case of older delinquents. Here also one usually finds the intermediate steps of self-consciousness and affected cynicism or sophistication. The high-school senior girl or the college freshman girl is particularly likely to show this state of affectation. Being thrown in with groups who look with amusement and disdain on passionate love scenes and pictures, she is likely to affect the same attitude, although she still may experience much of the old thrill while witnessing such pictures. On hearing further remarks about the absurdity of such scenes and the childishness of one's emotional reaction to them, her affected sophistication may become genuine. With such an attitude she strips away the glamor of the picture and thereby reduces the possibilities of her succumbing to its emotional appeal.[1]

The transition from naïveté to sophistication is usually not only slow but frequently imperfect; in other words, the individual may witness certain pictures to whose emotional appeal he may yield, while he may remain immune to the influence of others. The former is likely to happen when witnessing scenes presented with vivid artistic mastery.

Male, 19, white, Jewish, college sophomore.—When I was in my last year of high school, my attitude towards the movies had changed and my two years at the University have made me realize that these movies are not representative of real life, but rather portrayals of the unusual, something which will sell and bring profits. Thus I go to a movie now with a sort of antagonistic mind. I know that many of the scenes are false, and probably never would happen so I enjoy them for the time being, but I forget them usually after the film has ended. I feel inclined to disbelieve that some of the screen portrayals could ever have happened. Yet in spite of all my antagonism I cannot at times resist the urge to imitate certain actions and to desire many things I see on the screen.

[1] Incidentally, this very attitude of sophistication may on occasion be fostered by certain kinds of motion pictures. This has been the experience of the writer of the following account:

Female, 21, white, college junior.—During my senior year in high school I very consciously acquired an excess of sophistication, or what to my mind at that time I termed sophistication; it consisted of dressing in a certain type of clothing, being bored with everything and everybody, dropping squelching remarks to most people and above all being smartly cynical. This was my ideal, and though I fell far short of the mark I never gave up trying for it. The ideal was, to some extent, popular with the other senior girls, and on that account I was anxious to attain it; but the sophistication of certain actresses seemed to me to be perfect, and it was largely because of this fact that I acted as I did.

In concluding these remarks it is perhaps well to point out that one who views pictures with emotional detachment may still select out of them items for purposes of imitation. While he may be immune to the emotional appeal of the picture and so perhaps scarcely likely to experience awakened desire or to indulge in day-dreaming, he may in a detached fashion still be quite ready to copy certain forms of behavior.

This discussion of emotional detachment may throw some light on the problem of controlling conduct in the face of the influence wielded by motion pictures. At present, chief reliance is being placed on censorship as a form of control. Censorship is, of course, a negative kind of control, confined to deletion and rejection of pictures, and functioning under circumstances which make very questionable its effectiveness. The more effective and so desirable form of control comes with the development of attitudes of emotional detachment. The possibility of forming such attitudes in children and adolescents through instruction and through frank discussion of motion pictures instead of categoric condemnation of them is, in the opinion of the writer, very large. A greater willingness on the part of parent and teacher to talk about pictures with children and adolescents, to interpret them in broad ways and so to build up attitudes toward them, holds promise of better results.

CHAPTER X

SCHEMES OF LIFE

THE reader who has followed our previous discussion anticipates perhaps a treatment of the influence of motion pictures on ideas and attitudes. One would expect that movies would be effective in shaping the images which people form of their world and in giving form to the schemes of conduct which they come to develop. Motion pictures depict types of life which are unfamiliar to many people and consequently shape their conceptions of such a life. Further, many of the situations and kinds of conduct which are treated are shown very attractively. In witnessing them some people may develop longings for these forms of life. What is presented in the movies constitutes a "challenge" to the life of many. Out of the reflection may emerge attitudes, ambitions, dissatisfactions, desires, temptations, reënforced ideals, and so forth.

In this chapter we shall treat motion-picture experiences as an influence in the development of schemes of conduct. We shall limit ourselves to those lines of influence which seem to have been of major importance in the written motion-picture autobiographies collected for this study.

INFLUENCE ON GENERAL FRAMEWORK OF THOUGHT

LET us begin with a general statement of how motion pictures shape conceptions of life and influence subsequent schemes of conduct. Particularly in childhood we can detect the rôle of motion pictures in building up a

141

world of imagery used by children for purposes of interpreting and illustrating life. It is no misstatement to say that motion pictures fashion the minds of grade-school children in an appreciable way by providing both specific ideas and a general framework of thought. A large part of the average child's imagery used for interpretation of experiences in everyday life has its source in motion pictures. One may easily get an appreciation of this as the writer has done, by asking, on a number of occasions, classes of school children to draw pictures of action or of interesting life. Given no further suggestion but encouraged to use their imaginations freely, children will submit drawings showing unmistakably motion-picture imagery. The cowboy, the Indian, the airplane combat, mystery characters, and other familiar motion picture types or themes spring out of the children's sketches.

One appreciates further how motion pictures supply children with many of their images of life in the short stories or essays which they write. Usually the story submitted will be modeled after movie themes. The characters, the situations, and the plot conform very frequently to conceptions presented in motion pictures. School teachers are quite familiar with this condition. Many of them have striven on repeated occasions to free the minds of their students from such fixed patterns of thought.

There are other indications that many people carry, so to speak, a movie world in their heads. The great popularity of motion-picture magazines and the avidity with which they are read by many suggest how greatly people's thoughts and interests may be bound up with motion pictures. This is particularly true in the case of high-school students, perhaps chiefly in the case of high-school girls. It is very common to find the lockers of high-school girls profusely decorated with photographs and pictures taken mainly from motion-picture magazines. The keeping of motion-picture scrapbooks is again a common practice and further suggests the degree to which people may have their minds preoccupied with the movies. We may think also of the frequency with which the topic of motion pictures enters into the conversation of children and of high-school students.

A further significant sign of this general kind of influence is shown in the tendency of many boys and girls to invoke motion-picture images in visualizing the content of their reading. Very frequently they will conceive the characters and the plot of the book that is being read in terms of the conventional images of the screen. This in itself presents an interesting problem of imagination. We shall confine ourselves to two brief illustrations of the point.

Female, 20, white, college junior.—As we stopped imitating the movie tricks, my taste for movies changed. I didn't want to be the hero so much any longer. It was much more thrilling to be rescued and fought over. Then, the books that I read were not merely reading. They were stories acted out in my mind, as the movies would have them. Even now that persists. I can read plays and short stories and enjoy them as such, but there is always a subconscious picture of how they would look when produced.

Female, 21, white, college senior.—Sometimes the movies affected my appreciation of books. I think that my first acquaintance with Dickens was marred by the fact that I did not like the illustrations in the editions I read because the people were not drawn beautifully and were not made to look like stars in the movies. I expect certain types of characters to act as did those same types in the movies and often I was puzzled by differences.

The general impression formed by one who studies the minds of children and adolescents is that the content as well as the direction of the mental imagery derives in no small measure from motion pictures. It is rather difficult to estimate the extent of this general influence and even more difficult to assess its significance. If one turns, however, from this general manner in which motion pictures supply a framework of thought and interpretation, to more specific instances, the picture becomes much clearer.

STEREOTYPED VIEWS

ONE can see rather clearly the rôle of motion pictures in forming conceptions of the world in their stereotyped treatment of different people, different occupations, and different forms of life. In depicting villains, heroes, gangsters, nationalities, life of the rich, war, and other subjects, motion pictures may determine how people visualize these things. The following account suggests, in a general way, this kind of influence.

Male, 20, white, college junior.—A year or so ago I saw a picture in which a Jap was shown in a very brutal light, and I began to think that perhaps all Japs were that way. I realize now that I became prejudiced too early, but when a picture shows nothing but the evil side of a race, it is hard to believe them capable of good. Pictures of the World War used to make me very biased against all Germans. One or two of them I remember made me actually thirst to spill German blood. But more recent pictures have absolved Germany of these brutal charges, and enabled me to see their side of the question. I'm afraid that in all cases where a picture has been presented from a prejudiced point of view, I jumped too readily to the conclusion that it was all true.

Many of the writers of the motion-picture autobiographies tell of having their ideas of nationalities formed by the motion pictures. One of the chief of these types is the Chinaman. In many pictures he has been presented as a cunning, mysterious, treacherous person and has come to be regarded as such by some movie-goers. The examples which follow speak for themselves. The first three refer to the way in which the Chinaman was presented in serials.

Female, 19, white, college senior.—One thing these pictures did was to establish a permanent fear of Chinamen in my mind. To this day I do not see a Chinese person but what I think of him as being mixed up in some evil affair. I always pass them as quickly as possible if I meet them in the street, and refuse to go into a Chinese restaurant or laundry.

Male, 20, white, college sophomore.—While still at a very tender age I followed one serial picture called "The Yellow Menace." It was a story of Chinatown with plenty of daggers and opium. For quite a while afterwards I had an inward fear of every Chinese laundry man I saw walking along the street with a bag on his back.

Female, 19, white, college junior.—But I shall positively say that Warner Oland, the oriental-looking villain of the screen, was responsible for my mortal dread of Chinamen. Whenever I saw one I would run as fast as my little legs would carry me and palpitating with fear would cling close to my reassuring mother. He, Warner Oland, was always wicked in his rôle of the canny, cunning, heartless mandarin who pursued Pearl White through so many serials. I carried over this impression to all Asiatics, so that they all seemed to conceal murderous intent behind their bland features, their humble attitude—merely a disguise until the time was ripe to seize you and kill you, or, worse yet, to make you a slave. I never passed by our Chinese laundry without increasing my speed, glancing apprehensively through the window to detect him at some foul deed, expecting every moment one of his supposed white slave girls to come dashing out of the door. If I heard some undue disturbance at night outside, I was certain that "Mark Woo" was at his usual work of torturing his victims. I have not been able to this day to erase that apprehensive feeling whenever I see a Chinese person, so deep and strong were those early impressions.

Female, 19, white, college sophomore.—The characters that I have seen portrayed upon the screen have left uneasy imprints upon my mind. I have seen so many pictures in which Oriental people quietly sneak up and stab a person in the back that I am suspicious of every Oriental that I come in contact with, from my laundry man to the cook. I have a distinct aversion to crippled beggars gained from Lon Chaney's picture that I saw several years back. It is that repulsion that so many of his pictures have given me that has made me hate to see them.

Male, 17, Negro, high-school senior.—I think all Chinamen are crooks because I have seen them in pictures of the underworld so often. I have seen a picture where the Chinamen almost burned a lady to death trying to make her tell a secret. This picture and similar ones have made me afraid of the Chinamen.

Let us continue with a few further instances merely to illustrate the point that conventional depiction of certain types in motion pictures may implant fixed images of these types in the minds of many people. The writer of the following account, a Negro high-school girl, protests against the way she feels the Negro is usually presented in motion pictures. Her statement suggests the stereotyped image of the Negro which motion pictures have formed in the minds of many.

Female, 17, Negro, high-school senior.—It seems to me that every picture picturing a Negro is just to ridicule the race. When a Negro man or woman is featured in a movie they are obliged to speak flat southern words, be superstitious, and afraid of ghosts and white men. They have to make themselves as ugly and dark as possible. The bad things are emphasized and the good characteristics left out. This is very unfair to the race. All Negroes are not alike; there are different types as in other races. Why must they be portrayed as ignorant, superstitious animals instead of decent people that are just as capable of doing great things as any other race; all they need is the chance. It is the same with other dark races besides the Negro. They are always the loser, the shrinking coward, and never the victor. It is very unjust of the white race to make every nation appear inferior compared to them.

The following instances show how in their respective experiences, the writers developed a stereotyped conception of a "villain."

Female, 22, white, college senior.—I remember that the villains usually wore mustaches, and to this day I heartily despise any kind of an upper lip decoration on any man. Even John Gilbert, Doug Fairbanks, and Conrad Nagel do not alter this aversion.

Female, 20, white, college sophomore.—It was when I started high school that I began to enjoy pictures in which the love theme was prominent. I'd put myself in place of the heroine always, never the hero. It was at this time villains would wear a mustache and I still can't dispel the idea that every man with a mustache is a villain. I used to enjoy going over the picture in my mind and day-dreaming about them. These pictures developed my imagination immensely.

Another instance of the development of a stereotyped conception is given in the following statement concerning the police:

Female, 20, white, college junior.—The movies have made me skeptical about our police force. The pictures depicting gangs, etc., have made an impression on me. Lately, in "The Racket" I came away saying to myself "And that is our justice!" Such pictures should not be shown because they make one doubt the thing we should be faithful to. I must confess that whenever I see a policeman, I smile and get a kick out of his authority.

One thinks also in connection with the point under discussion of the way in which the Germans were depicted during the World War. It is unnecessary to give any accounts (many are available) to appreciate how successful the movies were in helping to develop an intense attitude of hatred towards the Germans through such pictures as "Hearts of the World." More recently through the presentation of the theme of war from a different point of view the movies have helped change the earlier stereotyped attitude. Some indications of this are shown in the following accounts:

Female, 20, white, college junior.—The following pictures of to-day such as "The Big Parade," "Wings," "Mother Knows Best," etc., have increased my horror of militarism. No speeches or lectures or doctrines desiring war can ever convince me to change my opinion or hatred of the beastly human practice.

Female, 17, white, high-school senior.—The War Pictures, and I believe I am right in capitalizing what I did, have convinced me of the real evils of war, of the ideas that though war is a menace, disarmament can never be fully and thoroughly put into effect. "Barbed Wire" with Pola Negri, "The Legion of the Condemned," and "The Big Parade" served as the founders of those ideas. One incident from "The Big Parade" I would like to requote here. John Gilbert is in a shell hole, awaiting the return of his buddy from No-Man's Land. His nerves are on edge; the cannons roaring about him and the shells bursting in air arouse his hatred of the general's orders; he hates himself for staying there like the general told him to do instead of going out and finding and aiding his buddy. Then on top of all this tension a soldier from the trench crawls into the shell hole to tell him to quit standing there and pacing, but to lie down so that the enemy will not spy their dugout. "Orders from the general," the soldier said. And then John Gilbert arose, and jumping up out of the dug-out he pauses long enough to draw himself up to the stature of a real man and to fire back, "Orders! Orders! Who's fighting this war, MEN OR ORDERS?" And with that he leaves to seek out his buddy from God knows where. I shall never forget that bit of philosophy, nor shall I ever forget the incident causing supposedly that bit of wisdom.

Further ways in which motion pictures have developed stereotyped conceptions are suggested by the two following accounts dealing with conceptions of "formal" society:

Female, 19, white, college sophomore.—Some of my ideas about life in general—particularly those connected with association with the modern young man—were drawn from the movies. I shall never forget my disappointment upon discovering after having attended my first real grown-up dinner party that all grown-up dinner partners weren't clever, distinguished, worldly-wise, and charming individuals I had thought them to be after seeing a large number of society melodramas.

Female, 20, white, college sophomore.—So long as the vehicle was amorous, the cast was of secondary importance; and I would dote upon a tender love scene for weeks at a time. The height of my desire was to be of an age where fine clothes, parties, an ardent lover would not be out of place. I longed to be a society belle, and my ambitions seemed to be realized when I was able to see the objects of my fancy on the screen. Of course, I believed that life was exactly as it was painted and that at the age when I would be able to go out, life would be a sort of bed of roses.

Finally, we may give the following account which represents a protest of the writer against the distorted impressions which he declares the movies have given him. This document is given here not to incriminate motion pictures, but merely to illustrate further how influential they are in developing stereotyped conceptions of life.

Female, 19, white, college sophomore.—The impressions which the movies gave me as a child, had to be torn down by experience, by reading, and by contact with other people. I thought that only wicked women smoked; that criminals were hard and inhuman, and were to be dealt with accordingly. I thought that all society women neglected their children, had parties most of the time, and were untrue to their husbands; I got an idea that divorce was wrong and that people who were in love married and lived happily ever after, in a little rose-covered bungalow. The movies gave me a lot of foolish ideas which my imagination accepted as facts. I think that movies make adjustment to life and understanding of people and their problems more difficult, because of the wrong impressions which they give. The understanding should come first—then the movies. Also I think that the movies overemphasize the sex interest, and cause people's minds to dwell on sex out of all proportion to its importance.

The investigation to any thorough extent of the stereotyped conceptions built up by motion pictures is outside the range of this report. The instances which have been cited are given merely to indicate in a general way how such images may be formed. A few words of explanation may be in order. The depiction of certain characters, nationalities, races, forms of life, etc., in motion pictures is particularly likely to leave an impression on imagery because of their vivid visual presentations. One's images, so to speak, come ready-made. They are likely, further, to be simple and unambiguous, and to be clothed with certain emotional and sentimental qualities which, one calculates, make their appeal somewhat irresistible. In other words, the setting of the image as shown in the picture, and the emotional feelings which are directed toward it, give it a "catchy" character. These features can be easily perceived in the accounts which have been given, as in those speaking of the conceptions formed of the Chinamen through the witnessing of certain motion pictures.

Some other remarks may be offered. Motion pictures may treat certain types or phases of life which the rest of our educational system accepts as unquestioned, and in doing so implant images which may be contradictory to those assumed by educational institutions. Thus, the policeman may be shown in a way that lessens his prestige or respect—although the school, church, etc., take it for granted that he has these effects. It would be interesting to learn to what extent motion pictures do implant images, in a concrete, realistic fashion, which challenge the abstract conceptions tacitly assumed by the remainder of our educational institutions.

It is fit to make here another observation. In responding to transient states of public opinion, motion pictures may develop fundamental prejudices or conceptions which persist beyond the occasion to which they were devoted. Thus the images of the Germans formed during the period of the war hysteria were retained far beyond the period where they presumably rendered some national service.

Whatever be the value of these reflections, our central point is evident. It is clear that motion pictures may provide individuals with fixed views of certain kinds of life and of certain kinds of people. Where there is a recurrence of this fixed way of depicting a given type, as has been true in part in the case of the Chinaman, stereotypes are almost certain to arise. Of course, they are likely to be formed most easily by those people who have few other sources of knowledge of the given kind of life which is shown. The development of fixed images in such situations is inevitable and requires no explanation.

CONCEPTIONS OF MODERN LIFE

MANY motion pictures are devoted to the life of modern youth. They deal particularly with relations between the sexes but also present schemes of conduct with respect to family and community life. These forms of life are of genuine concern to many young men and young women. The schemes of conduct which they imply are likely to be shown in a romantic and entrancing manner and may frequently carry the weight of authority and correctness. Some young men and women, because of their attitudes and background of experience, regard the life of modern youth as it is shown in motion pictures not only as an "ideal" type of life but as the proper type of life. From such pictures they are likely to derive ideas of freedom, of relations to parents, and of conduct towards one's associates. In this way motion pictures give *sanction* to codes of conduct and serve as an instrument for introducing the individual into a new kind and area of life. We follow with a series of experiences taken from the accounts of the writers of the motion-picture autobiographies. These reveal the ways in which pictures of modern life may shape attitudes and implant ideas.

Female, 18, white, high-school senior.—I saw "Mother Knows Best" a few weeks ago and thought it was great. I think that Madge Bellamy is "darling" and Barry Norton is great. He sort of gets under one's skin. "Mother Knows Best" proves that she doesn't always. The problem of whether mother does know best is being discussed universally just now, and this picture made me feel that maybe if daughter or son did get a word in edgewise once in a while, parents and children would not be having so many difficulties.

Male, 18, white, high-school senior.—From my observations in high school, I think that the movies have played a large part in influencing the actions of what is called the fast modern of today. The high school students see these wild pictures of fast night club life then they think that it is smart to mimic these actions. I know of several cases right here in ———— high school, girls who think it is smart to smoke, drink, stay out all night at clubs that have not a good reputation. They see these things done in the movies; therefore they think that they are being very cute.

Female, 16, white, high-school sophomore.—When I go to see Greta Garbo and John Gilbert in a movie I feel disgusted, because I think they are carrying it too far, but when I go to see a modern picture like "Our Dancing Daughters" I am thrilled. These modern pictures give me a feeling to imitate their ways. I believe that nothing will happen to the care-free girl like Joan Crawford but it is a quiet girl who is always getting into trouble and making trouble.

Female, 16, white, high-school junior.—The movies have given me some ideas about the freedom we should have. For instance, in the pictures the wildest girl always tames down and gets the man she loves. Why not in real life? My notion of the freedom I should have, and I have it, is to go out and have a good time, but watch your step. I don't believe chaperons are necessary because if you don't know how to take care of yourself *now* you *never* will. One thing that gets my goat is to have someone

constantly harping about automobile rides and they don't mean
strangers either but boys you have known for years.

In another part of her document the writer of the last
account states:

> On the screen when it shows a party with the heroine included
> they are generally the life of the party and I believe that "when
> you're in Rome do as the Romans do." I used to think just the
> opposite but after seeing "Our Dancing Daughters" and the
> "Wild Party" I began to think this over, and I have found out
> that that is the best way to act.

Conceptions of Love

From the earlier discussion of love pictures and imitation and of the influence of love pictures in stimulating
emotions, one would expect young men and young women
to derive from these pictures ideas of love and of the behavior associated with it. The sample of 458 high-school
documents were checked with reference to the item "Did
the individual get any ideas of love from the movies?"
Definite indications that the writers had secured such
ideas appeared in 228 documents, or approximately 50 per
cent. Denial was made in 13 per cent of the documents;
while no information appeared in 37 per cent of the accounts.

Some individuals get much of their information on love
and sex from motion pictures. Such has been the experience
of the writer of the following account:

> *Male, 18, white, Jewish, college freshman.*—I was raised in an
> orthodox Jewish home where nobody dared to talk about sex,
> love, etc., and it was immoral to talk about kissing a girl. Until
> I was thirteen I never had a thing to do with girls because of my
> home background. High-school parties were my first introduc-
> tion to the fair sex. After that, when I went to see a movie or
> romance, I actually liked it. As I look back upon it now, I smile
> when I think of the horror and amazement and awe that I had

of myself when I found out that I, the pure virgin, actually
conceived of the idea of kissing a girl and actually enjoying it,
too! As far as I can remember, almost all of my knowledge of sex
came from the movies. There was no other place where I could
have gotten it. Ideas about kissing definitely came from the
movies. This is absolutely true; the first time I ever kissed a girl
was after I saw Greta Garbo and John Gilbert.

Let us give a few other accounts typical of those who
acknowledge getting ideas and schemes of love from motion pictures.

Female, 17, white, high-school junior.—I read a little and I went
to the movies quite often. From both I learned about the cus-
toms of other countries and some high lights in the history of the
United States. I learned something about the art of love-making
and that bad and pretty girls are usually more attractive to men
than intelligent and studious girls.

Female, 16, white, high-school junior.—Love-making for me
was greatly influenced by my older sister, but the many love-
making pictures naturally affected me some. The seemingly
free abandon to the fact that love-making is perfectly all right
came to me through them. In the movies the hero is always
everything good and trustworthy as is the heroine, and the idea
came to me that I could trust any boy too. I have been very
severely reprimanded for carrying out this idea, but I still feel
that most people are trustworthy.

Female, 19, white, Jewish college, sophomore.—Certainly the
movies have made me sharply aware of the fact that men place
a high premium on the physical aspect of woman, that primarily
a man's attention is drawn to a woman because of her beauty;
that a large degree of the proverbial "IT" may be attained by
pretty clothes, risque clothes.

Female, 16, white, high-school junior.—Love in the movies as
portrayed by the stars always made me squirm because I knew
nothing about it. Now I think it's all "applesauce." When I
was younger, though, these scenes always stayed longest in my
mind. I'd put myself in the girl's place and try to make-believe.
But after all the feeling was second-hand. No wonder girls of

older days, before the movies, were so modest and bashful. They never saw Clara Bow and William Haines. They didn't know anything else but being modest and sweet. I think the movies have a great deal to do with present-day so-called "wildness." If we didn't see such examples in the movies where would we get the idea of being "hot"? We wouldn't.

Female, 15, white, high-school sophomore.—Goodness knows you learn plenty about love from the movies. That's their long run. You do see how the gold-digger systematically gets the poor fish in tow. You see how the sleek-haired, long-earringed, languid-eyed siren lánds the men; you meet the flapper; the good girl; 'n all the feminine types and their snappy comebacks which are most handy when dispensing with an unwanted suitor, a too-ardent one, a too-backward one, etc. And believe me, they observe and remember too.

RELATIONS BETWEEN THE SEXES

FINALLY, let us quote two accounts which reflect the judgment of the writers concerning the way in which motion pictures present ideas or schemes of conduct between the sexes:

Female, 16, white, high-school junior.—The fellows get all their ideas of necking from the movies. The girls learn how to lead a fellow on from the movies. In that respect they are both out for the thrill. One thing I must admit. When I go to a love or romance movie, I wish some sheiky looking fellow would fall in love with me.

Female, 14, white, high-school sophomore.—From my observations in high school I think that the movies have played a large part in influencing the actions of the, what is called, fast modern of to-day. The high-school students see these wild pictures of fast night club life and then think that it is smart to mimic these actions. I know of several cases right here in our high school—girls who think it is smart to smoke, drink, stay out all night at clubs, that have not a good reputation. They see these things done in the movies; therefore, they think that they are being very cute.

MOTION PICTURES AND UNREST

IN presenting the life of modern youth in an appealing and romantic way amid a setting of luxury and freedom, motion pictures engender a certain amount of dissatisfaction with life as it is for most people. Young women and young men may be led to compare their own life with that which they see presented on the screen. Such a comparison may foster dissatisfaction and unrest on their part. The sample of 458 high-school autobiographies was gone over to ascertain the number of writers who wrote of having become dissatisfied with their home at some time or other as a result of what was witnessed in motion pictures. It was found that 22 per cent of the writers spoke of such experiences. There was a denial of any such influence in the case of 28 per cent of the writers, whereas in 50 per cent of the documents there was either no information or insufficient information to permit one to make a judgment. It is interesting to observe in the case of those who spoke of having become dissatisfied as a result of witnessing motion pictures that the percentage of girls was twice as great as the percentage of boys.

Some indication of the way in which motion pictures develop dissatisfaction in the case of high-school boys and girls is given in the following accounts:

Male, 18, Negro, high-school senior.—Often I get ideas of how much freedom I should have from the way in which fellows and girls are given privileges in the movies, because they can wear the best of clothes, make plenty of money, go nearly any place they choose, become well known throughout the country and enjoy all the luxuries of life.

Male, 20, white, college sophomore.—I have compared the life shown in society pictures to the life around me and have found it very misleading. It furnishes one with the wrong ideas of luxuries and tends to make one discontented with his surroundings. In this way the movies depicting social life at first disturbed me. I wasn't satisfied with my environment; I expect too much from my parents in the way of comfort and leisure.

Female, 16, white, high-school junior.—The movies have always made me dissatisfied with my neighborhood, but not with my life. I have always wanted to live in a beautiful bungalow like those you see in the movies.

Female, 15, Negro, high-school freshman.—Since I have gotten old enough to realize what good times really are I am dissatisfied with my clothes and my home. I see the girls in the movies going out in cars to roadhouses and to balls, cabarets, and many other things that put me in the habit of wanting to go too. Sometimes I feel like stopping school and going to work for myself so I can go any place I want, do anything and get anything. I think the young girls of to-day should be given privileges to go and have a good time, not all of the time, but very often so they can enjoy themselves as everybody else.

In the light of these accounts it is fitting to observe that motion pictures often present the extremes as if they were the norm. Further, it is an attractive norm. For many young movie-goers no discrimination is possible—the intriguing appeal of the picture, the seemingly natural sanction which it carries, and the simple vividness of its display combine to impress its content as proper and unquestionable.

RESENTMENT OF PARENTAL CONTROL

On occasion the dissatisfaction represented by the accounts given may take a more acute expression in a form of some rebellion against parental restraints. The rebellious tendencies may merely exist in the form of feelings of acute dissatisfaction, or they may break over into some actual form of complaint and rejection of parental control. In the 458 high-school documents there is definite indication of such rebellious feelings at some time or other as a result of motion pictures in 12 per cent of the writers. Denial is made of such influence in the case of 31 per cent of the writers, while no information is contained in the documents of the other 57 per cent of the writers.

IN order to give meaning to this type of influence, to show how the movies, in other words, may induce in certain individuals feelings of rebellion against parental control, the following cases are presented:

Female, 19, white, college sophomore.—Another thing that movies are responsible for, I am sure, is my resentment at times of too much parental restraint especially in the matter of how late I stay out and where I go. Young daughters in films seem to have such a gay time traveling from night club to night club either ignoring their parents' wishes or being blessed with the kind that do not object, and I am afraid at times I think I should have as much liberty as they seem to have. Very recently I saw "Dancing Daughters" which in a way strengthened my ideas stated above, as the girl in it who was held down too much by her parents turns out badly, while the one who is "the modern" and is allowed full freedom ends up the best.

Female, 16, white, high-school junior.—Of course the movies made me want to rebel against my parents' supervision. They still do. My ideas of the way to behave come some from the movies, but more particularly, when it came to treatment of boys, from my older brother. I think that girls should be treated the same as boys by their parents. They should tell their folks where they're going, but shouldn't be kept on a strict time limit.

Female, 15, Negro, high-school freshman.—The movies have often made me dissatisfied with my neighborhood, because when I see a movie, the beautiful castle, palace, stone and beautiful house, I wish my home was something like these. I sometimes get dissatisfied with my own life when I see movie stars with beautiful gowns, diamonds, gold, silver, and other valuable and beautiful things. And I always say when I marry I am going to marry some rich man so I can get all these rich things. The movies sometimes make me want to rebel against the strictness of my parents because I see what other girls in the movies do and have such a nice time. No one to say you can't go out, or say "no." Then I wish I could go when I get ready. I often think mother is too strict and doesn't give a girl enough privilege; I got this idea from the movies when I saw what privilege girls in the movies have. I think I should have more freedom in these ways, go to the movies often and once a week go to a party and then about every two weeks receive company—and a few other things.

Female, 17, white, high-school senior.—After seeing a wonderful picture full of thrills and beautiful scenes, my own home life would seem dull and drab. Nothing unusual would happen and I would become dissatisfied and wish I could run away. My clothes were never smart enough and I felt that my parents were far too strict with me. The girls in the motion pictures nearly always had far more privileges than I.

Male, 17, white, high-school senior.—One great desire that has risen from the movies has been the desire to own a car and to be able to go anywhere, anytime that I wanted. The movies have made me dislike restraint of any kind. They have also made me dislike work.

Female, 17, white, high-school senior.—Fashionable pictures made me long for fine clothes. I could not see why my parents were not able to buy me all the clothes that I wanted. I sometimes thought I would run away like the girls in the movies and live on "easy street." But whenever I had these thoughts I would also have thoughts of what happened to girls that left home. They lived a high life for a time, but they always regretted having left home. So that was why I never had the courage to leave home.

I always thought that I did not have enough freedom. I remember one picture that showed the effects of being too strict which I will always remember. There was a young girl who had some very strict parents. They did not allow her any privileges. One night she came in late from a party and her father told her if she ever came in that late again he would put her out. The girl slipped out with a fellow that her father did not know anything about. She and the fellow went so far that she was afraid to go home. She would have gone on with the fellow, but she found out that he was a bootlegger. The fellow promised to give that up if she would marry him. But she would not think about marrying him so she left him and started to town on a lonely road. She did not go near home, but instead went to some place where girls were supposed to get on the stage. In reality they did anything the manager wanted them to do. When the father found out that his daughter was missing, he tried to find her. He went to the place where his daughter was, but they told him that she was not there. He looked until he thought that he had looked everywhere; then he broadcasted a message over the radio asking his daughter to come home. She heard his message and went home.

I think parents should take a lesson from that picture. I wished that mother had seen it. Maybe she would not be so strict on me if she had seen that picture.

I think a girl of seventeen should be allowed to go anywhere. I think she knows what to do and how to act. She should have the right ideas about right and wrong if she has had the right training.

Finally we may quote an account which presents another angle to these feelings of dissatisfaction with one's home and one's mode of life. The account stresses the element of temptation usually involved in such experiences.

Female, 16, white, high-school junior.—Although moving pictures have many good points, they also have their bad. They have suggested many temptations to me. Sometimes they have made me want to be a very bad girl, and do things that people would find hard to approve of. They have given me the idea I'd like to leave home, and go dance in some cabaret. I imagine I'd like the life in some night club. But upon reflection I have always decided that these things were not the best things to do, so I banished all thought of them from my mind.

It can be seen from the statements of experience which have been quoted how some young men and women may form their conception of modern life from the way in which it is portrayed in motion pictures; how, correspondingly, they may derive ideas of freedom, of privileges, and of rights from what has been seen; how, further, they may experience dissatisfaction, temptation, and unsatisfied desires. These may lead, in some, to a tendency to rebel against confining influences, particularly against parental restraint. The entire discussion indicates how motion pictures may generate and give content to new schemes of life; and in doing so, change attitudes and awaken desires to conform to these schemes.

Travel and College

Some further understanding of the way in which motion pictures may develop conceptions, attitudes, and desires can be derived from considering experiences with pictures showing adventure in foreign lands, and with those dealing with college life. Pictures treating such themes are of noticeable influence in developing desires, respectively, to visit other lands or to go to college. Writers of the motion-picture autobiographies speak very frequently of having been so affected. We may confine ourselves to the mention of a few typical cases.

A college girl whose early life was spent in a small Arkansas town declares:

Female, 16, white, college sophomore.—Life in a small town such as mine was not so thrilling after I passed the age of twelve, and oftentimes I went to the Friday night show and sat in a daze, picturing myself in the places I saw on the screen. My world was very small, for up to this time I did not know what existed outside the small circle I had been traveling in. When I would see the great open spaces of the desert and the cities with great buildings, my heart would yearn to break away from the surroundings I had always lived in and to get out into the world and see what it was all about.

The next account, to select one with a very different setting, comes from a college boy who lived during his childhood in one of the slum areas of Chicago:

Male, 20, white, Jewish, college sophomore.—I had and still have one ambition that has been developed primarily by the motion pictures. That is a desire to travel and see the world. The conditions under which the traveling would take place would be no barrier to me. I had that desire when I was young and have it now. I hope that I may soon be able to fulfill this ambition. It is common for the children to develop ambitions to become policemen or movie stars or the like, but I never did have any ambition like that. The desire for travel was so strong in me that when I used to quarrel at home, I always wanted to run away from home. The temptation to run away from home is due both to the fact that I desired to travel and to the fact that in the movies I saw scenes of how the wealthier class lives, and was dissatisfied with the life I was leading. It never occurred to me that if I did run away I would lead a worse life than that at home. Coming from surroundings of squalidness, dirt, thievery, missing meals often, and limited space to travel in always brings forth in one the socialistic attitude when he sees scenes of the rich and how they squander money. So it was with me. When a big beautiful car went through our streets we threw stones at it, having in mind that the rich were no good. The occasion to see the life of the wealthy was the only time when pictures made me dissatisfied with the life I was leading or perhaps dissatisfied with the life the rich were leading.

Finally we may give an excerpt from the document of a high-school girl. This is a typical example of the kinds of statements that one finds in the motion-picture autobiographies:

Female, 17, white, high-school junior.—I have always wanted to travel extensively and movies have strengthened that desire. Having seen the warm swept sands of the Sahara, the cold barren lands of Russia, and the white, snow-laden Alps portrayed in the pictures I have a keen longing to visit each and all of them. I am planning now to save sufficient funds to go abroad in about ten years.

In tabulating the 458 high-school documents being used as a sample we found in 59 per cent of them evidence that motion pictures have helped develop a yearning for travel. This was denied in 7 per cent of the documents, and not touched on in 34 per cent of them.

Somewhat of a similar distribution appears in the evidence in the documents bearing on the item, "Have the movies developed a desire to go to college?" Affirmative indication of such influence is given in 51 per cent of the documents and denied in 7 per cent. There was no information on the point in 42 per cent of the documents.

We follow with some accounts which show the rôle of motion pictures in engendering or reënforcing desires to go to college. The accounts, incidentally, call attention to the very attractive way in which college life is usually depicted and suggest the kind of stereotyped picture of such life that motion pictures help to form.

Female, 20, white, college sophomore.—When I was about twelve years old, college pictures had a particular fascination for me. I had a beautiful mental picture of college life and an ambition to be allowed some day to attend one. I used to get the biggest thrill when I saw pictures of young people having such glorious times at college, entering into athletics, being in dramatics, going to "proms," and having midnight escapades. After these shows I used to go home and study with renewed vigor so that I might get to college all the sooner. Alas, college is not all that I saw it to be on the screen or even imagined it to be in my wildest dreams. But that only proves that my imagination and my emotions overshadow my sense of reality.

Female, 17, white, high-school senior.—Like most students, college pictures gave me a longing for college days. I know all college life can't possibly be as it is portrayed, but it must be fun anyhow. I intend to go to college after I work a few years.

Female, 16, white, high-school junior.—When I saw "The Campus Flirt" I was determined to go to college and try to become the heroine of the campus activities. I was athletically inclined (at least people told me I was) so I was positive I'd be a great success.

Male, 18, Negro, high-school senior.—When I saw Clara Bow in "The Wild Party" it gave me a desire to go to college; so much so, that I had to go to see the picture again; because I realized that if the girls get along so nicely and have so much fun, the boys would have much more fun than that.

Female, 16, white, high-school sophomore.—College pictures have always made me ambitious. After eeing one o them I always feel like I would like to go to college and do everything the pictures show. An example of inspiring college pictures is "The Collegians."

Female, 18, Negro, high-school senior.—I feel that I've wasted a good deal of my time in high school, but I intend to go to college and make up for that mistake of getting out of all the work I could. Sometimes I give up the idea of going to college, but when I see a movie of that glorious life that little flame starts to burning again. For to me college life seems divine, not all work, but some good wholesome play. It would be more thrilling to attend a college football game than a high-school game. Track meets, socials, and class work would be very enjoyable.

In motion pictures college life is shown very attractively. Such pictures are likely to awaken yearnings, stir ambitions, and sometimes lead to resolutions. They are likely, also, to lead young men and women to build up "ideal" images of college life which are far-fetched or distorted. It is perhaps not improper to add that a good part of the general public's conception of college life is derived from the way the subject is depicted in motion pictures. Many college students speak and write of the disillusionment which they experience after coming to college or a university. The following is an account of a conversation, as verbatim as possible, between four college girls living in a dormitory. It will convey some idea of the stereotyped picture of college life which many derive from the movies.

"—Her idea of college is Bebe Daniels and Richard Dix."

"*One Minute to Play?*"

"Yes, that combined with *Flaming Youth.*"

"Well, you know a lot of us have that in mind when we come away to college."

"It doesn't take us long to get rid of it, though. But the ones who never get here are the ones who idealize the rah-rah stuff. They really believe college is nothing more than a big house-party."

"High-school kids are like that."

"Yes, and working girls. I worked in at Macy's one summer, and I learned a lot. When they discovered I was a college girl, you should have heard the questions they asked me. They were *pathetic.*"

"What, for example?"

"Well, the girl that worked beside me was particularly thrilled. She asked me if I lived in a sorority house, and if there were a lot of good-looking men, and did we drink much."

"I wondered the same things myself, when I was in high school."

"But that wasn't all. This girl wanted to know if we had dirt sessions, and did the college students pet all the time. Not a word about classes or studying, just the social side. She said, 'Oh, do you really go to houseparties? And do the men and girls wear their pajamas when they're together?'"

"Good Lord, where did she think of that?"

"Movies."

"She might have gotten it from these sizzling books—*Unforbidden Fruit* and so on."

"No, these girls don't read much. The movies are about their only source of enlightenment. They dote on college pictures, too. The University campus—Youth's Playground!"

"You know I had a few of those ideas myself, somewhat toned down. And I lived in a college town."

"I think we all have, to a certain extent. After seeing every collegiate show from *The Freshman* to *Varsity* we're all ready

to have just one big frolic through the fields of higher education."
"Yeh, and we find out soon enough—."

AMBITIONS

FURTHER instances of how motion pictures may help to shape schemes of conduct is shown in the development of ambitions. Adolescents may witness motion pictures which portray attractively a given life and may develop ambitions to experience that life or to emulate some character within it. It would seem from the autobiographies that motion pictures are of quite minor significance in the formation of ambitions since indications of such an effect appear in less than 7 per cent of the accounts. We shall content ourselves with listing a few of the descriptions of this effect as they appear in some of the documents.

Male, 19, white, college sophomore.—The pictures that I enjoy most now, though, are those centering about the law court. Films of this type are rather rare, in fact I have seen but two pictures in the last five years that I could place in this class, and as a consequence I always look forward to them. When I do see one, it has a more substantial and lasting effect on me than any other kind in that for many days after, whenever my mind is free, my thoughts wander back to the scenes of the courtroom. I picture myself in the position of the presiding judge, a source of justice, then in the rôle of the prosecuting attorney, freeing society from the scourge of gun-play and violence, and finally as the counsel for the defense, successfully maintaining my client's innocence. The effect of all this is to cause me to wish that I was through with school and out in the world covering myself with glory by virtue of super-attainments in the field of law. Again, these pictures seem to occur at a time when I am rather depressed, and they serve in the added capacity of refiring my ambition and giving it an entirely new birth. This, I believe, has been the most lasting beneficial effect that I have derived from motion pictures.

Female, 19, white, Jewish, college sophomore.—The picture

"Humoresque" has also influenced me. I always wanted to be a musician and that picture made my desire stronger. I seemed to "feel" music since that picture, and I still see the actor holding his violin and making facial expressions with every feeling of the tone. I might add that to this day I study music and have aspirations of becoming a concert musician in the near future.

Male, 21, white, college sophomore.—I firmly believe that my going to college was the result of the influence of motion pictures. Upon my graduation from high school I had no thought of going to college, because my commercial course had not provided me with all the subjects necessary to fulfill the entrance requirements. I was short two entire years of mathematics. That I had given up all hope of ever receiving a university education is shown, by the fact that I had enrolled for a course at a business college. One evening I attended the theater alone. A college picture was being shown, which was different, however, from most pictures of this type in that it did not stress football and the inevitable campus romance unduly. Instead, it was a really worth-while story of a young man's struggle to get a college education and his final success. The picture showed both the value of a college course and the pleasure derived from the social life.

I did not have to ponder over this picture after I had seen it. Instead, the answer to my problem came very suddenly while I was watching the screen. One thought flashed through my brain: "I've just got to go to college." Then I realized that I had wished to do so all the time, but that the thought of the work I lacked had held me back. Upon my arriving home I announced my new decision (to the surprise of everyone!) and within a few days had planned my future course of action!

Male, 20, white, college sophomore.—If it had not been for a college picture that I saw in my senior year in high school, I might never have gone to college. It was in the spring of my senior year, and graduation time was nearing. My friends and teachers asked me whether I was planning to go on to college. I told them that I would like to, but that I didn't see my way clear. About this time a college picture was in town, and I went with a friend of mine to see it. I cannot remember the name of the picture nor of the actor who played the part of the college boy, but I remember the story perfectly.

A young man was getting ready to go to college. It was during the summer time when the story started and the young man was employed in a machine shop in his town. It was hard work and he had long hours but he stuck it out, and made considerable money. At the end of September he bid his folks good-by and was off. As soon as he had registered in school and had gotten settled, he looked around for jobs. It was not long before he had a job in a cafeteria wiping dishes, for which work he received his meals. Then he found a job for his room. He took care of a Doctor's residence, raking leaves, washing porches, tending furnace, etc. He received his room in exchange for this work. Then after a few weeks of this, he got a job on Saturday in a grocery store and with this money he bought his incidentals. He got along fine in school also, mainly because he studied nights when the other fellows went out for a good time.

I thought about this picture for a long time. It had come just at the time when I was contemplating going to college myself and it was a remarkable help. I day-dreamed about going through college like this fellow had done. I saw myself wiping dishes, carrying out ashes and everything else, and getting an education at the same time.

I graduated from high school that June and was employed a week later in a door factory. I worked for 35c. an hour, but it was the only work to be had in the town. I worked all summer in that factory and by fall I had enough means to go to school. When I arrived, I immediately inquired about work at the University, and I received a job in ——— Hall serving meals. In this way I earned my board. About three weeks later I had another job checking men's clothing and with this money I paid my room rent. Then on Saturdays I picked up odd jobs, and with this money I purchased my incidentals.

Male, 20, white, college sophomore.—One ambition which I got from the movies has become a part of my daily life. In some circus picture (I forget the title) a few years ago, I saw Joe

Bonomo perform some wonderful feats of strength. At the time I was a physical weakling, suffering from lung trouble which it seemed could never be cured. The picture fired my ambition to become a strong man. I do not intend to say that the movie was responsible for that desire, for I had always wanted to be strong. But that picture was the event which made me decide to do something to realize my ambition. I tried weight lifting as Bonomo did on the screen, starting with light weights and adjusting them as I grew stronger. This exercise put me on the road to recovery, cured my lung troubles, added about forty pounds of muscle to my frame, and put me in perfect health and physical condition. I suppose that even if I had not seen that movie, I would some day have started on an exercise program, but I have the movies to thank for deciding to get busy when I did.

Female, 16, white, Jewish, high-school junior.—I always wanted to be a dancer and I believe the movies influenced this idea very much. Such a picture as "The Broadway Melody" helps to tempt one to be a dancer because it showed how a poor girl could become famous as a dancer if she worked hard enough. The fame and beautiful clothes and luxuries always appealed to me. I always thought that after I was a famous dancer I could travel and see the world as many pictures show how, after one is famous and has plenty of money they could travel around the world.

Female, 16, white, high-school junior.—I can remember very distinctly that when I was thirteen years old I saw a moving picture in which the heroine was a very young, pretty girl. In school she had taken a business course and after working hard she had been promoted to the position of private secretary. To this very day I would like to be a private secretary. I used to sit and dream about what my life would be like after I had that position. For quite some time after I had seen another picture in which the girl was a very talented dancer, my greatest ambition was to be a dancer. Then at other times I've wanted to be a motion-picture star, but that ambition didn't last quite as long as the other two did.

Female, 17, Negro, high-school senior.—As a result of my frequent trips to the movies I have had one ambition. That ambition has remained throughout the two years up to the present. I want to be a wealthy society lady! So often I sit and think of the many things which I would do if I were in the position of the ladies I see on the screen. Pictures showing a great deal of travel on the part of the heroine always arouse that old longing. How I would love to see Paris, Spain, aristocratic England, and the tropics.

We are omitting from this brief treatment discussion of the ambitions aroused in young children by motion pictures, and of the desires to become movie stars in the case of adolescents. In both instances one can detect markedly the play of motion pictures. The desires and hopes of becoming cowboys, aviators, detectives, and motion-picture stars are by no means infrequent. However, since these ambitions are almost always outlived and do not seem to enter significantly into actual life careers, we have consciously refrained from dealing with them.

INSPIRATION AND THE DESIRE TO BE GOOD

OTHER evidence of the influence of motion pictures in outlining views of the world or in developing schemes of conduct is offered in experiences of emotional inspiration and in the mingled desires and intentions "to be good" which people may sometimes form as a result of seeing motion pictures. Such experiences, as they appear in the accounts of high-school and college students, usually arise in response to motion pictures which play up themes of family affection or religious duty. Before considering instances of this sort, let us pay brief attention to the more casual ways in which inspiration may be aroused and moral conceptions reënforced.

These effects may be attained on occasion by the use of motion pictures which have a "propagandistic" character.

The following account written by a college girl of the Catholic religion describing her experiences as a student in a parochial school will illustrate the point:

Female, 20, white, college sophomore.—I was a student at a parochial school and the church gave a movie one afternoon. What an impression that picture left on me! It has only been within the last few years that I have been able to cast it entirely off. The picture was to emphasize the seal of the confessional. It opened with a murderer making a confession to a priest and while confessing he managed to get some of the blood of his victim on the hands of the priest. After the man has gone, the priest calls the police and they accuse him of the crime and his knife is found alongside of the body of the victim stained with blood. Because he will not break the seal of the confessional the priest is doomed to the electric chair. Before the electrocution the murderer confesses on his deathbed and thus the priest is saved. I realize now that this was to impress the seal of the confessional on our young minds. For some time after this I held the ecclesiastics in awe. What a wonderful and yet in some respect how terrible a life they must lead. I resolved that I would do anything possible to make life happier and easier for them. I did try helping the nuns after this, but after a short time the novelty of it wore off and I drifted back into my old ways.

Another experience of a somewhat similar character appears in the following account:

Male, 20, white, college sophomore.—The only outstanding case of this period that I can definitely recall which played an important part in my moral life of the future, was the attending of a show called, "Sowing Wild Oats." I was but sixteen years of age, but the impression this show left upon me still lingers in my memory. I was not taught anything dealing with sex matters prior to this and to see the condition of those people who did not live morally clean lives filled me with fear. A doctor about forty years of age, a resident of the city, having a good reputation, made a speech after the picture pleading for clean living and acting, especially when in contact with the opposite sex. I

believe this influenced my future life in regard to living a morally
clean life as much as my early Lutheran parochial school training.

In addition to such pictures which are probably consciously designed to implant definite kinds of attitudes,
more casual pictures may call forth incidental responses of
this nature in certain movie-goers. Some understanding of
how this or that picture may fortuitously stir the desires
of individuals and awaken within them resolutions towards
good conduct can be inferred from the following accounts:

Male, 20, white, college junior.—Then came a film of Abraham
Lincoln's life. He has always been my hero. I have never been so
aroused as I was at the portrayal of the death of Anne Rutledge.
I cried. For a whole week I was a Galahad. I could not entertain a
mean thought (nor a happy one) and I purchased Herndon
and Week's two-volume biography of Lincoln and read and
re-read it.

Female, 19, white, college sophomore.—I remember a certain
picture of a little boy running away and who got into a good deal
of trouble. Ever since that picture I held my tongue every time
I felt like saying, "I'm going to run away." A picture like that
should be shown to every child because in his life every child
gets the idea that he "wants to run away from home."

Female, 19, white, college sophomore.—When I was about fifteen years old, Mary Pickford and her curls in little girl parts
attracted me. I saw "Pollyanna," and cried and responded to
her emotions as though it were myself. I can remember vowing
to myself that I would be real good, too, and make everyone like
me for my politeness and self-effacement. I lived with her
through her trials and tribulations in orphanages and in poverty,
and I'd be so delighted at a happy ending for her. I was so impressed because she played the parts of girls as old as I was, and
I could appreciate their feelings.

Female, 20, white, college junior.—The love interest also was
extremely interesting to me. To what adolescent isn't it? Didn't
Elsie Ferguson play in a little skit once called "Forever" in
which she and her lover were separated for a period of some

fifty years by dreary prison walls, only to be reunited by death? I remember thinking that such a sad love would be the sublimest type of trial a woman could bear. Oh, yes! I believed in trials for the human race, on the grounds they were character building. For weeks I went around with an Elsie Ferguson expression of sweet self-sacrifice spread all over my countenance. A little premature, but nevertheless real to me.

Female, 20, white, college sophomore.—One evening mother, dad, and I went to see "Humoresque." I don't recall who the players were, but I think that Vera Gordon played the part of the mother. I sat through the entire picture without even stirring once, and my interest was so intrigued that I was utterly immune to everyone and everything around me. For the rest of the evening I thought I heard violins playing, and that beautiful melody kept running through my mind. I was going to make mother and dad as happy as the boy in the picture had made his folks. That night I went to bed with a determined fact in my mind. The following morning I arose, at least an hour earlier than I usually did, dressed in a hurry and without any breakfast I started to practice. I was going to prove to my instructor that I had talent and that if I wanted to I could become a great violinist and play "Humoresque" as well as did the boy in the movies. Unfortunately, my sincere motives were not recognized, for instead of being commended, I was reprimanded for making *so much noise* at such an early hour.

These accounts deal with experiences of emotional inspiration which are somewhat casual and fleeting. They are, perhaps, of little significance except in so far as they hint at the ability of motion pictures to cultivate some good intention or aspiration of the spectator and to increase its vigor, even though temporarily.

Family Affection and Loyalty

A MORE distinct appreciation of the rôle of motion pictures in fortifying moral ideals and in inducing individuals "to be good" should be conveyed by the series of accounts presented below. The experiences described have been evoked by sentimental pictures centering around the theme of family affection.

Male, 16, Jewish, high-school junior.—It is very rare for me to cry over something I have seen in a movie. It has always taken something very severe to start me crying. The first movie that I cried over was one I saw at the age of twelve and was entitled "Eli Eli." This movie was a very good idea about Jewish home life. I have my own ambitions which I will try to fulfil for my own sake and most for the sake of my mother, my best pal in life. I didn't realy feel the love of a mother until I saw "Eli Eli" and now I know that nothing is too good for her.

Female, 16, white, high-school junior.—I remember once I had had trouble with my mother. I said that everything that was done in the house I had to do. I was very downhearted and thought how cruel they were to me. That night I went to the movies. I do not remember the name of the picture but it hit the nail on the head. It concerned a girl who did not get along with her family and one who did. The one girl was so good that everyone loved her and her life was very happy. The other girl was not happy and people did not like her because she was not sweet, good, and kind to her mother like the other girl. This made me think that I was just like the girl who was not good. I always wanted to be liked by everyone and to be happy so I went home that night with the intention of being as good as possible to my mother and of trying to make family life as happy and pleasant as possible both for myself and mother and father. It has been a good many years since I saw this picture and I am still trying to be that kind of a girl. I have succeeded some, but not enough yet.

Male, 19, white, Jewish, college sophomore.—Movies do change my moods. They affect my behavior in certain channels for about a week after I have seen the movie. The best example or instance of how a movie has affected me is the following: I once saw a movie treating the theme of how a mother raised her children in poverty, but worked hard to keep them on the right path. After the children grew up they left home, became tramps, and the mother became a dependent of the state. For some time after this picture I was as helpful around the house in saving my mother work and in doing a lot of things that were never asked of me. Before going to bed, I'd repeat my goal to myself that "I'm going to make good." This feeling comes over me after sentimental pictures only. I do not believe that any other type of pictures has affected me in this manner, excepting the sentimental type.

Female, 19, white, Hungarian parentage, college sophomore.— I think of one picture which really made a lasting impression on me. This, of course, was "Over the Hill," with Mary Carr. I saw it with my mother, and during the picture I cried profusely and promised mother that Mrs. Carr's fate would never be her own as long as I was alive and able to do my share. I don't believe the effect of that picture will ever wear off.

*Female, 19, white, college junior.—*I also liked to see girls my own age acting in the pictures. If any misfortunes happened to them like their mother dying or if they were taking the part of selfish girls, I would start thinking if I was like that. I would appreciate my mother more than I had ever before and I would say that I would never disobey her again. I would try to be sweet and pleasant at home so these types of pictures had a very good effect on me.

The picture "Beau Geste," which dwells upon the theme of brotherly affection, had an influence on many similar to that of "Over the Hill." The accounts suggest how a picture of this sort may awaken good intentions and reenforce resolutions. Instances of boys and girls having changed their fraternal attitudes as a result of seeing certain motion pictures are presented in the following statements:

*Female, 17, Negro, high-school senior.—*Last year I went to see the picture called "Beau Geste," and the love the brothers had for one another was remarkable. Their love was different from the love of brothers and sisters I have seen. The love that I saw was distinct; the love for one another in the picture was great. From that night on I made a promise to have the same kind of love for my sisters. I am still trying to keep my promise and hope to continue.

Female, 18, white, college freshman.—"Beau Geste" on the other hand did wonders for me in regards to my brother. Brother and I always loved each other as much as any sister and brother ever did. Incidentally, there is a year and a half difference in our ages, his being $19\frac{1}{2}$, mine being 18. After seeing "Beau Geste," though, our love turned into something more beautiful. One seemed more willing to sacrifice something for the other. If I asked my brother to do me a favor it seemed that he did it with much more willingness. Possibly this was imagination on my part, but I know that I for one was changed and could "go through anything" for my brother.

Female, 17, white, high-school senior.—Words cannot describe "Stella Dallas." As far as realism is concerned that picture had "IT" in capital letters. Belle Bennett as the gay, frivolous, but loving and good mother will always be remembered by me. "Stella Dallas" taught me several things, but the one I can never forget I cannot really put into words. This lesson, though I guess it is more of a prayer, is that by God's grace and benevolence my mother will never have to suffer those pains which Belle Bennett suffered, that she may never need to wear that wretched, that remorseful, that uneasy and hunted and pleading look that Belle Bennett wore, and last, that she may never see the day when a son or a daughter of hers is unable to come to her at the time she needs them most. "Beau Geste," that beautiful story of brotherly love, really did influence my home environment. I became more considerate of the feelings of my older brother, I treated him with more respect, I lost my love for pestering him and for wanting to go where he goes, and consequently although he never saw the picture he changed in his ways toward me, so that now, about four years since the showing of that picture, my brother and I are the ideal brother and "kid sister."

Religious Influence

Motion pictures centering around religious themes are the other kind which seem effective in supporting schemes of moral conduct, and inducing intentions and vows to follow such schemes. Let us turn our consideration to some accounts which show this sort of influence.

Female, 20, white, college junior.—"King of Kings" from the beginning to "Lo, I am with you always" was an inspiration. Its portrayal of Christ's passion was splendid and brought every heart in the audience into sympathy and perhaps deeper understanding with the greatest figure in world history. I went in the mood of one desirous for peace and I received it. The words of the Master, the sight of Him and His disciples in work and in solitude lifted one out of this world into a different realm. It made me dream of a time and day when strife shall be no more and men shall live together as brothers. I rejoiced that all of my idealism has not yet been destroyed. My faith brings hope eternal.

Male, 20, white, Jewish, college junior.—Probably no other single factor influenced the spiritual side of my life as did the picture "The Ten Commandments." I am Jewish but no one in our family is orthodox and we do not make much of religion in our home. I can remember how I hated to go to Sunday School—"What's the use?" I always asked. When I was sixteen years old, I saw the picture mentioned above, and from that time on I have never doubted the value of religion. The many, many hardships which my people went through for the sake of preserving our race were portrayed so vividly and so realistically that the feeling of reverence and respect for my religion was instilled in me.

Male, 20, white, college sophomore.—Two or three pictures have been a great influence in strengthening my ideals. Of these, "Ben Hur's" influences were the greatest. I saw the picture three times, and I'll probably see it the next time I get an opportunity. That picture made me want to live an unselfish, self-sacrificing life. Each time as I left the theater I was intensely desirous of showing my new attitude by performing some noble, gracious deed. I dreamed of saving a life at great risk to my own, of dying a martyr's death, or of sacrificing my dearest possession for someone else. These ambitions usually last for two or three weeks, and during that time I was a model youth. Everybody noticed the change in me. But after several weeks I'd gradually lapse back into the normal again. "The King of Kings" also gave me high aspirations. It made me want to be a great religious leader, and I dreamed for quite a while of playing the rôle. Mother always wanted me to be a preacher, and these two pictures very nearly decided me. In fact, I am, at present, rather wavering between law and the ministry, and a few pictures like those would probably make me decide to become a minister. Not that I would allow just any picture to so summarily change my whole future, but I am so torn between the two ambitions that a little influence thrown to one side of the scale would turn the balance in favor of that occupation. The noble aspirations aroused by these pictures are still present, though in a less intense form, and I still feel the desire to lead an unselfish life.

My home ties have been strengthened by such pictures as "Sorrel and Son," which taught me to appreciate my father. There is a host of pictures which show a mother's love, many others show how strong are the ties of blood, and all these have made my home ties more binding. Still other pictures have shown me the true value of friendship, and enabled me to appreciate more fully the friendship of a pal who is very dear to me. Friendships don't flourish unless the friends are willing to sacrifice for each other. That theme was shown in some picture I saw several years ago, and it has helped me to keep my friendship with this pal of mine.

Female, 17, Negro, high-school junior.—After I saw "Over the Hill" I made up my mind to always respect my parents and try to do all I can for them. It was a sad picture, but I think it was a great one to teach children to obey and respect their parents. The "Ten Commandments" was another great picture. The man in the play broke all the commandments and to make things worse killed his mother although he didn't know it. It made me want to try to keep the commandments as best I could and to think about the next world. I think the movies are wonderful for if you would only try to do the things some of them try to teach, I think you would never go wrong.

Female, 16, white, high-school junior.—Pictures such as "Ben Hur" and "The King of Kings" awaken the higher emotions in me. They just thrill me. When I see such pictures I can't help wondering why everyone can't be good. I think those pictures are wonderful and there should be more of them.

Female, 19, Negro, college sophomore.—"The Ten Commandments" was a very impressive picture and I spent much time worrying for fear that I might break some of the commandments in my future life and bring a world of suffering upon myself. In order to prevent such a disaster I tried my best not to misbehave.

The reader who has read our discussion of Emotional Possession will of course recognize in the accounts which have been given some of the characteristics discussed in that chapter. The feelings of inspiration and the accompanying vows "to be good" may, and perhaps usually are, short-lived, although this remark should not cause one to forget that in certain cases the individual may maintain a lasting resolution. Usually, as the memory of the picture is lost the accompanying intentions disappear unless they are thoroughly assimilated into a life-organization which is in general possible if reënforced by other influences. In most cases, however, the experience is like that given in the following statement:

Female, 16, white, high-school junior.—Movies have in some respects affected my resolutions, although they were seldom carried out, as had been the case with the rest of my resolutions. After seeing Janet Gaynor in "Seventh Heaven" and "Street Angel" I resolved to be as kind and sweet to everyone as she was. But before long the picture died from my thoughts—also my resolution.

DIFFERENCE IN INTERPRETATION

IN order to fill out properly this sketch of how movies outline schemes of conduct, it is necessary to call attention to the different interpretations which people may place upon what is seen. There is a wide variety in what people may select out of a picture. Its influence, consequently, is dependent not solely upon its content but also upon the sensitivity and disposition of the observer. A picture which to one may be quite devoid of stimulation may be highly exciting to another. A picture which some may regard as highly moral may be construed in an opposite light by others.

The differences are not merely matters of age and sex, but of cultural background and personal character. Moreover it is often found that while a picture as a whole may have a certain dominant atmosphere, specific scenes and episodes may stand out unexpectedly in the experience of an individual because of specific reference they may have to his personal career. Consequently, in order to assess the significance of motion pictures in providing schemes of conduct, it is necessary to consider the other variable— the line of interest of the observer.

Sometimes the meanings which movie-goers may get from the same picture are diametrically opposite. A few cases of such difference in interpretation seem in order to illustrate the point.

We may choose as our first example "The Birth of a Nation." To many, perhaps to most, of the observers, this picture awakened some feelings of antipathy or hostility towards Negroes. One perhaps may recall the opposition of many groups to it on the score that it tended to fan racial hatred. The following account from the motion-picture autobiography of a college girl represents somewhat this sort of reaction:

Female, 22, white, college senior.—The pictures of the South that were in my mind were those given by Harriet B. Stowe. D. W. Griffith's production, "The Birth of a Nation," made me see the Negro of the South as he was and not as the Northerners have always portrayed him. I believe that many people were influenced as I was to realize what the Negroes thought freedom meant. It is only when a Negro demands the marriage of the abolitionist's daughter, who is white, that he, the father, can realize what all his agitation has meant. This picture did not make me an advocate of slavery as it existed but it made me see things from a Southerner's point of view.

We may follow this account with the remarks of another college girl with reference to the same picture showing a markedly different response:

Female, 20, white, Jewish, college sophomore.—In "The Birth of a Nation" I felt my first feeling of rebellion over a racial question. I remember coming home and crying because the poor colored people were so mistreated. I expressed my view of the "terrible" white people saying, "How would they feel if they were colored?" For weeks I looked with sympathy at every colored person and got eleven cents together within two weeks and gave it to a little Negro boy.

Let us illustrate the point further by considering the reactions to another picture, "The King of Kings." The reader will recall from our earlier discussion the influence of this picture in inducing emotional inspiration and a resolution to conform to certain moral standards of conduct. Another instance of this sort is given in the brief remarks of a high-school girl who writes:

Female, 16, white, high-school junior.—The religious picture "King of Kings" made me feel that I was wicked and it awakened in me a resolution to try to amend.

A Jewish high-school girl, however, has this to say about the picture:

Female, 17, white, Jewish, high-school junior.—I believe that pictures such as "The Passion Play," "King of Kings," and so on, should not be permitted on the screen, as there are many weak-minded people who bring up subjects that should have been forgotten centuries ago, such as the subject of the Jewish people killing Jesus Christ, which is not a fact.

It happens that the writers of the last two accounts were students in the same class in the same high school. Let us follow with the verbatim conversation taken from a group of university girls showing a still different interpretation:

"That's what I said, that I went for relaxation. No worry, no thinking. You just sit back and listen to the music and know for sure that everything will turn out all right. I suppose you go to be educated?"

"Well, I like a little thought. They're all so d—— superficial. No moral or anything.

"What about the *Ten Commandments?* and *The King of Kings?* There you have H. B. Warner dressed up like Jesus and running all over the place. Couldn't find more moralizing in the Bible."

"Those were exceptions."

"I'll say they were, thank God! They came the closest to making me an atheist since *The Golden Bough.*[1] I'll bet God got a big kick out of them."

Such instances as have been given are not at all rare. They show that the way in which an individual responds to a motion picture depends considerable on his own attitude. Let us give other instances showing this point. The following account is from a high-school boy aged sixteen from a highly religious background and with the ambition to "serve the Lord in some foreign land as missionary." He is expressing his attitude towards love pictures in a way that makes it markedly different from the points of view of many other boys of sixteen.

Male, 16, white, high-school junior.—When I was about 13 years old I gradually ceased going to movies and therefore I have gathered nothing from the modern love scenes. One cannot help seeing the many ads and signs and billboards and I have gathered that the movies now shown are composed of nothing else but love. Many of these shows, to my way of thinking, are

---

[1] Editorial Note: This refers to the book by Sir James Frazer.

not fit to be shown. For the most part, I think, they are composed of a lot of mushy love scenes. How anyone can go to a movie and sit there for several hours and enjoy himself watching a lot of other people make love is more than I can see. The signs advertising these various pictures are disgusting enough in themselves.

Some incident in the experience of an individual may cause him to construe pictures from a rather unusual point of view and consequently to react in a way which would not be ordinarily expected. Response of this sort is evident in the following experience written by a college girl in her twenties:

Female, 23, white, college senior.—But fate had something else in store for me. A broken engagement upset the whole world. Tragic pictures for the next few months helped me to weep it off. Youth doesn't cry long over spilt milk, and then what a kick I got from pictures where some vamp led some fool man on and got the best of him. Even in cases where a wife and family suffered I enjoyed it. By the time I tired of this type of picture I had forgotten the sting of the whole affair. In this case I think the pictures made me remember long, but they furnished a different light by which to look upon my troubles. To my people and friends I never intimated how badly I felt, and those pictures took the place of a confidant. After seeing the picture I felt better. It was just as though I had told them the whole affair, and they had mapped out an explicit bit of advice. I wasn't alone; somebody else had had similar experiences and we were strangely akin.[1]

Very frequently one can detect a distinct difference in the interpretation of the same kind of picture on the part of elders and adolescents. A picture which on the part of one may be regarded as chiefly salacious may carry a distinct moral to others. An interesting example was "Our

[1] This account exemplifies the not infrequent experience in which the spectator feels that the picture has a special message or meaning for him, and then feels a peculiar kinship with the actor and, in a sense, builds up an intimate world of two in which he gets approval for his attitude or latent conduct.

Dancing Daughters," featuring Joan Crawford. Many adults in conversation with the author impressed upon him their judgment that this picture was harmful and would likely lead to immoral attitudes and thoughts in high-school boys and girls. These informants included a number of high-school teachers, an editor of an educational magazine, and two college professors. In the experience of a number of high-school boys and girls, however, the picture tended to emphasize other values.

Some of these descriptions are of experiences which are illuminating:

Female, 14, white, high-school sophomore.—I should say that movies are taken at their value—according to the modern standard. For instance, "Dancing Daughters" was modern as could be and everybody (I mean the students) liked it. It portrayed petting and the evil consequences of drink and of taking people at face value. In other words, it was an educational picture, if one could take the example to heart, clothed in modernism.

Female, 17, white, high-school senior.—The last show that I am going to mention is the show that so accurately pictured the viewpoints of the younger generation—"Our Dancing Daughters," starring Joan Crawford. In Joan Crawford the true spirit of the younger generation was shown. No matter what happened she played fair. She even lost her man, and in the eyes of the older generation they think that when a modern young miss wants her man back she'd even be a cutthroat, but Joan Crawford showed that even in the crisis like that she was sport enough to play fair! And "Play Fair" is really the motto of the better class of young Americans, and even in the best products there is always a blemish so why must the younger generation be so shamefully thought of. I hope many of these women who are scandalized at the actions of the modern miss saw that show— and, if they did not change their beliefs after seeing it, well, then, it does not mean that the movie was a failure, but that they are the failures, not to recognize a truth so obvious.

Female, 20, white, college sophomore.—I am very emotional by nature and perhaps no pictures have played on them quite so much as some of these modern pictures which portray, with exaggeration, the modern generation. I remember seeing "Dancing Daughters" and "Dancing Mothers" not so long ago, both of which influenced me a great deal. These pictures emphasized the harm that can result when daughters do not confide in their mothers. Now, mother and I had never been each other's confidantes; I couldn't seem to confide in her as other girls did in their mothers, although I knew that she longed for me to do so, so that we might be pals; it just didn't seem to be my nature, but I realized that I was wrong and that I was making mother unhappy. During the performance of each of these pictures I seemed to live the whole story myself, oblivious of all around me. And when I saw how happy a mother was made when her daughter *finally* confided in her, and how so many misfortunes resulted from not doing so, I immediately decided to change my tactics even if I had to force myself. Ever since mother and I have been the closest pals.

Another instance of what some may regard as an unexpected response is given in the following account of a girl's reaction to the picture "The Wild Party." The reader may recall from instances previously cited how certain individuals experienced impulses towards passionate love from this picture. The following account represents a different angle of interpretation—the selection from the picture of a different feature.

Female, 18, white, high-school senior.—Cinemas have indeed strengthened me in my ties of friendship. My girl friend and I were raised in the same community. We never quarreled or fought as the other children of our age did. As we grew older we began to drift apart. We were forced to separate when we reached high-school age. She left the city and I did not keep up the correspondence, although she would write often. When I saw "The Wild Party" I determined to write more often and "stick by her" as a pal.

Importance of Conversation in Defining
One's Interests

Let us conclude this phase of our study by calling attention to the rôle of conversation in defining what an individual will see in a picture—the aspects that he will select to pay attention to. An individual's sensitivity and perception are built up very frequently in response to what his associates think and say. We have already touched upon this point in the consideration of emotional detachment. Here let us merely suggest that the different interpretations which are made of pictures are explicable to some degree in terms of the interests of one's group. The process by means of which individuals may be sensitized to certain phases of motion pictures, previously ignored, is brought out in the following series of accounts:

Male, 20, white, college sophomore.—There was a time, however, at about the age of sixteen, when I took more of an interest in this sex part of movies. This interest was developed largely through the comments of other boys who suggested that a certain actress was beautiful, or had a nice figure, or that it would be fun to kiss her, or that they envied the actor playing opposite her, etc. In this way I started to take an interest in love pictures and kept my eyes open for such scenes.

Male, 19, white, Jewish, college sophomore.—As far as adopting habits in one's childhood, I doubt very much if any lasting habits can be acquired through the seeing of movies in one's childhood. In my age, however, is when one can pick up ideas and use them. I know a fellow from the high school from which I came, he is a graduate of the reform school, and an alumnus of the city jail. I have heard him say time and time again "I'm going over to my 'Babe's' house and put on the John Gilbert act." Other fellows in the crowd, I for one, soon went to a show to see what is meant by a "John Gilbert act."

Female, 15, white, college sophomore.—I believe the reasons that brought about my change of interests were first, the fact that I went with older girls and heard them discuss the different moving pictures. They expressed their ideas of some different pictures concerning love. They aroused my curiosity and I went to see these pictures for myself. I finally grew more and more to their way of thinking.

Some idea of how girls may become interested in certain features of love pictures can be secured from the two following accounts which reflect the kinds of conversation which take place among some groups of girls:

Female, 17, Negro, high-school senior.—My girl friends and I have sometimes sat for hours talking of love scenes from various pictures. It seems we get a better thrill after it's about two days old. The general trend of these conversations was: "Oh, wasn't he handsome when he rescued the girl from the villain"; or "She was so beautiful; no wonder he fell in love with her," etc. That is the way our conversations run on, and sometimes we talk so long and so much, until my mother says, "Girls, isn't there anything of interest happening at the school now?"

Female, 14, Negro, high-school freshman.—When I am with a group of girls we always talk about love pictures. We tell how we like to see certain actors kiss and how they hold you when kissing. We also talk about how much effect the kiss has on the actress, whether she closes her eyes or whether she faints away, or whether she refuses such love-making.

These few accounts will suffice to suggest how the conversation of one's group or of one's companions may direct the line of interest and determine in part what one will seek to select out of the conduct presented in the movies.

CONCLUSION

THE discussion in this chapter has been given to indicate the ways in which motion pictures may affect conceptions and attitudes, views of life, and possible schemes of

conduct. Even without evidence it would be easy to understand that the witnessing of movies would leave such effects
on certain kinds of people. Reflection on both the content
of pictures and the manner of its presentation should make
this clear.

For one thing, motion pictures cover an extensive range
of topics. Even though the dominating themes be few
(as they are), their setting, the country, the epoch, the
characters, and the backgrounds of life vary. Much may
be shown which is outside of the previous experience of
individuals; it is natural that their conceptions of the objects and areas of life which have been treated should be
formed out of the images presented in the pictures. There
is no problem here. One may appreciate this influence of
motion pictures in providing people with images of life
previously unknown, particularly in the case of children.

The area of knowledge and experience in children is
usually more limited than in the case of adults, their objects
are fewer, and their acquaintance with life more circum-
scribed. The screen and depictions of objects in motion
pictures not only expand their world in new directions
but also determine how it is seen or viewed in these new
areas. In the early part of the chapter some attention was
given to evidence reflecting the influence of motion pictures
on the structure of imagination of children. They secure
from the movies not only images of this or that object, of
this or that form of life, but also of plot, of action, and, so
to speak, of the movement of life. To be true, their images
may be recast or rejected as they gather fresh experience
through either motion pictures or through other sources.
Yet as long as they are introduced by motion pictures to
objects or forms of life which are new to them, their views
will be made up out of the images presented in such pictures.

This point can be better appreciated when we realize that the display in motion pictures is a visual display. Images are supplied, so to speak, ready-made. They have a vividness and a clean-cut character which makes easier their absorption in "whole cloth" fashion. This it may be inferred is particularly true in the case of those who are visually minded.

The question may also be raised why motion pictures are such a favorable source of stereotyped conceptions of objects and forms of life. The answer may in part be sought in the clean-cut and unambiguous way in which such objects and forms of life are usually presented on the screen. The declaration that motion pictures have to be leveled down to the intelligence of a twelve-year-old may or may not be true. However, that they are usually simple in plot, with the characters usually depicted in a definite and easily recognizable manner, observation shows to be true. This simple and decisive form of the characters, rôles, and plot conduces to the easy formation of images which become elements in the views and conceptions formed by certain movie-goers.

In addition to the facts mentioned that motion pictures may present characters, objects, and modes of living which are new to the experience of certain people, that the presentation is in the form of vivid visual images, and that what is presented is decisive and unambiguous, there is a further point, namely, that what is shown may carry authority and the conviction of correctness. It is this latter mark which explains frequently the displacement of conceptions which people already have, by those shown in motion pictures. We have seen something of this effect in the ideas of modern life formed by high-school boys and girls.

By providing people with images motion pictures obviously, then, shape their views and influence their interpretations—that is, in those areas of life where people do not already have definitely shaped images. The image has a double use; it determines how an individual will conceive things, and it serves as an implement of interpretation. An individual uses the images which he has to fill out and make intelligible to him what he sees or hears, as in the case of the children who depict the Chinamen in their minds in a definite way on hearing reference to them.

If one understands that motion pictures may furnish certain people with conceptions, one can appreciate their influence on schemes of conduct. To develop a certain view of an object or mode of living is to form a corresponding disposition or tendency to act towards it. Conception and attitude are linked together. However, we may view motion pictures more specifically from the angle of attitude or projected activity.

It is easy to see, for one thing, that many kinds of life presented in motion pictures are shown in an attractive and appealing way. This is likely to be true particularly of those forms of life which are of momentous concern to young men and young women, those to which they look forward. In particular the life of modern youth as presented in the movies is full of romance and adventure, freedom and excitement.

In view of the likelihood of many young men and women being latently disposed to such possible experiences, that movies of this type should implant schemes of conduct is to be expected. Those affected may extract ideas as to their rights, ideas of what they come to believe they are privileged to enjoy. They may become dissatisfied or discontented with their own community control, may indeed actually rebel. Such results are likely to occur where the discrepancy is greatest, *i.e.*, where one's own life seems very drab and confined in contrast to the pleasures and freedom of that portrayed on the screen. From this point of view, one can understand the seemingly greater effect of this sort in the case of girls, rather than in boys, and in girls of the poor and immigrant families than in girls of wealthier and more emancipated families; awakened desires and family control are greater in the first instances than in the latter instances.

In the latter part of the chapter attention was called to the rôle of one's sensitivities and experiences in affecting what one will select from a picture. This principle should be kept in mind in any consideration of the aid which motion pictures may give to the development of schemes of life and conduct. It is quite possible, as it was shown, for people to place entirely different interpretations upon the same picture and to derive from it quite different lessons. The implication is that if one is to foretell the effects of a motion picture one must know, in general, something of the interests and experience of those to whom the picture will be shown.

CHAPTER XI

CONCLUSION

SOME REMARKS ON METHOD

THIS study is regarded by the author as exploratory in character. It arose in response to an effort to see what could be learned about the influence of motion pictures by inquiring into personal experiences. The procedure employed has been as simple as possible, for the only task involved was that of inducing people to write or relate their motion-picture experiences in an honest and trustworthy fashion. Efforts were always made to secure the frank and sincere coöperation of the informants.

The writer is not unaware of the criticisms which are often made of autobiographical statements. Without seeking to treat categorically these criticisms in so far as the present study is concerned, in the writer's judgment they do not apply significantly to the material which has been collected. The accounts of experiences which have been secured are numerous. They have been written independently of one another. The fact, therefore, that on major items they substantiate one another can be taken, in the writer's judgment, as a substantial indication of their reliability and accuracy.

The study has been confined to experiences with motion pictures. No effort has been made to compare or to contrast these experiences with those which arise through other influences. We are not in a position, consequently, to make any remarks of an evaluative character concerning the rôle

of motion pictures in comparison with other agencies playing upon the lives of people.

The writer feels that the statement of findings in this
report errs, if at all, on the side of caution and conservatism.
To an appreciable extent the people who have furnished
their experiences represent a sophisticated and cultured
group. This is perhaps not altogether true of the high-school
students who have furnished autobiographies, but it is quite
true of the university and college people whose experiences
have been employed. Our findings suggest that motion
pictures are less influential in the case of people who have
had access to higher institutions of learning. To this extent
the picture which is presented by this study is underdrawn
if it be regarded as depicting the action of motion pictures
on the lives of the greater mass of the American population.
However, these remarks are not meant to imply any substantial differences in the kinds of experience which people
of different strata of our society have as a result of witnessing
motion pictures; they are meant merely to suggest that the
degree of influence of motion pictures is less in the cultured
classes than it is in the case of others. With this one qualifi-
cation the writer believes that his findings apply to the bulk
of movie-goers.

STATEMENT OF FINDINGS

A SUMMARY of the more important of the specific findings
of this study is given here. We have indicated the great
influence of motion pictures on the play of children. We
have shown that motion pictures serve as a source for considerable imitation. Forms of beautification, mannerisms,
poses, ways of courtship, and ways of love-making, especially, are copied. We have shown the influence of motion
pictures on fantasy and day-dreaming. We have treated

at some length the ways in which motion pictures may
influence the emotions of the spectators, showing in particular how they may arouse terror and fright in children,
sorrow and pathos among people in general, excitement and
passions of love chiefly among adolescents. We have indicated how motion pictures provide people with schemes of
life, fixed images, and stereotyped conceptions of different
characters and modes of conduct. We have called attention
to the way in which motion pictures may furnish people
with ideas as to how they should act, notions of their rights
and privileges, and conceptions of what they would like to
enjoy. We have indicated, finally, how motion pictures may
implant attitudes.

Interpretation of Findings

These effects which have been discovered are not to be
considered as separate and discreet. They invite interpretation. We have introduced some statement of their significance while treating them in the separate chapters. Here
we may endeavor to offer a more embracing explanation.

Since the overwhelming bulk of our material has been
drawn from adolescents, or young men and young women,
it will be convenient to view our findings with respect to
their situation and problems.

In our society, the girl or boy of adolescent age is usually
being ushered into a life which is new and strange. It is
frequently at this period that the boy or girl begins to feel
the attractions and the pressure of more adult conduct.
New situations arise in their experience for which they are
not likely to be prepared in the way of previous instruction.
It is a time when new personal ambitions and hopes and
new interests appear, particularly those which involve association with the opposite sex. In the case of the girl, in

particular, desires for beauty, for sophistication, for grace and ease, for romance, for adventure, and for love are likely to come to the fore.

The influence of motion pictures upon the mind and conduct of the adolescent is more understandable if we appreciate this condition—to wit, that he is confronted with a new life to whose demands he is not prepared to respond in a ready and self-satisfying way; and that he is experiencing a new range of desires and interests which are pressing for some form of satisfaction. →

In the light of this situation it is not strange that motion pictures should exert on the adolescent the kinds of influences which have been specified. Motion pictures show in intimate detail and with alluring appeal forms of life in which he is interested.[1] Before his eyes are displayed modes of living and schemes of conduct which are of the character of his desires and which offer possibilities of instructing him in his own behavior. In a sense, motion pictures organize his needs and suggest lines of conduct useful for their satisfaction.

It is not surprising that the boy or girl should copy from motion pictures forms of conduct which promise to serve immediate interests. Some attractive way of dressing, some effective form of make-up, some gracious mannerism, some skillful form of making love may catch his or her attention and be imitated because of the possibilities which it promises. When such forms of conduct are clothed with romance and attended by successful consequence, as they are likely

want to be accepted

---

[1] It is important to consider that the movies do not come merely as a film that is thrown on a screen; their witnessing is an experience which is undergone in a very complex setting. There is the darkened theater—itself of no slight significance, especially in case of love or sex pictures; there is the music which is capable not merely of being suggestive and in some degree interpretive of the film but is also designed to raise the pitch of excitement, to facilitate shock and to heighten the emotional effect of the picture; there are the furnishings—sometimes gaudy and gorgeous, which help to tone the experience.

to be in motion pictures, their appeal is apt to be particularly strong. Further, since these forms of life represent experiences which the adolescent yearns for, that they should profoundly incite and color his fantasy is to be expected. Likewise one can understand how life as it is displayed in the movies may yield the adolescent a picture of the world as he would like to experience it and so give direction and focus to desires and ambitions. And finally, that motion pictures should grip the attention of the adolescent and stir profoundly certain of his emotions, as that of love, is not puzzling in the light of our remarks.

These considerations establish motion pictures as an incitant to conduct as well as a pacifier of feelings. It is insufficient to regard motion pictures simply as a fantasy world by participating in which an individual softens the ardor of his life and escapes its monotony and hardships, nor to justify their content and "unreality" on this basis. For to many the pictures are authentic portrayals of life, from which they draw patterns of behavior, stimulation to overt conduct, content for a vigorous life of imagination, and ideas of reality. They are not merely a device for surcease; they are a form of stimulation. Their content does not merely serve the first purpose, but incites the latter result. What might be intended to have the harmless effect of the former may, on occasion, have the striking influence of the latter.

These remarks should make clear that motion pictures are a genuine educational institution; not educational in the restricted and conventional sense of supplying to the adolescent some detached bit of knowledge, some detail of geography or history, some custom, or some item of dress of a foreign people—but educational in the truer sense of actually introducing him to and acquainting him with a type of life which has immediate, practical, and momentous significance.[1] In a genuine sense, motion pictures define his rôle, elicit and direct his impulses, and provide substance for his emotions and ideas. Their modes of life are likely to carry an authority and sanction which make them formative of codes of living. Despite their gay and entertaining character, motion pictures seem to enter seriously into the life of young men and women, particularly of high-school age.

Because motion pictures are educational in this sense, they may conflict with other educational institutions. They may challenge what other institutions take for granted. The schemes of conduct which they present may not only fill gaps left by the school, by the home, and by the church, but they may also cut athwart the standards and values which these latter institutions seek to inculcate. What is presented as entertainment, with perhaps no thought of challenging established values, may be accepted as sanctioned conduct, and so enter into conflict with certain of these values. This is peculiarly likely in the case of motion pictures because they often present the extremes as if they were the norm. For the young movie-goer little discrimination is possible. He probably could not *understand* or even *read* a sophisticated book, but he can *see* the thing in the movies and be stirred and possibly misled. This is likely to be true chiefly among those with least education and sophisticated experience.

Where, as in disorganized city areas, the school, the home, or the community are most ineffective in providing adolescents with knowledge adequate for the new world into which they are entering, the reliance on motion pictures seems to become distinctly greater. Where the molding

[1] The movies may also acquaint the person with aspects of life which, in his own age group, he probably would not have any notion about until later. Their promotion of premature sophistication seems significant.

of thought and attitude by established institutions is greater, a condition of emotional detachment seems to be formed which renders the individual immune to the appeal of much that is shown in motion pictures.

It seems clear that the forte of motion pictures is in their emotional effect. This is to be expected since in the last analysis they are a form of art—even though popular art—and their appeal and their success reside ultimately in the emotional agitation which they induce. To fascinate the observer and draw him into the drama so that he loses himself is the goal of a successful production. As we have sought to show, while in this condition the observer becomes malleable to the touch of what is shown. Ordinary self-control is lost. Impulses and feelings are aroused, and the individual develops a readiness to certain forms of action which are foreign in some degree to his ordinary conduct. Precisely because the individual is in this crucible state what is shown to him may become the mold for a new organization of his conduct. This organization, of course, may be quite temporary, as it frequently is. However, as our cases have shown, occasionally it may be quite abiding.

Another observation is in point, an observation which, in the judgment of the writer, is of major importance in seeking to estimate the rôle of motion pictures. We refer to the conspicuous tendency of commercial motion pictures to dull discrimination and to confuse judgments. One of the chief reasons for this effect lies in the variety, the inconsistency, and the loose organization among the emotional states which are stimulated. This is to be expected in view of the fact that the aim of motion-picture productions is merely that of provoking emotion whether it be done by playing on the themes of horror, excitement, romance, adventure, particularly passionate love, or what not. In contrast to other educational institutions motion pictures have no definite goal of conduct. They are not seeking to establish any definite set of values. They are not endeavoring to provide a consistent philosophy of life. Their aim, as stated, is essentially mere emotional stimulation.

Just because they have at hand in such an effective fashion the implements of emotional stimulation yet do not employ them consistently towards any conscious goal, their effects, ultimately, are likely to be of confusion. The movies generally play upon the whole range of human emotions, frequently with such realism and intensity as to leave the youthful person emotionally exhausted. The kaleidoscopic change that is involved in mood and receptivity of the spectator is so great that emotionally it may put demands on him which make him callous, or leave him indifferent to the ordinary requirements of emotional response made upon him in his workaday world. As far as his mind is concerned the result of this scattered emotional indulgence is confusion. A variety of impulses may be awakened, a medley of feelings aroused, a multiplicity of day-dreams engendered, a mass of ideas suggested —all of which, at best, are likely to hang together in a loose organization. It seems that such a multiple and loosely integrated reaction is typical of the impressions left by the ordinary movie—more typical when movies are considered collectively. In so far as one may seek to cover in a single proposition the more abiding effect of motion pictures upon the minds of movie-goers, it would be, in the judgment of the writer, in terms of a medley of vague and variable impressions—a disconnected assemblage of ideas, feelings, vagaries, and impulses.

We recognize two other conspicuous ways in which motion pictures confound discrimination and dissolve moral judgment into a maze of ambiguous definitions. One is the sanctioning of questionable or unexpected conduct by running a moral through it. Although the general tenor of a movie, or even its *leitmotif*, may be of an "idealistic" sort, so much often has to be taken into the bargain in the way of trimmings that discrimination becomes confused and the effect is lost. The ideal of the theme may stamp its character on the details of the setting which are meant to be kept apart.[1]

We conclude by directing attention to the other source of confused discrimination and judgment—the possible divergence between the standards of the directors of the pictures and the perspective of movie-goers. What may be intended by the producer and the director as art, may be accepted by the movie public, or significant portions of it, as pornography. The difference, if it exist, is obviously a matter of interpretation. But the standards and codes of art which transform things into aesthetic objects may be limited to a select number. Other people with different standards can scarcely be expected to view these things in the same light. To justify the depiction on the ground of aesthetic character, or "art for art's sake," seems to overlook the major premise of the situation. It circumscribes the area of judgment to the perspective of the director and those whose attitudes he represents. What may evoke aesthetic satisfaction on their part may stimulate others in an unmistakenly contrary fashion. Unless the aesthetic values and interpretation of the movie public are changed to conform to those of the directing personnel, it is anomalous to defend commercial depictions on the basis of their art value, and to charge unfortunate effects to the basemindedness of people.

[1] A good example of a picture of this sort was *Our Dancing Daughters* where, in the experience of many, the qualities of fair play and good sportsmanship tended to envelop and give sanction to forms of conduct such as freedom in relations between the sexes, smoking, drinking, petting, etc.

APPENDIXES

APPENDIX A

MOTION PICTURE INQUIRY

THIS study is part of a national inquiry into motion pictures by a group of specialists in physiology, psychology, and sociology. It seeks to find out the influence of motion pictures on conduct. One way to find out how people are influenced by motion pictures is to ask them. This method is adopted in this study as the best approach. Each student is requested to write an account, or autobiography, of his motion picture experiences, beginning with his earliest recollections and carrying the life history down to about a year ago. The student need not write about his contemporary experiences. Two thousand life histories are to be collected.

To insure frankness in writing one's experiences it is suggested that a complete anonymous relation be established. The following scheme may be used: the class appoint a committee of two or three students who assign a number to each student in the class; each autobiography is turned in without the student's name but under his number; the teacher returns to the student committee the student numbers with the grades given; the committee returns to the teacher a list of the students with the grades given. In this manner each student receives credit for his work—yet the teacher will not know the authors of the separate biographies.

This is a scientific study. Its value depends upon the accuracy of the material gathered. The student is asked to be conscientious, truthful, and frank. Do not try to dress up your account in a literary fashion—write naturally. Do not be concerned about English usage. Do not exaggerate in any of your descriptions; do not invent or make up experiences. Be scrupulously honest. Do not feel any restraints in writing fully and frankly your intimate personal experiences—arrangements are made to preserve your anonymity.

Guidance Sheet

Write about only those items on which you have had experience.

1. a. *Trace the history of your interest in the movies.*

How did you first become interested in motion pictures? What kind of pictures did you like at first? When did you lose interest in them? What kind of pictures did you like next? Trace in this way the different kinds of pictures you have liked, and mention about how old you were at each change. Explain as fully as possible the conditions under which each change occurred.

Who were your earliest movie favorites? Who next became your favorites? Who are your present favorites? Explain why you like the movie stars you mention.

As a child, with whom did you usually go to the theater? (Alone, with parents, older brothers and sisters, chum, gang, etc.). What time of day did you usually go? How many times a week? Whom do you usually go with now?

Were you interested in serials? If so, describe your behavior.

Explain how movies influenced your play. Give concrete instances. What parts did you usually play (cowboy, policeman, Indian, etc.)? Did you engage in any escapades as a result of what you saw in the movies? Did you do any damage, or harm anyone as a result of doing something suggested by the movies? Did you do anything which you now feel to be wrong or improper? Describe.

What day-dreams did you have as a result of the movies? Explain fully what you imagined yourself doing. Do you believe that your day-dreaming in childhood was aroused especially by motion pictures, or more by other things? What other things?

b. *Describe how motion pictures have affected your emotions and moods.*

Were you ever severely frightened or horrified by any motion picture or scene? Describe as fully as you can the experience. How long did the fright or horror stay with you? How did it show its effects in your behavior?

Have you ever cried at pictures, or felt like crying? Give instances. Do you like to cry at pictures?

Do you find it hard to control the emotions aroused by motion pictures? Do you get more enjoyment from a picture by letting your emotions go?

Do you find that the movies easily change your moods? How long do the moods last? Give specific instances.

2. a. *Write fully about what you have imitated from the movies.*

Have you adopted any mannerisms (any gestures such as the use of the hands and arms, the inclining of the head, walking in a certain way, etc.)? Any ways of dressing, any ways of beautification? Any poses? Give concrete instances of what you have imitated.

What have you learned about love-making from the movies? About how to behave with the opposite sex at parties and elsewhere?

Describe anything else you have imitated from the movies.

b. *Describe your experience with pictures of love and romance.*

When did you first become interested in love pictures? Tell how this interest developed. Was interest in boys or girls awakened through motion pictures? Did you ever fall in love with any of your movie idols? Describe. Did you ever imagine yourself playing a part with them in the pictures? Did you ever day-dream about them? Describe your experiences along this line as fully and concretely as you can. Did you ever write any love letters to your movie favorites? Did you ever practice love scenes in your play, as a result of the movies?

Write fully your experiences with love pictures and love scenes. Have you been thrilled by love scenes? Describe your feelings and actions on seeing such love scenes. Have you felt stirred as a result of seeing them? Have such pictures or scenes made you more receptive to love-making? Describe any experiences you may have had of this nature. Have any of your ideas of love been formed by the movies? Have you and your associates been accustomed to talk much about love pictures? What was the nature, in general, of your conversations?

3.   *Write fully about any ambitions and temptations which you have gotten, from the movies.*

What kind of picture or pictures did you get your ambitions or temptations from? What did you day-dream about when you had the ambitions and temptations? Write about each ambition and temptation separately.

Did the movies ever develop in you a yearning for travel? Did you ever want to leave or run away from home as a result of the movies? Have the movies ever made you dissatisfied with your neighborhood, or with your own type of life? (House, clothes, manners of your parents, etc.). Have the movies ever caused you to rebel, or want to rebel, against the strictness of your parents? Against school discipline? Did you get ideas of how much freedom you should have, from the way in which fellows and girls are given privileges in the movies? What is your notion of the freedom you should have?

Did you ever want very much, to become a movie star, or go into the movies? What kind of movie star did you want to become? What kind of life did you imagine you would lead in the movies? Did you ever feel tempted to go to Hollywood and seek a career? Describe.

Did the movies ever give you any vocational ambitions— to become a lawyer, a nurse, a soldier, etc. Have they ever reënforced some vocational ambition which you already had? Describe such instances. Have college pictures ever given you a desire to go to college? War pictures to become a soldier? Religious pictures, to become a religious leader or saint? Describe.

Indicate any other ambitions and temptations gained from the movies beside those suggested or mentioned.

Have any movies strengthened you in your home ties? In your friendships? Any movie experiences which led you to do kindly deeds, or any which made you resolve to lead a better life? Any movie experiences which inspired you? Describe.

Have you seen any pictures—such as racial pictures— which you feel developed prejudices in you? Describe such pictures and how you felt about them. Have you seen any pictures which made you more broad-minded? Describe.

Do you feel that the movies have made you feel more favorable toward crime? Did you ever have any inclination or temptation to engage in crime as a result of the movies? What kind of crime? Did you ever have the desire to become an honorable criminal—a benevolent criminal like Robin Hood?

APPENDIX B

Schedule filled out by 1200 sixth and seventh grade school children from twelve public grade schools in Chicago. Three of the schools were located in areas with high rates of delinquency, four in areas with medium rates of delinquency, and four in areas with low rates of delinquency. The other school was a special school for truants and boys with behavior problems.

MY REPORT TO THE MOTION PICTURE STUDY

Name of school _____ Grade _____

Boy or girl _____ Age _____

Nationality _____ Race _____ Religion _____

1. How many times during a week do you usually go to the movies? _____

   How many times during a week would you like to go? _____

   How many times do you usually stay through a show? _____

   What movie theater do you usually go to? _____

   How many blocks is it from your home?_____

2. Must you ask your parents for permission before you can go to the movies? _____

   Do you ever go, even though your parents don't want you to? _____

3. Place the number, 1, before the kind of picture you like best, the number, 2, before the kind you like next best, the number, 3, before the kind you like next, and so on.

   ( ) Cowboy pictures   ( ) News reels
   ( ) Airplane pictures   ( ) Serials or follow-up
   ( ) Love pictures   pictures
   ( ) Detective pictures ( ) Gangster pictures
   ( ) Spooky pictures   ( ) Comedies

4. I usually go to the movies   (Use check mark to show which)

   _____ By myself   _____ With other grown-up
   _____ With brothers or sisters   people

208

_____ With a bunch of boys _____ With a boy friend
_____ With a bunch of girls _____ With a girl friend
_____ With my parents

5. After I see a movie I usually (Use check mark to show which)
   _____ Start to play at what I have seen in the movie
   _____ Talk to my friends about the picture
   _____ Imagine myself acting like they did in the movie
   _____ Talk to my parents about the picture.
   (If you usually do something else after you see a movie, tell what it is)

6. Who are your three favorite men movie stars, and who are your three favorite women movie stars?

Men stars	*Women stars*
1. _____	1. _____
2. _____	2. _____
3. _____	3. _____

7. Place the number, 1, before the kind of movie scene you like best, the number, 2, before the kind of movie scene you like next best, the number, 3, before the kind you like next, and so on.

(   ) Sad scenes   (   ) Religious scenes
(   ) Spooky scnes   (   ) Fighting
(   ) Murder scenes   (   ) Funny scenes
(   ) Love scenes   (   ) Gun play
(   ) Scenes which show loyalty   (   ) Scenes of unselfish
        or true friendship.   action

8. Do your parents ever tell you that some movies are bad for boys and girls? _____
   What kind do they say are bad?_____
   Do you agree with them? _____

9. Which of the following kinds of life do the movies usually show in an interesting way? (Show by a check mark)
   _____ College life   _____ Honest life
   _____ Home life   _____ Hard work
   _____ Life of the criminal _____ Fighting
   _____ Wealthy or rich life _____ Having a good time

10. Do you always want the good man in the pictures to win? _____
    Do you ever want the bad or tough man to win? _____

11. Do you and your friends talk about what you see in the movies? _____ How much do you talk about what you see in the movies?
    _____ a lot   _____ once in a while
    _____ sometimes   _____ never

12. Do you day-dream about what you see in the movies? _____
How much do you do this?

_____ a lot   _____ once in a while
_____ sometimes   _____ never

13. Do you and your companions play at what you see in the movies? _____ How much do you do this?

_____ a lot   _____ once in a while
_____ sometimes   _____ never

14. Would you rather be one of the good people or one of the bad people in these games? _____

15. Show by an X which of the following are good men, and by an O which are bad men.

( ) Indians   ( ) Lon Chaney   ( ) A wealthy
( ) Cowboys   ( ) Tom Mix   bootlegger
( ) Policemen   ( ) Hack Wilson   ( ) A bold bandit
( ) Robbers   ( ) Detectives
( ) Soldiers   ( ) A rich banker
( ) Al Capone   ( ) A tough gang
( ) George Bancroft   leader

16. Show by a check mark which of the following you would like to be. If you are a girl, indicate which you would like to have as your friends.

( ) Indians   ( ) Lon Chaney   ( ) A wealthy
( ) Cowboys   ( ) Tom Mix   bootlegger
( ) Policemen   ( ) Hack Wilson   ( ) A bold bandit
( ) Robbers   ( ) Detectives
( ) Soldiers   ( ) A rich banker
( ) Al Capone   ( ) A tough gang
( ) George Bancroft   leader

17. Do any kind of motion pictures make you want to get a lot of money easily? _____
What kind of pictures, if any, do this? _____

18. When you see an exciting movie do you want to (Show by check mark)

_____ Do something brave and daring
_____ Act tough or fight someone
_____ Go out and have a good time
_____ Talk to others about what you have just seen
_____ Start to play an exciting game
_____ Imagine yourself having a lot of adventure

19. When you see a thrilling gangster, burglar, or bandit picture do you

_____ Feel sorry for the gangster or burglar

_____ Feel like you want to be a gangster or burglar
_____ Imagine yourself being one, doing big and daring things, and fooling the police
_____ Want to be a policeman
_____ Feel that every gangster and burglar ought to be caught and punished
_____ Think nothing about what you have just seen
20. Have the movies ever made you
_____ Want to stay away from school
_____ Want to run away from home
_____ Want to go out and have a lot of fun
_____ Want to break into a house and take something
_____ Want to take things from other people
21. Have the movies ever led you to do anything wrong, or that you feel that you shouldn't have done? _____
If so, what kind of picture did you see, and what did you do?
_____
22. Have you seen any pictures which made you want to be real good? _____ What was the name of the picture and what was it about?_____
For how long were you good? _____
23. Do you think that the movies make boys or girls do bad things? _____ What, for instance? _____
Do you think that the movies make boys or girls do good things? _____ What, for instance? _____
Do you think that the movies make no difference on how boys or girls behave? _____
24. Do you think that the punishment which the bad man gets in the movies stops boys from doing bad things? _____
25. What kind of pictures, if any, do you think are not true to life?
_____
Why?
_____
26. Place the number, 1, before the one you do most, the number, 2, before the one you do next most, the number, 3, before the one you do next, and so on.
    ( ) Reading stories
    ( ) Playing or talking about what you see in the movies
    ( ) Playing other games, such as baseball, or marbles, skipping the rope and so on
    ( ) Day-dreaming

(   ) Working around home for your family
(   ) Working for other people
(   ) Doing your homework

.   .   .   .

If you care to, you may sign your name here. _____

THANK YOU

APPENDIX C

THE following autobiography comes from a college senior, a girl of 22 years, of native white parentage:

Considerably influenced by the gospel of H. L. Mencken and George Jean Nathan, I have for the past few years held the complacent attitude that "the movies were made for morons," that they were an inferior order of entertainment, and that I was possessed of an intellect decidedly too keen to be swayed by such a low order of art. But as I detach myself from this groundless generalization and consider objectively my motion picture experiences, it appears that, on the contrary, I am at least temporarily very acutely affected.

The movies could not have wielded a very great or enduring influence over me, however, for the reason that I have never been a chronic devotee. All the eighteen years of my life I have lived in a small town whose only picture palace was a small, dark, ill-ventilated hole, frequented by every type of person. As I was rather frail, and an only child, my mother regularly discouraged attendance there; I do not recall ever seeing a movie unaccompanied by one of my parents until I was eleven years old. The theater was called the *Critic*, a name indicative of the types of shows presented to attract the ardent Baptist population.

My first recollection of a movie is still a very vivid one. I could not have been more than five at the time, when Mother took me to a matinée to see Charlie Chaplin. We arrived early, just in the middle of a "serial," which was shown in weekly installments. It was called "The Claw," and revolved about a villainous character whose right hand was replaced by an iron hook. I can still see this claw reaching out from behind a bridge to grab the heroine. Even the following antics of the famous comedian failed to soften

213

my terrified impressions, and for weeks after I slept with the light on at night and peered carefully under the bed each morning before setting foot on the floor.

I also remember seeing at a later date other "serials" in one of which a mother and her child, shipwrecked, drifted about the Atlantic Ocean clinging to a log, while the struggling husband and father drowned before their eyes; and in the other of which occurred a forest fire. All my earliest impressions were those of fear—very real and vivid.

A little later on, however, between the ages of about six and nine, the movies began to work their way into our play. At one period, our favorite game was "Sandstorm," an idea derived directly from some desert picture now forgotten. The two little boys with whom I played and I would hide in our caravan, the davenport, and watch the storm sweep over the horizon. When it reached us, we would battle our way through it, eventually to fall prostrate in the middle of the room, where we would lie until the storm blew over. Then we would get up and start the game over.

Another popular pastime, which was undoubtedly affected by certain "Western" pictures was "Cowboy." My father had at one time lived on a coffee plantation in Mexico and owned and provided us with all the necessary regalia—ten-gallon hats, spurs, 'kerchiefs, and holsters. The pistols which went with the outfit we were not allowed to have, but carried instead carved wooden guns. Stories of Father's own (fictitious?) experiences were combined with movie scenarios to form what was for two years our great game. I do not recall any specific instances of our imitating the two-reelers, but I do know that Father obtained and autographed for us greatly cherished photographs of the inimitable William S. Hart.

After I entered school, my tastes changed rapidly from the hairbreadth, wild and woolly Westerners and slap-stick comedies to more sentimental forms. Until the time I entered Junior High, I was interested in the actresses, the heroines. I preferred them sweet, blonde, and fluffy—everything that I was not. I doted on misty close-ups of tear-streamed faces. In the sixth grade, my best friend and I were constantly imitating Mary Miles Minter and Mary Pickford, respectively. Later on I became, in turn, Alice Calhoun and Constance Talmadge, but my friend remained true to her first crush. In classes we wrote notes to each other, and signed them "Mary," "Alice," or whatever names we had at the time adopted.

After the seventh grade, however, my attentions again shifted, this time to the male actors. I had become boy-conscious, and, affecting an utter disdain toward all boys of my acquaintance, I took delight in the handsome and heroic men of the screen. I liked nearly all of them, as long as they were neither too old nor too paternal (like Thomas Meighan), but I especially favored Charles Ray, Harrison Ford, and, above all, Wallace Reid. He epitomized all I thought young manhood should be—clean, good-looking, daring, and debonair. All the girls of my age and most of the boys liked him. We saw such pictures as "Clarence," "The Affairs of Anatole," and "Mr. Get-Rich-Quick Wallingford."

As a young high-school student, I attended the movies largely for the love scenes. Although I never admitted it to my best friend, the most enjoyable part of the entire picture was inevitably the final embrace and fade-out. I always put myself in the place of the heroine. If the hero was some man by whom I should enjoy being kissed (as he invariably was), my evening was a success and I went home in an elated, dreamy frame of mind, my heart beating rather fast and my usually pale cheeks brilliantly flushed. I used to look in the mirror somewhat admiringly and try to imagine Wallace Reid or John Barrymore or Richard Barthelmess kissing that face! It seems ridiculous if not disgusting now, but until my Senior year this was the closest I came to Romance. And then I fell in love with a boy that looked remarkably like Dick Barthelmess.

I liked my movies pure Romance: beautiful heroines in distress, handsome gallants in love, gorgeous costumes, and happy endings. "When Knighthood Was in Flower," "Robin Hood," "Beau Brummel," and "Monsieur Beaucaire" were favorites, although as a rule I didn't like screen versions of books I had read and loved. ("The Three Musketeers" was an example of an adored book grossly insulted.) In a life which was monotonous with all the placidity of a Baptist small town, these movies and books were about all the excitement one could enjoy.

I never liked pictures with a moral, unless it was so subtly expressed that I was unaware of its preaching. Such movies as

"The Ten Commandments," and more recently the "King of Kings," impressed me as gorgeous spectacles, but too flagrant in their moralizing, so that in parts I was bored to the point of antagonism. A renovated production of "Ten Nights in a Barroom" was so bad it bordered on a screamingly funny burlesque. Just recently, however, I saw "White Shadows in the South Seas," and was surprised to discover how deeply I was affected by the propaganda.

Over-sexed plays were always more or less repulsive. I remember especially "Flesh and the Devil" with the Garbo-Gilbert combination and an older one starring Gloria Swanson and Valentino. I liked neither. The former embarrassed and the latter bored me.

I have always been unrestrained in my emotions at a motion picture. My uncontrollable weeping at sad movies has been a never-ending source of mortification. I recall first shedding tears over the fate of some deserted water-baby when I was about eight years old, and I have wept consistently and unfailingly ever since, from "Penrod and Sam" to "Beau Geste." The latter, which I liked as well as any picture I have ever seen, caused actual sobbing both times I saw it. I weep at scenes in which others can see no pathos whatsoever. Recently I have refused to see a half-dozen notably sad shows because of their distressing effects.

I do not believe the movies have ever stimulated me to a real thought, as books have done. Neither have they influenced me on questions of morals, of right and wrong. They have given me a more or less fluctuating standard of the ideal man—in general, the good-looking, dreamy, boyish type—and the kind of lover he must be—sincere, thoughtful, and tender. They have given me my ideas of luxury—sunken baths, silken chaises-lounges, arrays of servants and powerful motors;—of historical background—medieval castles, old Egyptian palaces, gay Courts; and of geographical settings—the moonlit water framed in palms of the South Seas, the snow fields of the far North, the Sahara, the French Riviera, and numerous others. I suppose they have from time to time influenced my conception of myself; although I was not aware of this until recently when I saw "A Woman of Affairs," the film version of Michael Arlen's "Green Hat." For days after I was consciously striving to be the "Gallant Lady"; to face a petty world squarely and uncomplainingly; to see things with her broad, sophisticated vision; even to walk and to smoke with her serene nonchalance. I, too, wished to be a gallant lady.

On the whole, I doubt if the movies have wielded much of an influence on my life; not because they were incapable of it, but because they have had too little opportunity. In my youth, my family discouraged attendance at the local cinema, and as I grew older, I formed other interests. Since the first of October, I have seen no more than ten pictures. Two of these impressed me immensely; three of them I could not sit through. Last year I used to go mainly to hear the organ music, but with the advent of the Vitaphone, this attraction is dispensed with. I dislike the stage shows presented at the leading theaters, and also the "talkies." I usually attend a movie for rest and relaxation, and a bellowing, hollow voice or a raucous vaudeville act does not add to my pleasure. I like my movies unadulterated, silent, and far-between.

The following account is typical of those written by carefree, self-reliant high-school girls. A general description of life is given before her motion-picture experiences are discussed.

I am a girl—American born and of Scotch descent. My grandparents came to America from Glasgow, Scotland, and grandfather became a minister (Presbyterian). Mother was the youngest of nine children and was born in New York. Dad came from New York also; his parents were of Scotch and English stock. I was born in Detroit, July 1, 1913. I have one brother. Stating us in order of birth, we are: Mary, 16, and Edward, 12.

My religious denominations have been varied. Mom put me in the cradle-roll of a Congregational Church, but I have been a member of the Lutheran, Presbyterian, Christian Science, and Methodist Episcopal churches. All of which indicates that either I'm very broad-minded religiously or unable to make up my mind. The latter is more plausible. Was a member of a Camp Fire Girls group for several years and was greatly interested in its activities. I reached the second rank in the organization.

My mother has no occupation. One calls her a housewife, I guess, but she isn't home enough for that. She travels in the winter and fall. Dad is a Lawyer. My real father is dead. He died when I was very young. His work was in the appraisal business. My clearest picture of him is playing his violin. He played beautifully

Mother plays the piano and when she accompanied him I used to listen for hours. I love music.

My parents are dandy to me. They give me most everything I want. In fact, I'm afraid they have spoiled my brother and myself. But they are mighty nice and we appreciate them.

My very earliest recollections are of Christmas, my brother, my fondness for bananas, and my first and last spanking. The spanking was timidly, but none the less forcefully administered by my father who, when he had finished, gave me the impression of being sort of embarrassed, you might say; but at any rate, he heaved a sigh and acted as if he had done his duty. My other remembrances are of a very stout colored maid we had for many years and of having the measles. My mother created an early impression of herself on me. I had a great love of animals and insisted on carting home all stray kittens or cats to keep on the porch. Of course, this would be annoying to any housewife, and mother was no exception; so she took them "for a ride." I knew what she had done and my heart was broken. I wanted to run away.

Even while I was very little my play was not supervised by my parents. I enjoyed the companionship of several little girls and boys in the neighborhood; making mud pies, playing grocery store, school, and office were our most popular pastimes. I adored playing with dolls alone or I would play soldier with a boy cousin of mine ten months older, if he would play house with me next day. Later when I started kindergarten I didn't have as good a time playing. I remember there was a sand-box filled with lovely white sand and several tin steam shovels which I continually attempted to monopolize. One day when a little fellow wanted to share it with me I objected strenuously and threw sand in his hair. He came back with a handful very effectively, and the battle resulted in that I was compelled to sit in the corner while the other children grouped around the teacher for a story. I planned some awful mutinies on that occasion.

As to family relations, we always have been very congenial. All of us are endowed with a keen sense of humor and every mealtime is one of fun and laughter. Mother has a funny way of telling things; Dad was just a scream, and my brother is a perfect clown. He imitates anything and everything.

My early ambitions were to run an orphanage and help poor

people. Traveling held indescribable thrills! Dancing and piano also interested me.

When I was seven years old we were living in a large new home in a suburb, all very happy, and my father suddenly died. My mother was young and with two little children on her hands was unable to remain in the house; so we moved back to the city that we had left so gaily three years before. In the course of four years or so she remarried. I was terrified at the thought of the proverbial "cruel step-father," but he turned out to be wonderful and soon shattered any hostile feeling I held against him. After this marriage mother and "Dad" traveled quite a lot. I was beginning to grow up and I began to lose interest in dolls, doll-houses, and Tom Swift books. I took a great fancy to sewing and cooking, the latter causing my family much suffering.

Before I forget it—I was a very imaginative person and I lied unbelievably. My theme was usually telling the neighbors that someone had died in the family. Mother received many phone calls inquiring into such information. I remember one lady telling me that I should write books because I had such a vivid imagination. I followed her suggestion not long ago, and judging from the results the said imagination has made its exit.

About this time something humbled my spirit in such a way that even now I am afraid to argue or to have the slightest disagreement with anyone. I detest friction of this sort and will do anything to avoid an argument. When I am wronged and should stick up for myself I haven't the courage. At present no one knows the struggle I am having to overcome this. I've had two victories so far, however, and I feel very strong.

My interest in boys never came on at any special period that I can remember. As I said before, I always hit it off well with them and at grammar school fell very much in love (so I thought) with two ungainly lads who were classmates.   Since then I have had more comrades in the boys than in girls.   Girls I've known have been catty, jealous, tricky, and undependable. Many are pleasant to your face but are two-faced and turn against you when your back is turned. I am a poor judge of character, and people are always deceiving me in that way. I have had three real, true friends among my own sex.

My worries during adolescence were more or less family ones, if any. I knew babies didn't grow in cabbages, etc. Kids learn all that early enough now-a-days; so sex worries were not mine. The crowd began to attempt sophistication, blasé mannerisms, nonchalance, etc. I don't like people that are not natural, so I dropped out of the circle of friends I had been going with and resigned from the Camp Fire group I had been a member of. Then I made some so-called "ethics" that like New Year's Resolutions were a joke. I went to Junior High. We began trying to be "hot," "wild," or what have you and took to smoking, and we drank at parties once or twice. It was so superficial I soon got tired. This was a period of unsettled ideas, unrest, uncertainty. I fell in and out of love in rapid succession. We all entered High School then and are getting a bit more sensible. I haven't "fallen out" of love for nearly a year which is quite a record, and I have been going steady for six months, which is a mistake and a serious one on my part. I leave high school soon and am entering in the fall at a girl's school near Boston. The experience will be valuable and worth while, I'm sure. As I read this over, there is much, too much unnecessary detail, and I forgot to mention that at present my chief interests are in dancing, reading, swimming, tennis, and golf. I dislike card-playing. Singing is my "pet passion" and I have recently joined a Glee Club and church choir which I give a great deal of time to. Now I've told you everything!

I have tried to remember the first time that I went to a movie. It must have been when I was very young because I cannot recall the event. My real interest in motion pictures showed itself when I was in about fourth grade at grammar school. There was a theater on the route by which I went home from school and as the picture changed every other day I used to spend the majority of my time there. A gang of us little tots went regularly.

One day I went to see Viola Dana in "The Five Dollar Baby." The scenes which showed her as a baby fascinated me so that I stayed to see it over four times. I forgot home, dinner, and everything. About eight o'clock mother came after me—frantically searching the theater.

Next to pictures about children, I loved serials and pie-throwing comedies, not to say cowboy 'n' Indian stories. These kind I liked until I was twelve or thirteen; then I lost interest in that type, and the spectacular, beautifully decorated scenes took my eye. Stories of dancers and stage life I loved. Next, mystery plays thrilled me and one never slipped by me. At fifteen I liked stories of modern youth; the gorgeous clothes and settings fascinated me.

My first favorite was Norma Talmadge. I liked her because I saw her in a picture where she wore ruffly hoop-skirts which greatly attracted me. My favorites have always been among the women; the only men stars I've ever been interested in are Tom Mix, Doug Fairbanks and Thomas Meighan, also Doug McLean and Bill Haines. Colleen Moore I liked for a while, but now her hair-cut annoys me. My present favorites are rather numerous: Joan Crawford, Billie Dove, Sue Carol, Louise Brooks, and Norma Shearer. I nearly forgot about Barbara LaMar. I really worshiped her. I can remember how I diligently tried to draw every gown she wore on the screen and how broken-hearted I was when she died. You would have thought my best friend had passed away.

Why I like my favorites? I like Joan Crawford because she is so modern, so young, and so vivacious! Billie Dove is so beautifully beautiful that she just gets under your skin. She is the most beautiful woman on the screen! Sue Carol is cute 'n' peppy. Louise Brooks has her assets, those being legs 'n' a clever hair-cut. Norma Shearer wears the kind of clothes I like and is a clever actress.

I nearly always have gone and yet go to the theater with someone. I hate to go alone as it is more enjoyable to have someone to discuss the picture with. Now I go with a bunch of girls or on a date with girls and boys or with one fellow.

The day-dreams instigated by the movies consist of clothes, ideas on furnishings, and manners. I don't day-dream much. I am more concerned with materialistic things and realisms. Nevertheless it is hard for any girl not to imagine herself cuddled up in some voluptuous ermine wrap, etc.

The influence of movies on my play as a child—all that I remember is that we immediately enacted the parts interesting us most. And for weeks I would attempt to do what that character would have done until we saw another movie and some other hero or heroine won us over.

I'm always at the mercy of the actor at a movie. I feel nearly every emotion he portrays and forget that anything else is on earth. I was so horrified during "The Phantom of the Opera" when Lon Chaney removed his mask, revealing that hideous face, that until my last day I shall never forget it.

I am deeply impressed, however, by pathos and pitifulness, if you understand. I remember one time seeing a movie about an awful fire. I was terrified by the reality of it and for several nights I was afraid to go to sleep for fear of a fire and even placed my hat and coat near by in case it was necessary to make a hasty exit. Pictures of robbery and floods have affected my behavior the same way. Have I ever cried at pictures? Cried! I've practically dissolved myself many a time. How people can witness a heart-rending picture and not weep buckets of tears is more than I can understand. "The Singing Fool," "The Iron Mask," "Seventh Heaven," "Our Dancing Daughters," and other pictures I saw when very young which centered about the death of someone's baby and showed how the big sister insisted on her jazz 'n' whoopee regardless of the baby or not—these nearly killed me. Something like that, anyway; and I hated that girl so I wanted to walk up to the screen and tear her up! As for liking to cry—why, I never thought of that. It isn't a matter of liking or not. Sometimes it just can't be helped. Movies do change my moods, but they never last long. I'm off on something else before I know it. If I see a dull or morose show, it sort of deadens me and the vim and vigor dies out 'til the movie is forgotten. For example, Mary Pickford's movie—"Sparrows"—gave me the blues for a week or so, as did li'l Sonny Boy in "The Singing Fool." The poor kid's a joke now.

This modern knee-jiggling, hand-clapping effect used for accompanying popular music has been imitated from the movies, I think. But unless I've unconsciously picked up little mannerisms, I can think of no one that I've tried to imitate.

Goodness knows, you learn plenty about love from the movies. That's their long run; you learn more from actual experience, though! You do see how the gold-digger systematically gets the poor fish in tow. You see how the sleek-haired, long-earringed, languid-eyed siren lands the men. You meet the flapper, the good girl, 'n' all the feminine types and their little tricks of the trade. We pick up their snappy comebacks which are most handy when dispensing with an unwanted suitor, a too ardent one, too backward one, etc. And believe me, they observe and remember, too.

I can remember when we all nudged one another and giggled at the last close-up in a movie. I recall when during the same sort of close-up when the boy friend squeezes your arm and looks soul-fully at you. Oh, it's lotsa fun! No, I never fell in love with my movie idol. When I don't know a person really, when I know I'll never have a chance with 'em, I don't bother pining away over them and writing them idiotic letters as some girls I've known do. I have imagined playing with a movie hero many times though; that is while I'm watching the picture. I forget about it when I'm outside the theater. Buddy Rogers and Rudy Valentino have kissed me oodles of times, but they don't know it. God bless 'em!

Yes, love scenes have thrilled me and have made me more receptive to love. I was going with a fellow whom I liked as a playmate, so to speak; he was a little younger than me and he liked me a great deal. We went to the movie—Billie Dove in it. Oh, I can't recall the name but Antonio Moreno was the lead, and there were some lovely scenes which just got me all hot 'n' both-ered. After the movie we went for a ride 'n' parked along the lake; it was a gorgeous night. Well, I just melted (as it were) in his arms, making him believe I loved him, which I didn't. I sort of came to, but I promised to go steady with him. I went with him 'til I couldn't bear the sight of him. Such trouble I had trying to get rid of him, and yet not hurt his feelings, as I had led him to believe I cared more than I did. I've wished many times that we'd never seen the movie. Another thing not exactly on the subject but im-portant, I began smoking after watching Dolores Costello, I believe it was, smoke, which hasn't added any joy to my parents' lives.

The following account is of particular interest in showing the rôle of motion pictures in the play life of a child. It suggests the close relation between play and reverie. It shows how an individual may construct a world out of motion-picture characters and themes. The account has been written by a Jewish college student, a boy aged 20.

I. My Family and My Surroundings.

Up to ten years of age I was the only child of poor, young, lit-erate (*i.e.*, they could read, write, and speak Russian, Hebrew, and Yiddish), Russian immigrants. When I was only fifteen months old, the small family moved from the Halsted Street Ghetto district where I was born to the northwest part of the city at L—— and

D—— Streets. Here my father bought a small two-story building in which he used the first floor as a retail store and the second as the living quarters of the family. It was in this neighborhood and even in this same building that I stayed up to my graduation from high school when sixteen years old. This period of my life which I spent on L—— Street and which immediately preceded my university days is the period I shall discuss in its relation to the motion pictures.

I said that I was the only child in the family. It would be natural to expect, therefore, that I was pampered, petted, and spoiled by my fond parents. This was only true to a certain extent. On the one hand, both my father and my mother tended to the small business, which on some days, notably Thursday, would not close until twelve and even one o'clock in the morning, while the store was opened as early as six o'clock on Friday morning. Consequently, my mother was unable to devote as much time as she would have liked to my upbringing. But on the other hand, this keeping a store with the flat just upstairs also had its advantages. Business was not always so rushing as to constantly require the help of two people. Therefore, not only did I have my mother with me a great deal of the time, but I was also accustomed to see my father all day long and to heed both parents' admonitions; for if I didn't, why, mother would temporarily take care of the store while father would run upstairs and explain to me, with the aid of a leather shaving strap, the value of obedience. Besides, when I was five or six years old, we hired an extra man to help in the store, so that I had both my father and mother to contend with a great part of the time. Further, my parents, disliking extremely to see their boy playing and associating with rowdies on the street, had an instructor come to the house and teach me flute. I was required to practice one hour daily and had both parents present to enforce the rule. My father, being able to hear the sounds of the flute in the store, knew when I stopped and was thus able to check up pretty carefully on my conduct. Finally, I was not very strong physically. Being afraid of getting lickings from the older boys and being afraid of the name "Mucker," which was very distasteful to me, I stayed very near the store all the time and was consequently very much under my parents' strict influence.

It can be seen from this short, sketchy account of my family life and my surroundings that mine was a peculiar position, quite different from that of the average boy. Although I was closely bound to my parents because I was an only child, because of economic reasons, because of the flute, because of my physical weakness, and because of that obnoxious nickname, nevertheless both my parents had so much work to do in the house and in the store that they did not get a very good opportunity to spoil me— much. Because of my necessary aloofness, I was regarded by both the grown-ups and the children of the neighborhood as somebody different. The grown-ups expressed this difference in the phrase, "a fine boy," the children in the word "sissy."

II. First Stage.

On Friday evenings the store was closed as early as six o'clock. The only pleasures my parents had were either occasional visits to and from relatives living in other parts of the city or going to the movies. Being an only child I necessarily had to be taken along even if against my will. I can just dimly remember those evenings in the small, poorly ventilated neighborhood movie house when I sat on my father's lap.

I was only four years old when I was taken to a movie for the first time, and this first attendance was a decided novelty. Seeing apparently real characters moving about on the stage in a pitch-dark room was indeed a strange sight to see. But the movie at this time had only a momentary attraction. My interest would wane after I had been in the theater only ten or fifteen minutes and from that time on I would pester my father by tugging at his sleeve and begging him to leave. It was only natural that the movies should have no meaning for me at this time. I could neither read the explanatory notes of the movie nor could I understand the meaning of the characters' actions. Plot and sequence of events were meaningless to me at this time. Consequently, motion pictures had no positive effect on my mind or my actions in this early period of my theater-going. Negatively, perhaps, they did have an effect in that the mere mention of the word "show" was enough to make me hide, so great was my dislike for them.

III. Second Stage.

This very early period of my life when I was only four years old was a period which I spent almost wholly in my own and in my parents' company. Outside of my father and mother I did not know any other people's reactions to the movies; and even with regard to my parents, the reactions weren't particularly favorable, for my father, tired from the week's hard work, would invariably fall asleep in the theater. Even when he did view the picture, he was unable to understand fully what the various points were, for he could not read English. Consequently, my own personal ideas remained unchanged with regard to the motion picture.

But the next year I was sent to kindergarten and thus came in contact with many other children, learning to my surprise of their enthusiastic liking for the movies. It made me feel ignorant and inferior to hear Jack and John and Jane glibly speaking of various stars of whom I knew nothing. Slowly my ideas and thoughts regarding the movies changed from dislike to tolerance and then to interest. As I advanced in school, I gradually learned to read so that by the third grade I was able to get about halfway through the explanatory notes of the movie before they were removed. Through my contact with other children I also knew just what pictures to see. Formerly my parents had taken me to society movies with men in full dress suits and women in gorgeous evening gowns. Now, since I was permitted to go to a movie with a group of boys or even to go unaccompanied, I went to see three kinds of movies, each of which had different effects on me. I saw cowboy pictures, mystery pictures, and comedies of the Charlie Chaplin and Larry Semon type. The first two had by far the greater effect on me, partly because they appeared in serial form, one episode each week, while comedies (many reel, feature picture comedies) were few and far between, and partly because they appealed more to my boyish, romantic imagination; so that gradually in conversations with other boys about "Didja see William S. Hart do this?" and "Ya gonna see Tom Mix?", and in talk about Douglas Fairbanks and Harrison Ford I actually began to like the movies.

This interest was stimulated rather than suppressed by my parents. If I would be a good boy and practice my flute or eat my soup then I could go to the movies. That was one means of inducement. But my parents were happy to send me to the movies for another reason. I mentioned the fact that Thursday nights were very busy ones for my parents. Because I would constantly trouble them with various trivial matters in front of a storeful of customers and because, being an only child, they had no one to leave me with, they thought it best for themselves and for myself if I were sent to a movie on those evenings. Again, Saturday and Sunday weren't school-days. Consequently, they thought it best for me to go to a movie in order that I should be kept out of mischief and out of contact with the bad boys in the neighborhood. It can be seen, therefore, that my parents in many ways encouraged my going to the movie house. In this stage, therefore, the movies played a very important part in my life.

Of course, the general effect of the cowboy pictures was to awaken in me the desire to be a cowboy. There was a natural glamor about this open-air, manly type of "Wild West" picture with the wonderful horses, colorful cowboy suits, guns, and lariats which made this kind of life seem absolutely ideal to me. Since the actual attainment of these hopes was out of the question at that time, the desire manifested itself in my reveries and day-dreams.

For the various reasons named above I seldom played with other boys. Being the only child and with both parents intermittently busy, I was left alone to my own resources. The place where I spent almost all of my time was in our backyard which was rectangular in shape and inclosed on all four sides by buildings in this manner.

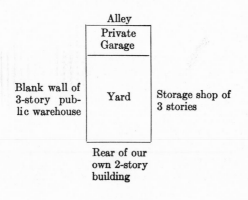

I emphasize the importance of the yard being inclosed because it made me feel alone and away from any prying eyes. I cannot adequately explain how dear this feeling of solitude, this feeling of privacy, this feeling of being a million miles away from the nearest inhabitant, was to me, for it was here that I put into dramatic action all of my innermost thoughts and desires, with the knowledge that nobody could see what I was doing.

Taking an empty barrel from among the many empty barrels and boxes which my father had neatly piled up in a corner of the yard, I would straddle it as though it were a horse and would play that I was a cowboy chasing the Indians or that the Indians were chasing me. A small "cap" gun lent realism to my actions. I remember playing in this manner for hours at a time, making various antics with my "horse," or falling down dead, etc. In fact, during the summer time I played in this manner from the moment I got home from school at three-thirty until seven or eight o'clock, when my mother would call me in for dinner, always intently interested in my impersonations. Whenever I saw anything in the movies which particularly appealed to me I would go into my yard the next afternoon and actually go over the entire action from start to finish, putting in many variations of my own which would strike me on the spur of the moment. So much did I enjoy this form of playing that my mother had to coax and cajole me into eating my dinner. I would even go into the yard on a Saturday afternoon or Sunday morning and jump on my "horse" and go chasing after the Indians, shooting at them with my "cap" gun.

The mystery pictures did not lend themselves to impersonations as well as the cowboy pictures. Fighting was the chief single factor that I got from these pictures. I was always the hero who was beset with six or seven imaginary thugs that were trying to kidnap or kill me. I would ferociously go through the motions of a terrific struggle, even to the point of rolling on the grass with my imaginary opponents upon me. Since I always tried to play my games in a realistic manner, I so arranged it that sometimes I would lose and at other times I would win in my struggles. If I lost, I pretended that I bound was up by the demons and that I was carried away to their villainous chief, who usually wore a black mask. Now we come to another interesting point. If there were several important characters in my sketch, I would impersonate each in turn. Thus, for example, imagining myself to be bound hand and foot, and thrown at the feet of the villain, I would bravely act the part of the hero—that is, look with contempt on the poor fool and valiantly, with a reckless bravado, talk back to him even though I was handicapped with my bonds and outnumbered ten to one. Then I would spring up and assume the gloating position of the sneering villain and would kick the imaginary prostrate form of the hero. I would pant, drop dead, fight, run, climb (there was a tall tree in our yard)— in short, do anything that each part called for; and in all these actions, it must be remembered that I felt myself alone, unobserved, and very, very happy because I forgot myself, who I was, forgot everything but the part I was playing.

I continued this solitary type of playing until I was well in my eighth grade; that is, until I was eleven years old. As I look back now, the surprising point to me is the fact that in all those early years I never tired of the backyard or of playing my childish games. Meanwhile, the indirect effect that the movies were having on me in relation to school was, on the whole, a very wholesome one. I remember my fourth-grade teacher, Miss K——, once asked me privately if I was sick or wasn't feeling well because I never talked or made any noise in the room. My answer was, "I do all my talking in my yard at home so that I am all out of words and haven't anything to say by the time I come to school." Miss K—— kissed me and when passing time came, she skipped me. In school I never, even for one moment, thought of cowboys and Indians. I took my work seriously and very seldom associated with other boys or became a party to their pranks. But the moment school was out I would slowly walk home alone, thinking whether I would be Douglas Fairbanks or Tom Mix or William S. Hart that afternoon. In this stage of my life, therefore, I was absorbed in movies and in acting (the movies furnishing my themes) and associated with others only when absolutely necessary. I remember walking home from school once, thinking as different boys passed me, "If they only knew who I really am and what a wonderful cowboy I'll be when I grow up!"

IV. Third Stage.

With high-school days a new world opened up before me and my mind was turned in an entirely different direction. After classes were over in high school I could not go immediately to my yard and start playing my old games, for now I had home-work to attend to. Besides this, there were many activities in school to which I belonged—societies, clubs, athletics, and or-chestra—all of which absorbed my attention and energies. After attending various meetings I would not get home until five or five-thirty o'clock, and then after dinner I had my home-work to do; and after this I had to practice my flute. Conse-quently, I was compelled to give up my backyard playing. One would think that this sacrifice of a daily habit would have hurt me keenly, but this was not so. I had such a good time in school with my meetings and athletics, and I was so busy when home with my home-work, flute, and an occasional movie, that I didn't even think of the matter. However, I would still indulge in my old pastime on an isolated Saturday or Sunday afternoon, but these moments grew rarer and rarer as I grew older.

In the meantime, there was a corresponding change in my taste for movies. It must be remembered that I had had little, prac-tically no, social contact with either boys or girls. Now, with so many student activities, I was necessarily thrown into their company and I learned many things from them which were en-tirely new to me. The boys spoke of sexual matters, and the girls spoke of love. I began to appreciate pretty girls and to be a crit-ical admirer of their figures. An entirely new class of movies began to appeal to me. I turned away from the childish cowboy movies ("only kids go to see those," I was told) and began to see Clara Bow, John Gilbert, Rudolph Valentino, etc. I was in an adolescent stage.

I was in a position now where I had plenty of time to think and to dream about various matters, but I had no time to put these thoughts and dreams into dramatic action. My reveries consisted in thinking of all sorts of situations in which this or that pretty girl that I knew was the heroine while I was the hero who saved her from the villains. Strangely enough, I never thought of these situations in relation to a movie heroine but always in relation to a girl of my acquaintance. I tried to conduct my first love affair on a romantic, movie-like basis. I thought of witty, gallant things to say. I conceived of my girl in all kinds of terrible positions, about to be tortured or deprived of her virginity (it is impossible to believe or conceive the many, many situations I concocted with regard to her virginity), or some such thing, and I, the hero, would always be on time to save her. Such were the subjects of almost all of my reveries during my high-school career. There seems to be a certain sameness to them now, but as I look back, I see that my mind, aided by plots and stories from movies I had recently seen, was continually busy with various compromising situations in which I hoped to find my girl placed while I was conveniently at hand.

Dramatics was my goal, my aim, my ideal in high school because it was so much like the movies. To be a real hero of the annual high-school play, which was performed before thirty-two hundred people, was the height of my ambition. But I was afraid to ever try out for a part in the play. The members of the dramatic society seemed to be such a wordly, sophisticated lot of students that I was actually afraid to associate with them. Although many minor plays were produced, I refused to even think of trying out for a part in one of them. I aimed high, but meant to stick by that aim. Finally, in my senior year, just before I was to graduate, there came the try-outs for "The Way Things Go," the big play and chief social event of the season. Here was my last chance and in desperation I took advantage of it. I remember how, after I had tried out for the hero's part, nobody wanted to even attempt to compete with me. I was immediately accepted. In the play I put in all the results of my early backyard training and the result was that I was voted and accepted by all as the greatest actor R—— ever had. At last I had had some definite results—some concrete facts to show for my long training. At last, the movies had shown their practical effects on my behavior and on my mind.

V. Conclusion.

Now as I look over my life and its relation to the movies, I see that the movies have exercised a profound and, on the whole, a decidedly good influence on it. In the first place, the motion pictures gave me something to think about. On the one hand,

I had a group of rough, thoroughly bad boys (three are at present members of E——'s gang and one is in jail serving the second
of a ten-year sentence) with whom to associate. My associations with them would not have been on the basis of an equal
because I was weak, different, and a sissy; it would have been
on the basis of a dependent, a slave, a parasite whose will would
never be consulted and who would always have to fawn on and
be subservient to the others. On the other hand, being alone
with just my flute to keep me busy would have been equally bad.
I would have been continually thinking of my weaknesses and
would have been wishing that I were like other boys. In the end,
out of sheer need for some sort of companionship, I would have
been driven into their company anyway. Now the movies came
into my lonely life—lonely, for I had no playmates, no brothers
or sisters—and gave me a healthy subject to think about, a subject which completely occupied my mind and made me give no
thought whatsoever to the other boys. Ideas common to average boys of my age, such as running away from home, never so
much as entered my head. Further, the movies built up my
confidence, and instead of looking with envy at other boys, my
look was one of disdain. My sincere thought, when called a sissy,
was "They should see what I can do in my yard and then they
wouldn't call me a sissy." I never thought of asking the boys to
share my yard with me and to play with me. The yard was mine
and I resented any trespassing.

The effect of the movies in my early life, therefore, was to keep
away from bad ideas and bad associations long enough so that
by the time I went to high school I had built up some definite
resistance and had permitted my habits and ideas to be somewhat set with regard to other boys' actions. Instead of being a
mollycoddle and as weak as a jellyfish, the movies had instilled
into me a certain self-sufficiency, an imperviousness of manner
which caused boys to follow me and to elect me president of their
clubs and societies rather than my following them meekly just
as one of the crowd.

However, in another manner, the movies were a cause of my
deficiencies. By giving me a subject to think about, I was content to be physically isolated from the group. Naturally, therefore, by the time I went to high school, girls were to me a very

strange species of humanity and I had a hard time getting accustomed to my associations with them. I had no difficulty at all with the boys, but with the girls it was another matter. Mine was chiefly a romantic reverie (in high school) which never expressed itself in action directly. The movies were not only the source of my reveries and of my magnanimous and bombastic thoughts regarding girls, but they were also the cause for my regarding and thinking of girls as only from a distance. I never learned how to dance, for cowboys don't dance, in fact no he-man dances. Consequently, I have never, even up to the present, had enough courage to ask a girl on a date. My relations with the girls have always been restrained and formal. I hold the movies chiefly responsible for this.

The following account was written by a girl, age 21, of native white parentage—a senior in a university:

Whether or not movies have had a great deal of influence on my life is a subject I cannot discuss in any matter-of-fact way. I can only make certain suppositions and recall some reactions.

One of my first conscious desires was to follow a serial every Saturday afternoon from beginning to end. Other children in the neighborhood did it, but my parents refused to let me go unless one of the family took me. I had no young brothers and sisters who could enjoy such movies with me; and because I could not go as often as I wanted to, my idea of a perfect life was one which might be spent seeing every movie in town. I heard the folks speak of the movie critics who wrote for the newpapers, and my ambition was to do likewise, in order that I might see all the shows.

I cannot recall at just what age I began to receive a weekly allowance, but I remember I resolved at the same time to save enough of it to enable me to see at least one movie a week. I was one of the proudest girls in the world when I was able to accompany the neighborhood crowd every Saturday afternoon.

The first and only serial I remember was Houdini in "The Iron Man." I thought it was wonderful. I do not remember anything about it except that the Iron Man was a very mysterious character. He was a huge form of iron with a great square head that had eyes like tiny lights. It could not talk, but would signal with these eyes. Because of its strength and the impossibility of wounding it, it was able to walk through walls and doors, and by a mere tap on the head of a person kill him or her instantly. Of course, the last episode revealed the den of a gang of thieves and a man was found with the complete outfit of iron beside him; and the mystery was solved. This is the only serial I saw through to the end.

I believe my interest was completely attracted to war pictures for a while after that. I loved them. I was always prepared with several handkerchiefs of my own and sometimes one of my father's, for the sadder they were the more I enjoyed them. I would weep profusely for the girl whose lover was killed as he begged his buddy to tell his mother and sweetheart good-by. This was the first stage.

Then I began to observe the attitude of my playmates towards the Germans and was greatly perplexed. They talked with bitterness about them and the young boys told me of their desires to be old enough to kill "hundreds of Huns." I couldn't understand it. I couldn't hate them. I couldn't see that they were different from Americans. They were fighting for their country and we were fighting for ours. If they killed our soldiers, surely ours killed theirs. I remember this troubled me a great deal, but I would never voice my opinion because I was afraid of being ridiculed by my playmates. I finally decided that they were cold-blooded and unsympathetic; that if they couldn't see it as I did and sympathize with the Germans as well as with the Americans, they couldn't sympathize with my troubles either. It seems to me now that from this time on I told very little of my own affairs to friends and always tried to see both sides of a situation before judging it. I do not know whether movies were directly responsible for this attitude, but I am convinced they were at least influential.

When war pictures became less popular, I preferred society pictures. At that time I was of an age at which I was beginning to be extremely conscious of my personal appearance. I longed for the gorgeous costumes shown in the movies. After seeing such a one, I would go home and dress up in mother's dresses and try to arrange my hair after a fashion I had seen in a movie featuring Theda Bara, the Talmadge sisters, or some other actress of note at the time.

I remember having a girl friend, Jane, who believed that at about eighteen every girl's father became president of a large company and she was sent away to school. She must always come home as a debutante and have a great many suitors. When Jane was asked why she believed this, she said because it "always happened that way in the movies." I thought she was dreadfully foolish.

However, I received one of the greatest disappointments of my young life, I believe, when I went to a movie that ended sadly. I cannot remember what it was, but it surely revolutionized my ideas. I had always believed that no matter how badly things seemed, everything would turn out happily in the end. Some people had a long period of difficulties, and others were more fortunate, but both at some time would finally "live happily ever after." I used to call that my philosophy (I liked the word) and I comforted my playmates at every opportunity by telling them that they just hadn't reached the turning point yet. I had quite a group of followers who were the same friends with whom I went to the movies. I could always refer to the movies to confirm my beliefs until that fatal day. They asked for explanations and I couldn't give any. I was almost heartbroken, and finally I went to mother and told her all about it. She didn't laugh. I often wondered why. She talked to me for a long time and told me I must not take movies seriously. They only showed a few experiences of lives of imaginary people, both pleasant and unpleasant. She told me I could pity people who must live as some did who were represented in the movies and at the same time by contrast appreciate my own opportunities. It was during this talk, too, that she impressed upon my mind that to obtain money was not the main aim of life—another idea I had gathered from movies. There were two parallel points she stressed: happiness for myself and happiness for others. I shall always remember that talk.

For quite a time afterwards I cared little for movies. If I went at all I usually went with mother, and we saw only shows that had been well recommended by critics or were starring some noted actress or actor, such as Mary Pickford or Doug Fairbanks.

Then came the time when I became interested in men. I had heard older boys and girls talking about "technique," and the only way I could find out how to treat boys was through reading books and seeing movies. I had always known boys as playmates; but having reached my freshman year in high school, they became, no longer playmates, but "dates." I didn't want it to be that way, but it seemed inevitable. I was asked to parties and dances and friends' homes. The boys were older and sophisticated. I felt out of place. I noticed that older girls acted differently with boys than with girls alone. I didn't know what to do.

I decided to try some of the mannerisms I had seen in the movies. I began acting quite reserved and memorized half-veiled compliments. I realized my "dates" liked it; and having laid the foundation with movie material I began to improvise.

Of course, I had a rival in the crowd. Every time she began to receive more attention from the boys than I, I would see a movie and pick up something new with which to regain their interest. I remember one disastrous occasion. She was taking the center of the stage and I was peeved. I could think of nothing to do. Then I remembered the afternoon before I had seen Nazimova smoke a cigarette, and I decided that would be my next move. The party was at a friend's home and I knew where her father's cigarettes were kept. I got one, lit it, and had no difficulty whatsoever in handling it quite nonchalantly. The boys were fascinated, and the victory was mine. Of course, the news reached home and I was informed that just because I had seen something in the movies I must not think it was necessarily the correct thing to do.

My early ideas of love may have been somewhat formulated under the influence of movies. I was extremely sentimental and am not sure but that I am now. My greatest ambition has always been to marry the man I love and make him happy. I cannot be a "gold-digger," though I admit I have tried to be one a few times; but I find I derive no enjoyment from it. I want to go out with men because I enjoy their company and not for the sake of the money they spend on me. I cannot say whether or not movies have had any effect on this characteristic of mine, but I am inclined to doubt it.

I have never worshiped movie stars such as Rudulph Valentino. I have talked to girls, however, who would have given most anything to have met him and become intimately acquainted.

The most disgusting display I have ever witnessed occurred one evening at the *Trianon*. A crowd of my friends and I went to see Valentino in person with his wife, the former Miss Hudnut. When he appeared, some of the girls simply went wild. (Not any in our crowd, thank goodness!) Some threw diamond rings from the boxes and others screamed, "Oh Rudy! just one kiss!" and fainted. And so I saw and realized the effect movies may have.

I do not think they have influenced my moral judgments, unless it has been in my perhaps extreme broad-mindedness. This is certainly a product of my own experience, but it may have been justified or confirmed by the movies. I believe my personal moral standards are fairly high and also my judgment of myself; but I am neither hasty nor scornful in my condemnation of others. It may be that movies show so many sides of life and so many examples of misunderstanding that I have been influenced by them in that way.

I do not remember that the news reels and educational films held much interest for me until about my last year in high school. Since then, however, I have enjoyed them equally as much, if not more than, the feature movies. I believe they are of great educational value.

I care little for movies now. I go only if I have read a favorable criticism or just to be sociable. They have ceased to really influence me, but I enjoy them if I do not go often enough to become bored with them. When I do go I find myself criticizing the acting and production, lighting effects, direction, etc. This has been fostered by my study of the legitimate stage. I do enjoy going to movies once in a while now, though, because from that point of view most of them are bad—amusingly bad—and it is a surprise and a satisfaction to see one that is really good.

The following autobiography was written by a girl, age 17, native white—a senior in high school. She was the honor student of her class:

Though but sixteen years old now, I have been attending movies for the past ten years at an approximate average of twice a week. Movies have always been a part of my existence, a part of my education—verily, a part of me.

Perhaps the best way to continue this simple narrative will be to divide the photoplays into six classes: namely, comedies, serials feature pictures inspiring horror and mysterious sensations; the "sob story" type, the humorous kind, and, last of all, a miscellaneous section; I shall attempt to deal with each of these classes in their respective order.

Those old, gone-but-not-forgotten slapstick comedies with their pie-throwing versatilities never appealed to me. In fact, very few comedies at that period of my life did. Charles Chaplin in "Over the Top" was the first one that met with my approval, but now, as I recall some of the scenes, I have to laugh at my taste, because they were just as silly, just as imaginary, just as ridiculous as were those of the so-called custard comedies. Perhaps it was Chaplin's personality—nevertheless I saw all of his succeeding shows, in one of which, "The Immigrant," his acting so impressed me that upon my return home I donned my father's derby, took an umbrella and mentally labeled it "cane" and then began to practice Chaplin's walk and mannerisms according to my own interpretation. Gradually my potential sense of humor developed and I had other favorite comedians, foremost among whom were Baby Peggy and Wesley Barry. But with this growing list of favorites also unfolded a roll of disfavorites (if I may coin my own word for the sake of emphasis).

Ben Turpin, the Mack Sennett girls, and Lupe Lupino headed this list, and, as I grew older, my lists remained the same with the exception of a few additions on the favorite side; Our Gang with special mention to Farina, Snookums, and Felix the Cat of Aesop's Fables being the additional ones. But practically all these comedies never affected my being and character in any way, except perhaps to augment my store of wise-cracks.

But serials, on the other hand, went so far as to turn my daydreams into nightmares. Of course I was only so influenced when I was in that stage of childhood where seeing, whether it be on the screen or on the street, is believing. Pearl White in "The Precious Diamond" was the first serial I ever viewed. Not one installment of it did I miss, and while witnessing it, I went through the processes of biting nails, standing up and sitting down, breathing quickly and holding my breath, and last of all, poking my loving brother who always accompanied me to these exciting

Saturday and Sunday matinées.   Then the movie world gave
birth to a new and more unreal, more sensational, and more
blood-curdling type of serial, the picturization of the Tarzan books,
Tarzan, half-man, half-animal, impressed me as being something
of a demi-god, always arriving at places at the crucial moment
to rescue the fair damsel in distress. At night I'd dream of Tarzan,
of the jungle, of animal life. Often I'd wake up in the middle of
the night thinking I was in the clutch of a baboon or some other
carnivorous animal.   But Tarzan pictures as all other serials
gave me a beautiful outlook on life. My theory was that in life
as in movies everything always turned out right. The hero and
heroine always lived happily ever after. But how I ever disposed
of the villain still remains a subject of discussion. I felt that as
long as I was good, and my childish conceit led me to believe that
I was always good even if I was reprimanded occasionally, nothing could ever be injurious to me because wasn't there a hero for
every heroine?   Thus, even if serials did give me bad dreams,
their good influence so overcame their bad influence that to see
them was an advantage and asset rather than a disadvantage or
liability.

My third section I have classified under the head of feature
pictures inspiring horror and mystery. I was about twelve years
old when I first saw a picture giving a feeling of extreme dread
and terror—namely—Lon Chaney in "The Hunchback of Notre
Dame." A shiver still runs through me at the mere mention of
it. 'Tis true, the historical settings, the superb characterization,
and the wonderful direction combined to make a never-to-be-
forgotten photoplay.   Nevertheless, that picture should have
been censored; not from a standpoint of immorality, but because
of the exaggerated horror inspired by the appearance of Lon Chaney, by the gloomy aspect of the theme, and by the revolting actions predominating. For a solid year I managed to avoid seeing
any of Lon Chaney's productions.   Then finally realizing that
Chaney was an artist in his line I went to see several of his pictures, one of which, "The Monster," inspired as much fear as
did his first horrible show. Those were the only hair-raising, because of horror, movies that I have ever seen. Because of mystery, I have once in a while been terrorized. The only pictures of
this kind that I can recall at the present are "The Bat" and

"While the City Sleeps." However, these gave a mysterious sensation rather than one of real horror.

And now for the "sob story" kind! "Humoresque" was the first picture of that sort that I ever saw. For some reason or other, although it left me with a lasting impression, nevertheless, as far as learning anything or developing anything from it is concerned, I gained nothing. Soon after, I saw Jackie Coogan in "Oliver Twist"—and for some reason or other, I decided that the moral of that picture was that one should never speak to strangers. In this day and age, that little lesson learned from a two-hour movie was indeed practical and helpful. I doubt very much that any experiences my parents might have told me about children speaking to strangers would have as thoroughly impressed me as this movie did where I could actually see what happened. Vivian Martin in "Old Curiosity Shop" left me with similar impressions as did "If Winter Comes" starring Alec B. Francis and "Orphans of the Storm" with Lillian and Dorothy Gish. Then soon after I saw "So Big" starring Colleen Moore. I gained from this show the knowledge of how to practice in real life the Fifth Commandment, "Honor thy father and thy mother." Then an interval of about two years elapsed during which I did not have cause for tears while at any movie. Then in rapid order I saw "The Count of Monte Cristo," "La Boheme," "Resurrection," "Camille," "Stella Dallas," "Beau Geste," "The Last Command." In the past year I have seen and enjoyed "Laugh, Clown, Laugh," "The Jazz Singer," "Sorrell and Son," "The Singing Fool."

Though all of the aforementioned impressed me greatly, nevertheless I will only give some details about a few of them. "Camille" was spoiled by excessive and much too detailed love-making. Instead of showing close-ups of the facial emotions of the characters, close-ups of all the kisses were shown. It's true one learns how to work their eyelids when in the arduous process of kissing one's beloved or boy-friend, but, though I am not considered a prude, why must the real moral of a picture be overshadowed and placed in the background in order to emphasize the correct kissing methods? It seems crazy to discuss "Stella Dallas" right after "Camille," but if I were to discuss each picture to its full length, this paper would turn into a book. Words cannot describe "Stella Dallas." As far as realism is concerned, that picture had "IT" in capital letters. Belle Bennett as the gay, frivolous, but loving and good mother will always be remembered by me. "Stella Dallas" taught me several things; but the one I can never forget, I cannot really put in words. This lesson, though I guess it is more of a prayer, is that by God's grace and benevolence my Mother will never have to suffer those pains which Belle Bennett suffered, that she may never need to wear that wretched, that remorseful, that uneasy and hunted and pleading look that Belle Bennett wore, and last, that she may never see the day when a son or daughter of hers is unable to come to her at the time she needs them most.

"Beau Geste," that beautiful story of brotherly love, really did influence my home environment. I became more considerate of the feelings of my older brother, I treated him with more respect, I lost my love for pestering him and for wanting to go where he goes, and, consequently, although he never saw the picture, he changed in his ways toward me, so that now, about four years since the showing of that picture, my brother and I are the ideal brother and "kid sister." "Mammy"—Mammy—who could forget the sensation of hearing Al Jolson singing Mammy over the then newly invented Vitaphone? In the "Jazz Singer" it seemed to me that death and religion, two really beautiful things supposedly, were emphasized. Until Death with his greedy claws seemed to threaten him indirectly and to knock on his door and call for Life, Al Jolson has practically forsaken the religion he had been inbred with. But Death brings to light all things— when Death is near, everyone speaks kind words, does kind deeds, and in the "Jazz Singer" Death brought to one, Al Jolson, reawakened filial respect as well as a true rather than a hypocritical spirit of religion, a religion which was not forced upon him but which he unconsciously was led to have uttermost faith in. "Sorrell and Son" also depicted a son's love for his father but in a different way. And now to return to Al Jolson. Those of us who have seen the "Singing Fool" recognize the fact that Al is a genius, but have we given enough credit to the type of movie, to the lesson taught by the show? I shall not say anything further about the last named picture, but about sob pictures collectively, I want to inform you that if there were more, no matter what the innermost qualities of the persons viewing it were, everyone would gain something advantageous. I will add that I picked up little trivial mannerisms. Some of these may seem foolish but as this seems to be a sort of confession anyway, I'll confess. I figured that when I ever want anything real badly and am almost at the point of tears begging for it, I should clench my fists; that when I go out for the evening, drop earrings are more becoming than the screw earrings; that my hair behind my ears, like Greta Garbo, emphasizes the facial contour; that when I cry, I should not even attempt to wipe away the tears as they are so much more effective rolling downwards; and then, there are a host of other similar trivialities.

Feature pictures having humor as the predominating feature is my next class. Roscoe Arbuckle in "Brewster's Millions" was the first picture of that type I ever saw and I was thoroughly satisfied. Who wouldn't be? To see a plump fellow of about thirty running around trying to get rid of it would amuse even the most serious-minded to laughter and hearty guffaws. The after-effect this show had on me was a very queer one; it was a dream. I dreamed that all this money was in my hands; that I had to get rid of it by a certain day; and that my method of getting rid of it was by buying a large department store and buying as much stock for it as my money could buy. Then after the date when all my money had to be gone, I could start selling this overstock at stupendously cheap prices to retail customers, thus getting a part of my money back. The day following my dream, I began to think that if I could puzzle out all by myself such a great economic problem that a man of thirty could barely figure out, I must be a child prodigy as far as the solving of various problems is concerned. Immediately I forced my parents to invest in numerous put-together puzzle games, and, to this day I enjoy any sort of a puzzle, no matter how childish it is; and in my school career thus far, the subjects that most interested me are those in which problems must be figured out and not where problems already solved must be memorized.

Then I saw Douglas MacLean in "A Connecticut Yankee in King Arthur's Court." Besides giving me two hours of delightful amusement, that show also led me to read the book by Mark Twain, and, as all know, the study and pursuit of good literature s the foundation of a cultured nation. "The Hottentot," "Up in the Air," and the Harold Lloyd pictures were all enjoyed by me. The present-day pictures of this type have more of the love element than formerly, but, of course, every picture for the most part has some love affair. Clara Bow in "It," Norma Shearer in "The Latest from Paris," Harold Lloyd in "Speedy," Williams Haines in "Telling the World," and Clara Bow in "Red Hair" are a few of the latter type.

My last section is a miscellaneous one; it is a combination of adventure, love and romance, war, the underworld, the younger generation, history, and humor. Mary Pickford in "Little Lord Fauntleroy" so impressed me that I made my Mother buy me a pair of black velvet pants with white buttons like those Mary Pick ord wore in that show. I realized later how foolish I was to wear such boyish garb, but then, I could at least have the satisfaction of saying that my clothes are modeled along the lines of Mary Pickford's. Douglas Fairbanks in "The Mark of Zorro" was a picture of adventure and so appealed to my childish adventurous instincts that I saw the picture four different times and would have seen it more if I had had the time. His grace in dueling always made me want to some day learn to fence, but this childish day-dream and illusion of mine had to be spoiled, because, you know, ethics (and now I am sarcastic) state that little ladies must not handle dangerous weapons, must not even dream of acting so tomboyish. "The Prisoner of Zenda" also gave me adventurous and dueling ideas; but it also served to give me a fairly-good idea of the English castle, drawbridge, and other characteristics of feudal times. "Scaramouche" left me spellbound; it served to give me a very elaborated idea of the French Revolution, but though exaggerated, nevertheless, four years later when I read a book for a book report on the French Revolution, I was more wont and ready to believe the gruesome but honest details of that period.

Rudolph Valentino in "The Shiek" was laughed at by me. I came home and told my parents that I had seen a marvelous actor who sure knew how to ride a horse but he was always mushing over a lady. At a later date, when I had matured by at least two years, I saw the "Son of a Sheik" and came home with a different report. A report very flattering to his ability and method as a lover. I often wondered what it would be like to be in his arms, if he gave wet kisses or dry ones, if he smacked his lips or merely held them tightly, but death took him away and now I've ceased wondering about these wonders.

"Three Wise Fools" starring Alec B. Francis afforded me much pleasure and took away that misconceived notion of mine that step-parents or guardians were very mean and would make you slave for them as in the story of Cinderella. "Black Oxen" with Corinne Griffith made me believe more in the extraordinary powers of chemistry as did "Tolerable David" starring Richard Barthelmess. "Bluebeard's Eighth Wife," featuring Gloria Swanson, greatly appealed to me and in one respect was very beneficial. Up until then, movie picture titles were ignored by me. But that title about Bluebeard, and I had read the fairy tale, developed my sense of why is a movie title and what is its relation to a movie. From that time on I have never yet seen a picture whose title I have not fitted to it to my own satisfaction. I will only skim over the historical pictures I saw, namely, "Paul Revere's Ride," "Abraham Lincoln," "Man Without a Country," "Covered Wagon," and the "Vanishing American," as I did not care for them in the least. The Duncan Twins in "Topsy and Eva" I will also ignore for the reason that my anticipation of the show was so great that I was doomed to disappointment in the realization of it.

William Haines in "Brown of Harvard" was the first really impressive college picture I saw, and I then resolved to refrain from molesting freshmen when I am an upper classman in college. However, I do not want the reader to get the idea that I am still of the same opinion.

William Boyd in "The Volga Boatman" was the realized movie ideal of my thoughts. That was the most perfect picture I have ever seen. Photography, direction, acting, subtitling, accuracy of details, truth of plot, truth of historical event, truth in scenic backgrounds, correct costuming—everything combined to make a truly perfect picture! I still don't know if I received anything of real value from that picture, but if anyone would quiz me on any detail, whether of action or description or detail, I could answer correctly. I only saw it once but I was so entranced by it that I overlooked nothing. I forgot nothing, I remembered everything.

The War Pictures, and I believe I am right in capitalizing what I did, have convinced me of the real evils of war, of the ideas that though war is a menace, disarmament can never be fully and thoroughly put into effect.

"Barbed Wire" with Pola Negri, "The Legion of the Condemned," and the "Big Parade" served as the founders of those ideas. One incident from the "Big Parade" I would like to re-quote here. John Gilbert is in a shell-hole, anxiously awaiting the return of his buddy from No Man's Land. His nerves are on edge; the cannons roaring about him and the shells bursting in air arouse his hatred of the general's orders; he hates himself for staying there like the general told him to do instead of going out to find and aid his buddy. Then on top of all this tension a soldier from the trench crawls into the shell-hole to tell him to quit standing there and pacing but to lie down so that the enemy will not spy their dugout. "Orders from the general" the soldier said. And then John Gilbert rose, jumping out of the dugout, he pauses long enough to draw himself up to the stature of a real man and to fire back, "Orders! Orders! Who's fighting this war—Men or Orders? And with that he leaves to seek out his buddy from God knows where. I shall never forget that bit of philosophy nor shall I ever forget the incident causing supposedly that bit of wisdom.

Underworld pictures such as the "Drag Net," "London After Midnight," "Twelve Miles Out," (this was not exactly an underworld picture, but inasmuch as it dealt with hi-jackers, rum-runners, etc., I have classed it as such), and "Streets of Sin" are in my opinion utterly worthless and in some cases ruinous for the unsettled youths. It gives too many ideas to become one of those gunmen because they believe they have found some new and ingenious method of outwitting the police, and then, wouldn't it be fun to realize their William S. Hart child ideals by going out and shooting and capturing and escaping and then not have to pay any penalty? Many people maintain that pictures of that type are instructive rather than destructive. They believe that youth upon viewing pictures of that type will profit by seeing that the gunman pays the penalty, but it has been proved time and again that youth loves to be inventive, adventurous—wants to always outwit somebody. And then people say that those underworld pictures are so instructive (and again I am sarcastic!).

John Gilbert in "Masks of the Devil" I would like to say several things about. By chance, the day after I had viewed that show my English teacher used it as an example of something I cannot just now recall, but then she started to tell what she thought of the show. She said it was immoral—immoral in the sense of truth, because, she said it was not true; it was a lot of "bunk." I then raised my hand, and upon being called on, said that if that show was not truth, then all fiction books are also immoral and every one knows that if fiction was so immoral, it would not be handed down from one generation to another. Her answer was that they were different sorts of truths. That was a teacher's point of view of that show. I, as a pupil, claim that it was immoral in the sense of pollution. If the reader has seen this show, I am leaving it to him to decide whether the younger generation or the older generation has a better interpretation of movies and their morals. "The Noose" and "The Wheel of Chance," melodramas in a sense, were exceedingly similar. "The Wheel of Chance" was adapted from the book, "Roulette," and its philosophy was that life is like the roulette wheel—one either wins or loses—there is no semi-loss and semi-gain; that we're just the little ball that spins around on this wheel of life, uncertain where we are to fall, yet always molding our landing places.

The last show that I am going to mention is the show that so accurately pictured the viewpoints of the younger generation— "Our Dancing Daughters" starring Joan Crawford. In Joan Crawford the true spirit of the younger generation was shown. No matter what happened she played fair. She even lost her man and in the eyes of the older generation they think that when a modern young miss wants her man back she'd even be a cutthroat, but Joan Crawford showed that even in a crisis like that she was sport enough to play fair! And "play fair" is really the motto of the better class of young Americans, and even in the best products there is always a blemish so why must the younger generation be so shamefully thought of. I hope many of these women who are scandalized at the actions of the modern miss saw that show and, if they did not change their beliefs after seeing it, then, it does not mean that the movie was a failure but that they are the failures not to recognize so obvious a truth.

And now, I hope I have convinced the reader of this: that movies are godsends, and to express my sentiments, long may they live and long may they stay in the land of the free and the home of the brave!

The following account comes from a college girl, aged eighteen, American born, and of wealthy Swedish parentage.

It is of interest in suggesting how one's "world" may be built up out of movie images and themes. The account also illuminates the influence of motion pictures on such sentiments as sorrow, and such emotions as passionate love.

My memories of the motion pictures as a child are vague, not because of age for I am only eighteen now, but because of my intense desire to remain away from them. This attitude was developed soon after I had returned from Europe. I was a child of five when I was pushed off grandmother's doorsteps in her country home by a goat, and received some unpleasant treatment. Barely three months later after we had been in Chicago about two weeks, my parents took me to a southside show. No sooner had we entered than I gave a piercing scream, for on the screen I saw a white beard jumping up and down. My thoughts were of the goat in Europe trampling me with his bobbing and threatening beard above me. And this dancing white haired and white bearded man was enough to keep me away from the shows until I was about ten years old.

When I was about ten years old, I received the grammar-school prize in the oratorical contest. That day after school there was much celebrating, and my parents took me with my friends to a movie. It was at this time that I became interested in the poor, and I think, Irish screen family. In this family besides great poverty, they had great courage. The two children in the picture worked hard and graduated from high school with honors, which the rich man's son and daughter failed to earn.

But not only these struggles interested me, for in my sophomore year in high school I went with my uncle to see a love picture. The heroine's kindness and courtesy to those below her, as well as her idealistic—very proper and yet loving attitude—toward her lover, or in other words, her absolutely non-petting nor cheap behavior, helped me in firmly establishing my conduct or at least ideals.

Now at eighteen what am I interested in? Love, beautiful and clean where the actors marry and remain married in spite of difficulties. Just about two years ago I saw a movie where a young mother sat by the window smoking a cigarette, and near her lay her tiny baby. It cried and cried. But she did not get up and give it its milk. Angrily she told it to wait until she finished her cigarette. Oh, I hate her, and her kind, and the movies which show such pictures. If the audience took the right attitude it might have been of value, but many howled with laughter and whispered here and there "She's not as dumb as her mother was." Just what they meant by "dumb" I am not sure, but the picture did not displease them; nor make them think why there was such a difference in the way the baby was treated and the way its thoughtless mother had been treated.

The first time that I really became interested in the movies was when I saw the poor family. Its struggles and experiences have lived with me since. Why it did interest me at just that time I do not know. I do know, however, it was this interest which led me to ask father and his friends to give part-time work to students. And this interest has become more and more intense because of my fondness for a poor boy whom, curiously, father likes too. He is studying at nights, but it will be years before he reaches his goal. Many an afternoon we have spent talking over this life and our problems. Many times we have cues or suggestions from this movie family, which incidentally we both saw. And I too, have been modeling my life according to the girl's in the picture, not in earning money but in helping others get part-time work, and by entertaining many of these poor students.

Sometime after I saw the beautiful love picture, I became conscious of the desire that I wanted to be loved, and love as the heroine did. But this consciousness of the desire was, I think, because of the attentions of a boy four years older than I. I was not quite sixteen years old when the idol of the school asked me to be his prom partner.

My interests haven't changed for they have become a part of me, and are becoming more or less important as my life changes. But they are still with me. I had been brought up as strictly as convent girls are brought up during my grammar-school days. I was very reserved and what few movies I saw while in high school were a dream world out of which I was getting patterns for life in novel experiences, especially when my human or aesthetic ideals failed me.

The actors and actresses whom I know are few. Among these I well remember Wallace Reid, Warren Carrigan whom I saw in a part of a serial; but he struck me by his kindness to an old woman whom he helped across the street; Laura La Plante, Barbara LaMar, and her perfect loves. Within the last two years I have been interested in Douglas Fairbanks, and Mary Pickford because of their experienced-like scenes. Gary Cooper and Janet Gaynor I like because of their youth and their skill in meeting life's troubles. Greta Garbo and Pola Negri have a personality that is intriguing and interesting and helpful in their charming, coy, and encouraging behavior toward their sweethearts. But far above all of these I place Dolores Costello. She embodies a spiritual beauty, something deeper and purer than any other actress that I have ever seen. To me she seems capable and desirous of helping the poor and downtrodden. Why? I don't know; but she has a soulful face so much like a nun, Sister Cecelia, whom I worshiped while she lived and taught me.

My childhood experiences in the movies, as seen from the reading above, have been extremely limited. That first frightening memory of that white bearded man on the screen could not then be clearer before me than it is now. About five years later I became acquainted with "my poor family." I remember the play, but neither the actors nor the name. I know it was played near my home. I remember the feelings within me as the boy and girl received their honors. All the way through the picture I felt what the girl felt. When she gained a victory over her proud, rich class-mates I, too, felt happy and victorious. When she had to stay home because of funds I worked with her helping the neighbors to earn the necessary few cents. The worst part was that after I got home I would react and relive these experiences in my room. To me it was something real, and even now when I go to a movie I feel such intense joy or sorrow as in "Resurrection" when Kaska may never marry her lover, and the shock of the discovery of the secret that she loved him; their separation, their last kiss, his mother's denouncing her were very much a part of me. Such a part of me that I did not realize I was in a show with people around me, until the orchestra played after the picture was over. Then with an odd unhappy and heavy feeling I left, because I could not understand why the orchestra played so happily while I suffered. I went to sleep with the same feeling and only gradually did it go away. But it stayed for several days. At times, I have lived the life of the actor if he appealed to my ideal. But how intensely I have suffered after a sad or tragic picture. And if it is a happy and pleasant picture its effects last for several days also. I will be happy, willing to do my sister's home-work, help my maid, and do almost anything unusual or out of the way to help others.

In a picture like "Resurrection" I feel more sorrow and happiness at first than in my actual life. For in real experience I have had but few infatuations which never went very far while I was in high school. They left me utterly cold after a short while, whereas the effects of the picture awaken similar feelings now as they did when I saw the picture. In times of joy, sorrow, troubles, or difficulties these scenes of sorrow from "Resurrection," or the struggles from the "poor family scenes" come back to me, and add to my joy or sorrow—make it more deep. In difficulties and troubles these scenes of struggles give me more courage to fight my battles.

I hate to go to a movie where people clap, talk, or make any noise which breaks the silence in the room. It has a very unpleasant and jarring effect when I am very excited or downcast to have someone bring me back suddenly to myself. I don't think I ever tried to foretell what would happen next, for I had no time. I lived in what was before me. I don't want others to tell me the story before I see it, nor to keep on talking about it after I see it. After I see the picture I want to go home and relive it in my room.

The movies, during the few times that I have seen them, have shaped my actual life more than my play. In reading, holding the book, turning the pages or in coaxing my father I would find myself using some of the mannerisms of the actresses which I like. Especially did I become aware of this in my treatment of father when he looked puzzled at my sudden changes, caresses, and attitudes whereas before I had asked to go somewhere and upon being refused I would remain reading or something in my room without speaking to anyone. Very likely I would react the sad parts of "Resurrection" and feel myself to be the heroine.

Upon going to my first dance I asked the hairdresser to fix my hair like Greta Garbo's. Of course I did not tell the hairdresser that I was copying this intriguing and fascinating actress or she would think I had gone insane. I, the "nicest" girl, whom mothers to this day set as an example to their daughters and young sons. Oh, the unconscious cruelty of father when he forbade me pleasures other children had and have, and I partly made up this injustice to myself by seeing a picture once or twice a year and living them over and over again. I lived the life of the heroine and used my little sister for the rival or unpleasant character, very seldom the good character. The rival afforded me more opportunity to be dramatic. In speaking on graduation day I did my best to finish with the swaying-like courtesy which Pola Negri taught me from the stage.

Somehow or other Dolores Costello has not taught me mannerisms, but what beauty is. When I see her I cannot help but truly believe that there is a God, creator of the beautiful. She brings to me that deep feeling of beauty and all that goes with beauty—love, truth, sympathy, etc.

Only at one time did the movies decide my yielding to a temptation which my better self condemned. I regret it very much. I had been fond of a dark boy, somewhat like John Gilbert, who had proposed many times while I was a sophomore in high school. He seemed perfect to me at the time. His family are among the best known aristocrats and he was supposedly intelligent. How I dislike him for this lack of the "supposed intelligence." He did not realize what he was asking me to do but they are not all of that type. One evening after he had built more alluring castles than usual, I decided it would be romantic to run away with him. No longer would I be under my dear but misunderstanding father's strict rules.

At that time we lived some distance from here in an enormous home with a beautiful garden surrounding it. My "hero" was to wait near the thick bushes, and to help me to get out through the windows as soon as it was dark. I had scarcely flashed the light as the signal, when father came into my room. He had been told by the gardener or someone else that somebody was lurking among the trees. He came to warn me about closing my windows, and found me with my clothes packed. No one outside of father, the boy, and I will ever know this, but it hurt all of us.

Because my father had been very strict in his beliefs, regarding marriage, rights of women, and these beliefs gave me many chances to rebel unsuccessfully, I was in a mood to listen and see other beliefs. Sometime before this again unsuccessful rebellion I had seen a runaway marriage which had impressed me tremendously. I did think that having a hero like this dark boy to protect me from father's anger and strictness would be heaven. Curiously enough I was more interested in the details of escaping—how the girl got her clothes down, how she got down, what he did to help her down —all these details I watched more carefully than the rest of the play in the runaway marriage.

My reactions toward the movies, so different from those of my sister, may be due to my desire to be above my friends. I have always been ahead, at least two years, in school. Before sixteen I was graduated from high school, and I did none of the things I would have liked to do. I have always been known as reserved and quiet among others outside of the family, or as a speaker among the various foreign clubs, or as a serious student, but at times I wanted to play with those of my age. I would have given all my toys or anything to be with others on the street. And all this pent-up grief, desire for play, anticipated joy in company with others of my age has been unfulfilled. Only after I had been to a movie did I release these emotions when no one saw me or heard me except my little sister. I felt so much better after having been naughty Pola Negri for a few moments, or Vilma Banky without being reprimanded by that old governess or father's sister. After being "naughty," undignified and unladylike, as father would say, I would see Dolores Costello or through her see Sister Cecelia and settle down again for a few days. I would not relive some old picture again until I had been thwarted in or refused my desires. Dolores Costello has an influence over me which is similar to that of father when he is sad and dreams of past days.

Do I day-dream? I think that my "confession" thus far shows much day-dreaming. I have (most of the time) imagined myself as someone above many, where others may come to me for help. I imagine myself advising parents in some big institution not to be too strict with their children, to allow them time to play even with the dirtiest little boy or girl. How would I have enjoyed to run down the street with even a colored girl or boy of my size. I have always dreamed of marrying a poor man, contrary to father's life plans, and through this poor man of meeting hard-working, honest people whom I shall be able to help with whatever I have. And because there is every possibility that these dreams may come true, I cling to my dream world woven about the movies I have seen. Just what I would like to do would be something like this: I should like to build a big factory of some kind, and enable students, children of laborers, to become well educated through their earnings, in part-time work.

Although I feel very intensely the pain, joy, sorrow of the heroine, or the struggling character, I do not, and cannot cry. I don't think that I have cried but twice, just dry, painful sobs, and that was days after the funeral when I realized what death at home meant. How many times tears would have been a blessing instead of those painful choking feelings in my chest somewhere. Scenes of sorrow, as in "Resurrection" where the lovers are in the power of love and by force are separated, and the girl is starving because she cannot find work anywhere; in the poor family scene, the struggles, joy, grief; in a picture "Divorce," or something like that, where the child dies of neglect because the parents are too busy fighting for a divorce to care for the child,—all these come back to me. These scenes become a part of me and teach me unselfishness, kindness, and sympathy. Many times these scenes or the recollections of them mean nothing until trouble or pain comes to me and I recall the pains or troubles which I saw in some picture.

When I discovered I should like to have this coquettish and coy look which all girls may have, I tried to do it in my room. And surprises! I could imitate Pola Negri's cool or fierce look, Vilma Banky's sweet but coquettish attitude. I have learned the very way of taking my gentlemen friends to and from the door with that wistful smile, until it has become a part of me. I have been disgusted with the flirting and vamping in the movies. And yet, haven't I done it to one? Yes, but I console myself, that it wasn't with anyone, or everyone, but the one.

Has anyone not admired a passionate lover? I certainly did when I was in high school; and John Gilbert gave me reason to admire a passionate lover. He made me wonder what it feels like to be loved in that manner. And this unconscious yearning became conscious when I met one who was almost my ideal. But this yearning, as many of father's "not nice" yearnings, had to be satisfied by living and experiencing them in the movies, until recently since I have been engaged. But if I see any more of these passionate fiery movies I will not be able to resist the pleas to become a wife before next quarter. These passionate pictures stir such longings, desires, and urges as I never expected any person to possess. Just the way the passionate lover held his sweetheart suggests so many beautiful and intimate relations, which even my reacting a scene does not satisfy any more. I cannot believe myself that I am "I" any more; because when I first entered high school these scenes gave me unpleasant and guilty feelings. I would determine that I would never see them again. And now they come back clearly to me, but in such a different light. I actually want to experience these scenes, and see beauty in them.

Negro male student in High School. Age—17.

I first became interested in the movies when I had started to kindergarten. I had gone to the theater before but I had not paid much attention to them while sitting on my mother's lap or down in what seemed to me a very low seat. In school I heard the other children talking about cowboys and detectives and policemen that they had seen on the screen. When I again went I saw an exciting serial and William S. Hart which made me clamor to come back on the same day weekly. I kept up with that serial and several others when that one had ended. I did not lose interest in these pictures until a few years ago when I took to a higher type and more refined picture. I learned through education to distinguish between a good picture educationally and a bad or poor picture. This led me to those dramas mostly, although I occasionally go to see a serial or a Western story.

The earliest movie stars that I can remember were Wm. S. Hart and Tom Mix who played entirely in Western stories. I liked to see them shoot the villain and save the girl and "live happily ever after." It caused me to shout as loudly, or louder, than the rest. Following them came Douglas Fairbanks, who seemed so carefree and light that he won nearly everyone with his personality. He would jump, use a lasso, thrust a sword, and fight in a way to satisfy any child's desire for action. Now I have no special star but I think Emil Jannings is a great actor because he seems to put his heart and soul into his work.

As a boy, I went with nearly every one to the theater; my mother, father, sister or brother, relatives, and friends. Usually I went in the afternoon or evening, anywhere from one to five times a week. Now I still go with my relatives occasionally but mostly with friends or alone.

I cannot recall anything that I have done that I had seen in the movies except try to make love. It happened that when I was small there were no boys in my neighborhood and I had to go several blocks before I could play with some my size or age. But there were a few girls in my neighborhood my size. Seeing Douglas Fairbanks woo his maiden I decided to try some of "Doug's stuff" on one of the girl friends. I know I was awkward and it proved more or less a flop.

Several times on seeing big, beautiful cars which looked to be bubbling over with power and speed, I dreamed of having a car more powerful and speedier than all the rest. I saw this car driven by myself up to the girl friend's door and taking her for a ride. (I was then eight years old and in my dreams I was no older.) Then too, I saw Adolphe Menjou, the best dressed man in the world, try in various ways to kill me because I had won his title. Perhaps the picture that left the most depressing picture on my mind was one in which a murdered man was thrown over a high cliff from a mountain top. I could see that dead body falling, falling to the rocky depths far below and squash into almost nothing. Some nights I dreamed of falling and other nights I had nightmares from dreaming of the same thing, awoke in a cold sweat, and was not able to go to sleep again till dawn. Whenever I saw anyone looking down from some rather high place or some workman in the precarious position, I had a sickly feeling in the pit of my stomach and averted my eyes.

The most heartbreaking picture that I ever saw and which caused me to shed uncontrollable tears was "Over the Hill," starring Mary Carr. She was ill treated by all her children except one and had to go to the poorhouse and scrub daily. This picture caused me to see my mother in a new light and make a vow that I would always protect and provide for her as long as I or she lives. This mood lasted until the comedy, when I soon forgot it, but I have always kept my vow.

I have not adopted any mannerisms from the movies but I have tried to act like the actors of a picture for a short time after seeing the picture. Such actions were trying to act like a screen drunkard, a hero cowboy who shot and killed the villain and rode triumphantly away with the fair one. I used to go to "wild western" pictures and observe the Indians grab their hearts, or put their hands over their hearts, turn all away around and fall dead after they had been shot while resisting the unlawful Americans. When my chums played cowboy or cops and robbers, I tried to imitate these Indians in falling. Of course, many besides myself, I suppose, have tried to imitate Charles Chaplin or Douglas Fairbanks but I became so proficient in imitating Charles Chaplin that I became to be known as Charles in the neighborhood in which I formerly lived which made me dream of the time when I, Charles Chaplin, would be the star of the silver screen. Douglas Fairbanks gave me an inspiration to jump, fight, use long whips, ride, use rapiers and to be as happy and as full of life as he seemed to be.

While imitating these stars I became interested in love pictures and went to see them as often as I could. This liking developed after seeing such stars as Wallace Reid, Norma Talmadge, Rudolph Valentino, Mary Pickford, and Pola Negri. These actors stirred within me a desire to do an ardent love scene with a girl. The first girl that I tried this on said that I was crazy. The second girl wasn't interested. But the third girl actually thought that I really meant what I was saying about her eyes and lips and she permitted me to try out everything that I had planned and this occasion proved successful in more ways than one.

Occasionally I used to think constantly of such actors as Wallace Reid, Rudolph Valentino, or Pola Negri; especially the latter whose bewitching eyes instilled within me many ungodly thoughts that never were voiced.

I cannot say that I received any temptations from the movies but I did get one real ambition. That being, to fly and be an aviator. This desire originated from such pictures as "Wings," "The Flying Fleet," and "Lilac Time," all of which featured airplanes. Now I visit all the aviation exhibits and "talks" possible. The most interesting show I have yet seen is the one that was at the Chicago Coliseum. I visit the municipal airport often and just the sound of an airplane's motor is enough to start one thinking of that time when I am going to have a powerful plane of my own and see all the world by means of it.

Another ambition that I had was to be a "Jackie Coogan" at the age of eight. I thought I would be more of a star than Jackie himself. I dreamed of the time when I would be a great star and have a great deal of money because of it. Then I could buy a tiny automobile, just my size, that would run as fast as any big car. I would also have some ponies, a beautiful home for my mother and myself and be a veritable "lady's man." (All this time I was eight years old.)

Sometimes from seeing such pictures as "The Birth of a Nation" I would not but feel the injustice done the Negro race by other races. Most of the bad traits of unintelligent Negroes are used in many pictures and a lovable or educated character is rarely pictured.

At other times, "West Point," a picture of college life and a military training school, stirs within me a desire to go to college or some military or naval school away from home and serve my country as best I can.

In crime pictures, as in real life, the criminal not only becomes the hero on the screen but outside the theater as well. At other times the criminal's life is such that the audience simply abhors being such a character. If there were more of the latter type of picture I am of the opinion that there would be far less crime.